THE WORKING CLASS IN ENGLAND 1875-1914

THE
WORKING CLASS
IN ENGLAND
1875-1914

EDITED BY
JOHN BENSON

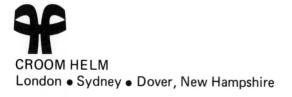

CROOM HELM
London • Sydney • Dover, New Hampshire

© 1985 John Benson
Croom Helm Ltd, Provident House, Burrell Row,
Beckenham, Kent BR3 1AT

Croom Helm Australia Pty Ltd, First Floor,
139 King Street, Sydney, NSW 2001, Australia

British Library Cataloguing in Publication Data

The Working class in England—1875-1914.
   1. Labor and laboring class—England—
   History
   I. Benson, John, *1945 July 23-*
   305.5'62'0942   HD8390
   ISBN 0-7099-0692-7

Croom Helm, 51 Washington Street,
Dover, New Hampshire, 03820 USA

Library of Congress Cataloging in Publication Data

Main entry under title:

The working class in England, 1875-1914.

   Bibliography: P.
   1. Labor and laboring classes — England — History.
I. Benson, John.
HD8399.E52W67 1984   305.5'62'0942   84-17672
ISBN 0-7099-0692-7

Printed and bound in Great Britain by
Biddles Ltd, Guildford and King's Lynn

CONTENTS

TABLES AND FIGURES

Tables

Figures

THE CONTRIBUTORS

JOHN BENSON is Senior Lecturer in History at
Wolverhampton Polytechnic. His books include
*British Coalminers in the Nineteenth Century: A
Social History* (1980) and *The Penny Capitalists: A
Study of Nineteenth-Century Working-Class Entre-
preneurs* (1983).

HUGH CUNNINGHAM is Lecturer in History at the
University of Kent at Canterbury. He is the author
of *The Volunteer Force* (1975) and *Leisure in the
Industrial Revolution* (1980).

M.J. HAYNES is Lecturer in European Studies at
Wolverhampton Polytechnic. His previous publications include studies of class and class consciousness.

ELIZABETH ROBERTS is a lecturer in adult education
and a Research Fellow in the Centre for North-West
Regional Studies at the University of Lancaster.
Her book, *A Woman's Place: An Oral History*, is published by Croom Helm.

F.B. SMITH is Professorial Fellow in the Institute
of Advanced Studies at the Australian National
University. His books include *The People's Health*
(1979) and *Florence Nightingale* (1982).

DAVID WOODS is Senior Lecturer in History at West
Midlands College of Higher Education. He has published articles on crime, policing, and the
magistracy in nineteenth century Britain.

ACKNOWLEDGEMENTS

John Benson is grateful for the advice of Stephen
Wood, for the typing assistance of Mary Barnett and
Rosemary Sproule and for the comments made by those
members of the University of Southampton History
Department and of the West Midland Group for the
Study of Labour History to whom he read an earlier
version of his chapter. Elizabeth Roberts wishes to
thank her colleagues in the Centre for North-West
Regional Studies at the University of Lancaster for
their support, especially Marion McClintock who read
her chapter, and Judish Haxby who typed it and coped
with her handwriting. She also wishes to express
her profound gratitude to all the respondents who
answered her questions and volunteered such useful
and illuminating information. M.J. Haynes wishes to
thank Sam Cameron of North Staffordshire Polytechnic
for his helpful criticisms from a different perspective. We are all grateful for the advice of W.R.
Garside and C.J. Wrigley and for the Nuffield
Foundation's award of a grant which enabled us to
meet together to discuss our contributions to the
book.

INTRODUCTION

Despite recent, well publicised setbacks, social and labour history have prospered in Britain during the past two decades. Social history has acquired its own university chairs and departments, its own professional organisations, conferences and journals - all the accoutrements which mark the emergence of a distinct academic discipline.[1] The progress of labour history has been less spectacular perhaps; but it too has thrived. Labour history's traditional institutional and political strengths (what one critic has dubbed 'the boring bureaucracy of trade unions and proletarian parties'[2]) have been supplemented by the successes of social history: by new studies of demography and kinship, class consciousness, economic and social mobility, popular culture, urban life, education, crime, social protest, leisure, religion, health, sexual behaviour and the lives of women and children. The list seems almost endless.[3]

Historians of the late Victorian and Edwardian working class have benefited enormously from this growth of ambition and achievement, from the growing volume of knowledge about almost every aspect of the lives of ordinary people. Yet this burgeoning historiography brings its own difficulties. Indeed the very proliferation of information, and the increasing specialisation which it encourages, drives even the most conscientious and critical of historians to take more on trust than they should; it forces them to accept uncritically too much about those many aspects of working class life about which it is no longer possible for them to possess an intimate understanding. Thus Poor Law historians have overlooked the importance of self-help and of private charity; historians of work have neglected many types of criminal and quasi-criminal activity;

trade union historians have ignored, or misunder-
stood, the attitudes, experiences and behaviour of
the rank and file.[4]

The contributors to this volume are profoundly
conscious of the dangers of such atomisation; only
too aware of the need to study the crucial, yet
complex and elusive, interrelationships between what
have been treated too often as distinct aspects of
working class experience.[5] What is needed is a new
synthesis. This volume, it must be stressed quite
clearly, is not that synthesis; neither does it aim
to be comprehensive; there is little here, for
example, about working class religion, education,
politics, poverty, or immigration.[6] Its aim is more
modest: to bring together a collection of up to date,
wide ranging and provocative studies on aspects of
late Victorian and Edwardian working class life to
which recent research has been able to add to our
knowledge and deepen our understanding.

Contributors have been chosen, not for their
likely adherence to any editorial 'line', but because they were known to the editor, personally or
by reputation, to be experts in their fields. Indeed
there is, it is hoped, a stimulating eclecticism
about this collection. Elizabeth Roberts examines
the socialisation of children and young people in
the family: 'it is only', she concludes, 'if the
deep abiding bond between the working class child
and his family is understood, that the position of
the young people in a wider society can be understood.' F.B. Smith explores some still neglected
changes in standards of health: the transition from
the traditional pattern of morbidity and mortality
based on endemic infections to the contemporary one
of widespread, chronic functional disorders in an
older population; the success of antisepis and the
rise of mass surgery; and the movement towards
smaller completed families and present levels of infant and maternal mortality. John Benson challenges
the view that the history of work between 1875 and
1914 was characterised by struggle and change. There
were present, he argues, 'in even the leading sectors of the economy ... major continuities in workplace organisation, experiences and attitudes.'
M.J. Haynes believes that previous accounts of class
consciousness have paid too much attention to membership of political organisations; he attempts therefore to analyse class and class conflict primarily
through strikes and industrial relations. Hugh
Cunningham takes issue with the way in which late
nineteenth and early twentieth century leisure has

been seen in one of two contexts: either as a 'golden age' or as the beginning of 'mass leisure'. Moving beyond a study of the opportunities for leisure within the working class, he examines various ideological constraints and concludes that the concept of the leisure class provides the most helpful context for the study of leisure in this period. Finally, David Woods seeks to estimate the extent of community violence in late Victorian England and to comment upon its forms and patterns. He concludes that 'From approximately 1880 onwards the indices of community violence showed a marked decline, suggesting a substantial change in public order in most areas.' Taken together, the contributions to this collection suggest that the everyday lives and values of late Victorian and Edwardian working people were even more varied, creative and complex than is generally suspected.

If the contributors to this volume provoke their readers into challenging the views expressed in it - or, better still, encourage them to undertake that sorely needed synthesis - they will have achieved their purpose.

NOTES

1. H. Perkin, 'Social History in Britain', *Journal of Social History*, 10(2), 1976; D. Smith, 'Social history and sociology - more than just good friends', *The Sociological Review*, 30(2), 1982; Editorial, 'Twenty Years On, *Bulletin of the Society for the Study of Labour History*, 41, 1980; E.J. Hobsbawm, 'From Social History to the History of Society', *Daedalus*, 100, 1971; Jay Winter, 'Introduction: labour history and labour historians', in Jay Winter (ed.), *The Working Class in Modern British History: Essays in Honour of Henry Pelling* (Cambridge, 1983).

2. Perkin, 'Social History', p.133.

3. Perkin, 'Social History', pp.136-9; Hobsbawm, 'Social History', p.12; R.J. Morris, 'Whatever happened to the British working class, 1750-1850?', *Bulletin of the Society for the Study of Labour History*, 41, 1980; K. Thomas, 'The ferment of fashion', *Times Literary Supplement*, April 30, 1982.

4. See, for example, the introduction to John

Benson, *British Coalminers in the Nineteenth Century:*
A Social History (Dublin, 1980) and A. Seldon (ed.),
The Long Debate on Poverty (London, 1972).
    5. P. Joyce, *Work, Society and Politics: The*
culture of the factory in later Victorian England
(Brighton, 1982).
    6. The *Bulletin of the Society for the Study*
of Labour History contains valuable bibliographical
guides: see, for example, J.S. Hurt, 'Education and
the working classes', *Bulletin*, 30, 1975; 31, 1975
and 43, 1981 and A.J. MacKenzie, 'The Communist
Party of Great Britain', *Bulletin*, 44, 1982.

THE WORKING CLASS IN ENGLAND 1875-1914

Chapter One

THE FAMILY

Elizabeth Roberts

I

This chapter will concentrate on certain aspects of
working class family life, notably the socialisation
of children and young people, and the interaction in
their lives of home, work and school. It is almost
impossible to define in terms of age who exactly was
a late Victorian or Edwardian child. There were no
recognised rites of passage between childhood and
adulthood; on the one hand, quite young children
adopted heavy responsibilities; on the other, young
people of twenty could be very much under their
parents' control. James Walvin in *A Child's World*
also had some problem in defining a child and finally settled on the age limit of fourteen. 'Yet the
age of fourteen, particularly at the end of our
period, has a more than arbitrary importance, it was
the predominant school leaving age and the limit of
childhood criminality.'[1] For many reasons which will
become apparent in the chapter, no precise definition of children and young people by age has been
attempted, although most of the evidence relates to
the under twenties.

The evidence used is drawn not only from
secondary documentary sources but also from oral
ones, and selections are used from an extensive
archive of oral evidence collected from 170 old
people in south Cumbria and Lancashire. This evidence is particularly useful in an analysis of
family life because so many facets of that life are
not recorded in official documents.[2] It must also
be apparent that the bulk of the oral evidence will
relate most directly to the last 25 years of the
period 1875-1914.

It has been suggested, both during the period
itself and subsequently, that the family was the

most important socialising agent in a child's life.
Helen Bosanquet, a prominent member of the Charity
Organisation Society, wrote in 1906, 'Apart from the
fact that no one has ever devised an adequate substitute for a parent, the further fact remains that
the family with its mingled diversity and identity
of interests is the best, if not indeed, the only
school of life of its citizens.'[3] Philip McCann
wrote in 1977 that 'The moderate functionalist
definition of socialisation is usually on the lines
of the transmission of culture, the process whereby
men learn rules and practices of social groups; the
family is considered as the primary agency and the
school or other formal educational institutions as
secondary in transmitting skills, values and social
norms.'[4] (Ironically, but possibly inevitably,
because of the difficulty of finding evidence about
socialisation within the family, other than from
oral sources, the book then concentrates on the
provision of education and the process of socialisation by formal educational agencies). Stephen
Humphries has written: 'It is difficult ... to
establish the precise significance of schooling as
an agency of socialisation ... legislators ...
severely underestimated the extent and intensity of
resistance to provided education. This opposition
was rooted in the values and modes of behaviour that
were learned from the family, the neighbourhood and
street culture. Indeed it is likely that agencies
of socialisation operating outside the school exercised a much more profound influence upon the morals
and manners of the working class child than the
school teacher in the classroom.'[5] While one might
wish to question the existence of *widespread* active
resistance to provided schooling, there can be
little question of the paramount importance of the
family in the socialisation of the working class
child and youth throughout the period under discussion.

It is of course obvious that no working class
family existed in either an economic, social, or
moral vacuum. It can be argued that virtually all
aspects of a family's background had some influence
on their behaviour whether as parents or as children.
There is much truth in this but an attempt has to be
made to analyse the more obvious influences and constraints on the ways in which working class parents
consciously socialised their children.

Firstly the economic standing of working class
families was very important. The studies of
Victorian and Edwardian poverty are well known and

demonstrate the extent of the problem.[6] Charles
Booth in his survey of life and labour in London in
the 1880s and Seebohm Rowntree's later study of York
showed that many working class people had their
basic needs unprovided for. Seebohm Rowntree developed the concept of a poverty line. He suggested
that any family of four or five persons with an
income of less than 21s 8d a week was below the
poverty line and unable to afford the basic essen-
tials of life.[8] There are no comparable data available for Lancashire, but in the north of the county
no unskilled man earned as much as 21s 8d before
1914, and many of course, had families larger than
four to five persons. From the oral evidence it is
clear that these families might not have been quite
as poor as Rowntree's hypothesis would suggest but
it is also clear that their poverty and ways of
making it less acute were one of their chief preoccupations.[9] Questions of budgeting and of making
ends meet affected many aspects of the working class
child's upbringing. Nor should it be presumed that
the spectre of poverty only haunted the families of
the lower paid. Skilled men and those in a super-
visory capacity could earn nearly twice as much as
a labourer in Edwardian England but that did not
make them and their families comfortably off. Many
men and women in this group remembered poverty very
clearly, either as children or as young adults,
before improved wages were achieved, and these
memories influenced the ways in which their children
were brought up.

Working class people were not simply economic
pawns, with all aspects of their lives dominated by
financial considerations. They acted according to a
complex set of moral and ethical rules handed down
from generation to generation. (These were obviously modified to some extent by each generation and
each family but there is a strong impression of
continuity and conformity in the late Victorian and
Edwardian period). The original sources for these
mores are of course difficult to ascertain. Much of
the moral philosophy of the working class can be
traced to the Bible, and the teaching of the churches. Religion, throughout this period, continued to
play an important part in working class life.[10]
Working class people did not however tend to be
concerned with theological debates, but followed
what was widely considered to be the basic Christian
teaching of loving your neighbour; added to which
was a widespread belief in judgement and punishment
for wrong doing and this sometimes resulted in an

observable (but unrecognised by those holding them)
ambivalence in attitudes to, and in relationships
with, others. Added to these basic moral standards
was an overwhelming devotion to respectability.[11]
Some observers have divided the working class into
the respectable majority and the rough minority, but
it is clear from oral evidence that while the rough
might not have followed or accepted *all* the standards of the truly respectable (they tended to swear
and fight for example!), they also had their own
pretensions to *some* respectability.

The characteristics of respectability are well
known: a devotion to the work ethic and to apparent
cleanliness; an avoidance of swearing, fighting and
discussion of sexual matters; and a respect for
other people and their property. Although the
features and existence of respectability are easy to
observe, their origin is difficult to establish.
E.P. Thompson saw Methodism as contributing to the
rationalisation of work through self-discipline,
whereby the labourer must be turned into his own
slave driver.[12] Many examples of a passionate devotion to the work ethic can be found in both
documentary and oral evidence but by the end of the
nineteenth century it was certainly not confined to
members of any particular religious sect but could
be found in them all. The other elements of
respectability can probably also be traced to
religious sources so that from the Bible and especially the Ten Commandments came the rejection of
stealing, swearing and adultery; from the Pauline
tradition came the suppression of sexuality and from
the Methodist tradition the idea of cleanliness
being next to godliness. From the by now well
established industrial discipline there flowed the
virtues of punctuality, obeying authority and self-
discipline. Some historians have suggested that
these standards were somehow imposed on the working
class child by external agencies, particularly
schools. Stephen Humphries argued that one of the
purposes of state education in the last decades of
the nineteenth century was the amelioration of
certain working class social problems 'through an
infusion of the bourgeois values such as hard work
discipline and thought'.[13] It is obvious that
schools, churches and the work place did reinforce
these values but it must be emphasised that these
standards had become, by the last quarter of the
nineteenth century, internalised within the working
class and were transmitted from generation to generation principally through the family. This chapter

examines how these values were transmitted and some
of the effects they had on the individual and on
family and working class life in general.

II

The ways in which children learned their standards
were complex and varied to some extent from family
to family. They learned through a mixture of pre-
cept, example, exhortation, reward and punishment,
and through the absorbing of unspoken but powerful
assumptions. Virtually all working class children
were expected to do as they were told by parents
(no exceptions have been found to this generalisa-
tion), and to conform to the parents' externally
imposed standards and rules. Obedience was the
prime virtue to be encouraged among the young.[14]
(This tradition did not disappear with the arrival
of the twentieth century and was much discussed by
sociologists in the 1950s and 1960s).[15] There
appears to have been no difference within the
working class between the skilled and unskilled in
their belief in the importance of child obedience.
Some contemporary observers and later historians
believed that there was. Alexander Paterson wrote,
'Parental discipline is in fact a sure sign of
prosperity or respectability.'[16] John Gillis
accepted this judgement: 'Obedience on the part of
the children was regarded as an especially important
status symbol.'[17] Standish Meacham wrote 'Segre-
gation was implied in the strict disciplinary
standards imposed upon working class children in all
but the most disreputable households.'[18] It is not
easy to define 'most disreputable' but it is clear
from the oral evidence (which included that of some
very rough families) that child obedience was always
expected and child disobedience invariably punished.
     Children were not of course angels and from
time to time either wilfully or unintentionally
transgressed their parents' rules or fell below the
expected standard of behaviour. The ways the mis-
demeanours were dealt with varied depending on the
perceived seriousness of the offence and on the
severity of the parents. Some children were never
physically chastised at all. Mrs W. came from a
family of fifteen and she said: 'I don't think any
of us ever got hit ... He just used to speak to us
and that was all.'[19] Unlike Mrs W., Mr S. was
more afraid of his mother than his father, 'Odd
times we might have been a bit thoughtless. She
should say, "Now that wasn't a wise thing to do. You

5

want to think a bit more." and she would point at
you just like that and that was enough. If you
merited a thick ear you got it. It wasn't half
measure, it was full weight'.[20] This reliance on
the reprimand, supported by an occasional blow, was
the most usual pattern. Some children were physically beaten frequently but these were a minority.
Mr T.'s father was a soldier and later a docker,
and in reply to a question about his strictness
replied, 'Very strict, there's many a time he's
kicked me under the table'.[21] (Robert Roberts
claimed that ex-regulars from the army or navy had
a bad reputation for the treatment of their children).[22] Other children were hit with sticks, cats
o' nine tails, belts and fists but it would be quite
wrong to suggest that the majority of working class
children were physically hammered into submission
by their parents. They were not. Paul Thompson,
surveying the national picture, wrote, 'The strictness of Edwardian parents did not necessarily imply
abundant physical punishment as is often believed.
It is not true that families in which children were
given a good hiding were common. The truth is that
they did not need to because their authority was
rarely openly challenged.'[23]

Many aspects of working class life cannot be
easily understood without a realisation that this
habit of obedience to parental wishes continued to
dominate the lives of working class children,
through youth to adulthood. Writing of working
class youth, Paul Thompson concluded, 'It is equally
striking how few children recall any systematic
challenge to their parent's authority at this stage
... It would seem that ... the habits of deference
towards parents acquired in the first years of life,
years of real and complete physical and emotional
dependence upon parents, could long out last the
power basis on which they were built.'[24] These
habits of deference and obedience towards parents
affected the working class child's schooling, his/
her job and even his/her adult life.

III

The standards to which children needed to conform,
the rules they were to obey have already been out-
lined, but it is also useful to examine their effect
on children's and young people's lives in more
detail. There was a very great emphasis on cleanliness, in the visible parts of the body, in top
clothes and in the home itself. Hands, faces and

necks had to be scrubbed; boys often wore white
celluloid collars (which inflicted very nasty burns
when 'accidentally' set alight) and girls very often
had immaculate white starched needlework pinafores.
Shoes and clogs were polished until they shone.
Houses too were scrubbed and polished; mothers spent
a vast amount of time and effort in boiling, mang-
ling, starching and ironing clothes and lace
curtains. Floors were scrubbed, mats beaten, metalwork polished, grates black-leaded, windows polished,
and steps were donkey stoned.

As a result of all this effort people and homes
may have looked clean but this cleanliness was more
apparent than real, since the immense difficulties
women had in heating and lifting tubs of water meant
that the thorough and frequent washing of both
bodies and underclothes was almost impossible. No
one remembered being washed more than once a week,
and thick top clothes (like trousers, jumpers, coats
and skirts) were washed even more infrequently.
Respondents and Medical Officers of Health alike
reported problems with fleas and head and body lice.
Following the 1907 Education (Medical Inspection)
Act data were collected on a national scale on the
state of both children's health and their cleanliness. Dr George Newman's first report as Chief
Medical Officer in 1910, recorded 30 to 40 percent
of children as having unclean heads or bodies.[25]

The almost total absence of bathrooms in working class homes before 1914 presented not only great
practical problems for the parents but also something of a moral dilemma. The rules of respectability were clear on nakedness; it was forbidden!
Consequently bath nights became a very complex
organisational feat when brothers and sisters were
not allowed to catch glimpses of each other (or,
even worse, their parents) in the bath tub. Decades
of Victorian puritanism had produced by the turn of
the century a generation of working class parents
who were extremely prudish about all aspects of sex
and sexuality. Some respondents were brought up in
such an inhibited atmosphere as children that as
parents they themselves found it difficult to discuss any sexual matter with their children. In
answer to the question 'Did your mother ever talk to
you about the facts of life?' Mrs W. replied 'You
just found out yourself and it was far better. Some
of these kids are being taught so much that they try
out what it is ... The only time I talked to B (her
daughter) was about her periods ... I expect she
found out at school.'[26] Another Preston woman,

asked the same question, replied, 'Nanny wouldn't speak like that because she was such a good living woman.'[27]

It is truly astonishing that in such small houses, so frequently overcrowded, working class children remained so uninformed and so naive about sexual matters. Mothers' pregnancies continued to be unremarked, or indeed unnoticed, even by quite old children. Mrs M.'s brother was away in the First World War when his mother became pregnant. On a holiday at home he remarked 'You want to get yourself a new skirt Mum, your figure's gone terrible.' His sister remarked 'He didn't know there was a baby on the way, he was 19 nearly.'[28]

And yet children, in emergencies, did become involved in confinements and their ignorance made the experience traumatic for them and was subsequently resented.

> Do I remember her having them? Don't mention it. I always remember mother but they always hid it from you. M'father had gone to work, and I'd be only about 10 or 11 ... and I had to run over for the midwife. I put a coat on top of m'nightie and I can just remember m'mother sitting on the bed with a towel pulling in the moans. As a child 'Oh m'mother's going to die.' Then we were put out of the road and we didn't get to know anything after that. My mother was awful, she never told us anything.'[29]

There are examples of ignorance of pregnancy and childbirth continuing into young adulthood for although respondents remember being told something about sex by contemporaries, it was sometimes surprisingly inaccurate. More than one young married woman found herself pregnant and expected the baby to be born through her navel. James Walvin overestimates the knowledge of sex gained by Victorian and Edwardian children: 'The sexual realities of adult life were inescapable ... for the poor sexuality was a feature of every day life.'[30] The ignorance recalled by so many respondents not only as children but as young adults too, would cause one drastically to question this conclusion

Girls of course had to be told something about menstruation. Many mothers forced themselves through what appears to have been a dreadful ordeal only once. They told their eldest daughter and expected her to see that the younger girls knew in turn. By their silence or alternatively by their curious lists of 'taboo' activities during menstruation (like not washing your hair or having a bath), mothers undoubtedly imparted to many girls a feeling of repugnance about this natural function, a feeling that it was something shameful. Girls tended to develop feelings of being unclean and of somehow at risk whenever they were unwell.

> We would probably have two or three pairs of
> knickers on, especially when we were unwell ...
> that was horrible work.
> Did you have to wash pieces of cloth?
> Yes we had proper towelling.
> Was she particular about not letting your
> brothers see?
> Oh yes, you hadn't to tell anybody or you
> hadn't to let anybody else see anything. Every-
> thing was kept out of the road.[31]

Examples can be found of the medical profession reinforcing these negative attitudes to menstruation. One Barrow woman related how she was excused school on medical grounds because of menstruation when she was twelve in 1901. 'The doctor gave mother a note, "Keep her at home because she is no sooner there than she's off"'. Carol Dyhouse examined medical views of menstruation and wrote, 'There was a view that during puberty the growing girl needed to establish a regular menstrual cycle. If this was not achieved because of energy being diverted into intellectual pursuits it was believed that permanent damage could be done to her repro-ductive system.'[32]

Not only was frank discussion of sexual matters seen to be undesirable for its own sake, but under-lying parental inhibitions about such matters as pregnancy and menstruation was the fear that girls might become pregnant before marriage and thus en-danger not only their own, but also their family's respectability. Whilst, however, the working class universally frowned upon premarital sex and claimed to be horrified by premarital pregnancies, there were interesting variations in attitudes, firstly about the relative degrees of responsibility for pregnancies between males and females, and secondly towards an actual, as opposed to a hypothetical, pregnancy. At one end of the spectrum was the burning of an effigy of a young man who had got a girl 'into trouble' while at the other was the public stoning of a pregnant girl as she walked to

church to be married. Some families accepted an
illegitimate child with love, but at the other
extreme there were cases of pregnant unmarried girls
killing themselves.

All families went to considerable trouble to
ensure that neither their sons nor their daughters
put themselves into situations which could be
morally dangerous. Particular emphasis was placed
on the importance of coming in at a proper time of
night. As will be seen from Mrs S.'s evidence, it
was not always the girls who were shamed for being
out late (although some terrible punishments were
inflicted on some who stayed out past the set time).

> Was she stricter than your father?
> Well m'father, he didn't have a lot to do with
> us really, I mean he was at work all day. It
> was mother really that brought us up. I always
> remember a young man, he was a fisherman, and I
> met him like, I mean to say we were very
> friendly, and there wasn't a right lot in it
> you know, but he brought me home and I was at
> the corner of the street you know saying ...
> just having a few words with him. My mother
> come to the corner of the street, she said,
> 'Come on, get yourself in. He's no better than
> he ought to be to keep you out after nine
> o'clock.' Nine o'clock! And when I was going
> to be married, this is gospel. When I was
> going to be married, I was twenty-three, and
> my husband and I went up to see his brother to
> tell them that we were going to be married and
> invite them to the wedding. I was rather late,
> and my mother was sick in bed. You know she
> died a month after I was married. I came in at
> night, I opened the door and he came in with me
> and my mother shouted downstairs. 'What time
> do you call this coming in. You know he's no
> better than he ought to be for keeping you out
> in hours like this.' You know, very, very
> strict.33

Not only were girls instructed 'not to get into
trouble' but so too were boys. Mrs M. was the young-
est of a big family, some of whom grew up before
1914.

> I've seven brothers and there wasn't one had to
> be married. I mean they'd know you know.
> He used to tell them about it did he?
> He'd have killed them. No, I mustn't say that,

> he must have told them and he would have
> mur.... you know, he would have seen there'd
> have been no shennakins. There wouldn't have
> been no flying their kites and then changing
> their minds. They'd have had to marry the
> girl, if she'd been good enough to do that
> with, she'd have been good enough to marry and
> that would have been dad's lot.[34]

The success of this parental strictness appears to
have had the desired effects if the illegitimacy
rates both for the local area and for the nation are
studied. The national figure in the period 1890-
1914 never reached five percent and was frequently
below four percent. It is impossible to know in
what percentage of couples the girl was already
pregnant when married, but the oral evidence would
suggest that it was not high, (only four out of 170
respondents said that either they or their mothers
were pregnant before marriage, although it is
obvious that others might well not have known the
truth about their parents unless wedding anniver-
saries were kept.)[35]

Respectability not only meant avoidance of
nudity, discussion of sexual matters and avoidance
of sexual activity outside marriage, but also avoidance of swearing, fighting and stealing, all of
which were regarded as forms of rough behaviour.
Whatever men may have said at work, swearing was not
permitted in the home. One old man from a very poor
home said, 'I never swear, even to this day. I
thought it fouled your mouth ... Never heard anything at all from us. If we did we would get a
rattle across the puss, it would do us good.'[36]
Robert Roberts too recalls that even in the roughest
families in the roughest of areas, there were considerable inhibitions about using bad language
especially in the home.[37]

Children did of course fight, especially boys,
but if they were discovered they could be sure of
parental disapproval. Respectable people did not
steal either, for were they not continually told how
wrong this was by their own standards reinforced by
the churches and the law? It is very difficult to
estimate to what extent working class children were
involved in theft or, if they were, whether or not
they regarded it as theft. There are no examples
in the oral evidence of respondents being involved
in house or shop breaking, or pickpocketing. Indeed
there were very few court cases involving juvenile
theft; Stephen Humphries suggests that the figure

rarely exceeded 0.5 percent per annum in any district.[38] He also suggests that the low rates of prosecution grossly underestimated the true amount of juvenile theft.

There is certainly an ambivalence about theft in many respondents. As is obvious from the oral and documentary evidence there was very considerable poverty in working class families and many had to develop strategies which would expand the family income with either goods or cash. Many families, especially outside the big cities, developed a variety of ways of living off the land, such strategies being invariably carried out by the males of the family. The produce thus acquired was usually consumed by the family but the surplus would be sold for profit. Many of these traditional activities had been carried out within families for generations and were not of course illegal. The most common form of living off the land was growing fruit and vegetables on a rented plot of land and this was clearly a legal activity. There, of course, were many other forms of living off the land, some of which were legal, and others illegal. Respondents well knew which came into which category but the law's apparent *moral* ambivalences were reflected in the attitudes of some respondents. It was legal, for example, to take eels from the River Lune, but not salmon; it was legal to take fruit from hedgerows but not from orchards; it was not legal to catch rabbits but most landowners welcomed this form of pest control, while prosecuting those who took game birds. Collecting manure from the streets for the allotment was legal, but collecting coal from coalyards was not. The vast majority of respondents and their children clearly understood the differences between what was legal and what was not and did not indulge in the latter. But this was not true of every family and it was in these rather grey areas that illegal practices of living off the land can be found. It is doubtful if the families who carried these out regarded them as theft and there is absolutely no evidence to suggest that the salmon and rabbit poachers ever considered serious crimes, such as housebreaking. It is not surprising that working class people were not prepared to label themselves as thieves, but it is significant that when discussing *others* who partly lived illegally off the land, respondents do not condemn them as thieves either. (This cannot be attributed to a reluctance to condemn crime or sin; such condemnations are all too frequent in other circumstances).

Stephen Humphries described these various illegal activities thus: 'It is significant that many people described their illegal activities as traditional customs ... all of which conveyed a belief in time honoured rights in opposition to property law'.[39] The local evidence does reveal an attachment to traditional custom but says little about opposition to property law. In conclusion it must be emphasised that although some families were driven by poverty to illegal actions, the majority continued to live off the land in a perfectly legal way.

Being respectable implied of course that one was worthy of respect and that in turn one respected other people. Children learned from parental exhortation and examples the duty of helping kin and neighbours' errands were run, babies minded, all kinds of help were given. Many children did their tasks either because they wanted to, or because it was expected of them. Others (usually unbeknown to their parents) did small tasks in the expectation of reward. Whether the child was calculative or generous, they were all learning the duty of helping neighbours. This lesson was well learned and mutual help continued to be an important function of working class neighbourhoods well into this century. There is little evidence, however, that adults expected such direct rewards as did the next respondent as a child.

> There was things that they would deem as important. An elderly person would insist on you doing a job for them without a reward. Sometimes you would see somebody standing on the step and you knew if she was standing on the step she wanted something doing so you didn't go that way, you went the other way.
> Neighbours, not a relation?
> Neighbours. Some of them you would knock and ask if they wanted anything because there was something about them, they were good.
> When you asked if they wanted a job, did they always give you something?
> They would give you a piece of cake or a bit of bread and jam.
> Did you go because you wanted to help or because you wanted the bread and jam?
> This was the inducement to go.[40]

Respect was not only due to the living but to the dead as well. The Victorian and Edwardian child,

innocent about sex, was very knowledgeable about
death. From their parents and neighbours (but probably rather less from improving books)[41] children
learned about the inevitability, frequency and
indeed naturalness of death. Between one fifth and
one quarter of all respondents experienced the death
of a sibling before they were fourteen (many more
babies and children died in the families concerned
but some did so before the birth of the respondents
themselves). The frequency with which children
encountered death tended to reinforce the fatalism
so often found in working class people of these
generations; the attitudes of 'what is to be is to
be...' and 'It's God's will'. Standish Meacham
wrote,'Many resorted to a kind of fatalism.'[42] It
was difficult to make plans or attempt to organise
one's life when death was such an ever present
threat. It is only rarely that one finds the death
of a child met with anger rather than a fatalistic
acceptance. Mrs G. remembered her father railing
against the death of a son and associating the
tragedy very directly with the social conditions of
the working class.

> He was a Socialist and a Trade Unionist and he
> told us what was wrong and what was right ...
> I remember him taking us up to the cemetery (to
> see the dead brother's grave). He said (over
> the grave) 'All you children what a future
> you've got ... Distinction, class distinction,
> unemployment, ... exploitation, ... how we were
> exploited.'[43]

This kind of outburst was totally unusual; death was
usually greeted with grief and acceptance but no
anger, no questioning. Miss T. was twelve when her
father died. 'He died a very good death, and when
he was dying he called them all round ... all of us
..., and said that if he'd ever done anything to
hurt us, or anything that was wrong, would we forgive him, and ask God to forgive him, and pray for
him when he was dead.'[44]

IV

Working class children and young people did not only
learn their families' *mores*, they also learned much
about their individual, familial and indeed their
class economic and financial status. They learned
from an early age that they were members of the
working class and grew up with that indelible self-

image. In conjunction with this they learned much
about poverty, budgeting and financial management.
The learning about their class and financial status
was obviously interconnected and began at an early
age.

Small children did not of course think of themselves as poor, but they knew from an early age that
little of anything should be wasted and that items
like bought toys were luxuries to be expected, if at
all, at Christmas. (Birthday presents were almost
unknown). One respondent, interviewed early in the
project, remembered being given a toothbrush by her
parents for her birthday. At the time I believed
this to be an indication of poverty. Subsequently
I recognised it as a sign not only of prosperity but
also of progressive thought; very few working class
people before 1914 had toothbrushes.

Children learned to improvise toys from
rubbish: footballs from old paper and rags, bats
from old pieces of wood; and traditional street
games required little if any equipment - endless
versions of hide and seek, races, chasing and gues-
sing games. Perhaps more significantly for their
adult futures, children daily witnessed their
mother's battles to make ends meet and to balance
her budgets. As they grew they were expected to
help in making something out of nothing - most sym-
bolically the winter's peg rug making, when the
whole family converted old sacks and old clothes
into a rag rug. Children did a substantial part of
the family's shopping and thus learned a lot about
budgeting. Some went to the cooperative shops and
learned the importance of the dividend whose growth
was visibly demonstrated by the ever increasing pile
of 'checks' stuck on the spike at home. Others
bought 'faded' fruit - fruit with the damaged parts
cut out and all learned where to find a good bar-
gain. Children from the poorest homes learned the
exact and sharp nature of their families' poverty by
having to ask for credit. Mothers presumably
thought shopkeepers would deal more sympathetically
with a child asking for credit than with an adult.
Respondents look back at the pre First World War
credit system with rather different views. Some
have sympathy for the shopkeepers whom they felt
were frequently swindled by their more dishonest/
impoverished customers who never settled their debts
and who regularly 'disappeared'. A large number
remember with bitterness the 'Belly Bibles' in which
their families' debts were recorded. They still
believe that the little corner shops which gave

credit made a fortune out of charging high prices
and cheating their customers by keeping inaccurate
records. One old woman said with considerable
bitterness about her local shopkeeper, 'I never
forgot her cheating me.'45 Rather fewer families
went to the pawnbroker's as compared to the shops
which offered credit. It was unusual for a child to
go on behalf of the family, and only a tiny minority
remember doing this. Usually mothers went, or
alternatively used a 'runner' who, for a small fee,
took several families' bundles, thus saving them
the embarrassment, or even disgrace of being seen
entering the pawnbroker's.

V

As children learned various ways of balancing the
family's budget they were learning, simultaneously,
about work. Fathers (and in textile families
mothers) worked a 55½ hour week before 1914, and
were obviously absent for long hours each day at
work. Mothers at home rarely ceased from their endless round of domestic toil. Children very soon
realised that just as their families belonged to the
working class so too they, as individuals, belonged
to a working social unit, the family. There was no
obvious division between the world of childhood and
the adult world of work. It was however, for
obvious reasons the world of domestic work which
first impinged upon children. It is difficult to
think of any household task which was not done by
some child in some family, at some time. Children,
according to their age and aptitude, were expected
to carry out a wide range of tasks. They learned
not only the importance of hard work if the family
was to be fed, clothed and kept clean, but also that
they, as individuals, had a vital role to play in
that work.

Did this work in any way condition working class
children into their adult roles? Certainly they
grew up with a belief in the value and importance
of work. It is also possible to trace the conditioning of girls into a female role and boys into a
male role. Obviously all children who had both
parents absorbed the model of father going out to
work and being the provider, while mother stayed at
home and was the manager. Even in the minority of
families where mother worked full-time (and she was
unlikely to work on this basis throughout a child's
life) she still carried the ultimate responsibility
for feeding and clothing the family and for keeping

it clean. Although in some families (especially where there were only boys) there was no obvious differentation between boys' and girls' tasks; in other families there were clear differences between the boys' roles and those of the girls. While girls acted as their mothers' apprentices or even their substitutes, boys were more likely to be out of the house doing the shopping, helping with the allotment or accompanying male members of the family on some expedition like walks, fishing trips or food gathering forays.

> You were saying about going out for long walks. Did the girls ever go out for these long walks or was it just the boys?
> No. The girls never seemed to go out for walks they were always busy sewing and one thing and another.[46]

It was usually assumed that boys would lead this freer, less home bound existence, but it was sometimes deliberate parental policy. One father, with five daughters and one son, said, 'I'm not having him growing up a cissy with all these females', and while insisting he helped with the cleaning also took him himself for long walks.[47] In other families not even a minimum of household work was expected from the boys.

> Did she expect the boys to do anything about the house?
> She didn't. She wasn't having her boys Mollies, she expected me to do everything, and I did.[48]

Mrs A.'s mother had very bad knees and the girls had to help:

> We all had our certain work, one would have the brasses to clean, and one would do the washing up ... we all had our work to do. We always had summat to do every night, each one of us.
> Did she make the boys do the same as the girls?
> Well the boys went out playing football and she didn't seem to bother with the boys. They used to chop the wood and fetch the coal in ... that was their work.

It is interesting that Mrs A. assumed that when speaking of 'all' in connection with housework she actually meant all the girls.[49]

While boys were learning, probably subconsciously, that their role was out in the world as a 'provider', girls were absorbing the message that their place was in the home; some enjoyed their domestic work, others disliked it. They were not of course simply learning their future roles, they were also absorbing a vast amount of practical knowledge, which would be of great practical value when they themselves became housewives and mothers. They acquired both confidence in the handling of small children and babies and they also learned to refer to mother (or her substitute) for advice in child rearing. Working class mothers can be contrasted with middle class ones as portrayed by Patricia Branca in *Silent Sisterhood*, the latter presumably being denied, by the presence of servants, the opportunity of bringing up small relatives when children themselves, and as adults appearing to rely a good deal on the advice offered in women's magazines. Working class women were more confident and relaxed but less free to innovate, being circumscribed both by the advice and example handed on by their mothers.

Contemporary observers and historians have not been in agreement about the value of this early training of both boys and girls in household work. Helen Bosanquet was enthusiastic about the value of domestic tasks for children. 'Little duties about the house, little services to other members of the family are possible from a very early age and contribute far more than any direct teaching can do to make the child realise how social life depends on mutual helpfulness.'[51] Possibly this observation was true *when* the duties remained little ones, but the burden of work and responsibility undertaken by some children, more especially girls, was very heavy and they appear to have had little childhood. Life was all work with little time for play or relaxation. Mrs G. said of her sister 'One had to do all the work, and that was the eldest one. She was a slave really and had to help.'[52]

In examining working class parents' attitudes to children, one is constantly surprised to see how much was expected in the way of work and responsibility. This assumption of adult responsibilities by children was an old tradition and has been commented upon by Pinchbeck and Hewitt. Although their comments apply to an earlier period they would still seem appropriate for late Victorian and Edwardian England. 'Children were expected to accept the hardships of life at a very tender age and at the

earliest opportunity to accept the responsibilities
of the adult.'[53]

VI

It was these working class attitudes and assumptions
which greatly perturbed an increasing number of
philanthropists and social reformers in the nineteenth century. These 'child-savers', inspired by
such writers as Wordsworth and Rousseau, saw the
child as an innocent being requiring protection and
indeed isolation from the cruelties and hardships of
the adult world. Increasingly young people also
came to be included in this group which required
special protection, guidance by, and total dependence upon, caring adults.
     This group of child-savers worked firstly to
keep children out of undesirable employment,
especially at a young age, and secondly to get and
keep them in schools for longer and longer periods.
By 1900 this group had an impressive array of
legislation to its credit; children were excluded
from the mines, the ages at which they could begin
and the hours worked in the mills were restricted,
and by 1899 the compulsory school leaving age was
fourteen (although there were several areas of
exemptions). This important movement of social reform has been extensively written about but rather
less has been heard from those who were the recip-
ients of the legislation.
     Working class poverty is a constantly recurring
theme in any study of the socialisation of working
class children and youth. Poverty obviously affected working class parents' attitudes to their
children working. In the presence of large
families and the absence of servants, children
obviously had to undertake many household tasks.
Because parental incomes were low, it was vital in
many families for children to earn wages as soon as
they were able. Added to these financial impera-
tives was of course the working class devotion to
the work ethic, which made work seem morally valuable for its own sake. Rowntree wrote 'The importance attaching to the earnings of the children in
the families of the poor, reminds us how great must
be the temptation to take children away from school
at the earliest possible moment in order that they
may begin to earn.'[54] It is clear that later
Victorian and Edwardian parents welcomed their
children's earnings and this undoubtedly produced at
best unenthusiastic attitudes towards continuing

education for working class youth. Legislation
whether about working conditions or compulsory
education did not of course prevent children from
working. It is clear that many children (possibly
as many as one third in the North West), almost
always boys, worked part-time out of school for
wages from as young as nine years. This estimate
comes from oral evidence and accords with that of
Reginald Bray who in 1910 calculated that 25 percent
of London children had jobs outside of school
hours.[55] This evidence contrasts sharply with that
of a report in 1908 which found only nine percent of
children working outside school hours.[56] Standish
Meacham regards this as an underestimate[57] as was
indeed that of the Schools' Medical Officer of
Health for Lancaster.[58]

Many of the boys were involved in some aspect
of the retail trade and will be familiar to readers
of Charles Booth and Robert Roberts: 'Well before
they left school, boys from the undermass had been
working part-time in shops or as street traders of
some sort.[59] What is notable about these young
part-time workers is their belief that they were
playing a valuable and important role in the economy of their families. One boy who delivered meat
in Barrow was partly paid with a joint and sausages
and he firmly believed that he was feeding his
family from Sunday to Tuesday every week.[60] A
Lancaster man cheated his employer (though not very
seriously), but justified his actions on the grounds
of providing essential help for his family.

> I used to count eggs coming in from the farm-
> ers. The farmers' wives used to come in with
> baskets of eggs. He used to say, 'Will you
> come and count Mrs. Jackson's eggs, Ernie?'...
> I used to say 'So many dozen and half a dozen
> chipped ones'. What I used to do, the large
> ones, I used to catch them on the side of the
> box. 'The old horse's done some jogging this
> morning!' ... I'd put any eggs away ...
> Did he give you the eggs?
> I got them cheaper, ... I thought I was doing
> something great for home, for mother.[61]

Part-time work usually meant that the boy worked for
a few hours a week, but it could mean in extreme
cases a virtually full-time job on top of his schooling. The most exploitative job and one regarded as
such by the respondents was selling newspapers.

> I started at 6 a.m. and met the newspaper
> train. After sorting out bundles of papers I
> set out on my round ... and then back to the
> station to run alongside the trains to sell
> papers, cigarettes and sweets. I was set free
> at 8.50 to go to school ... After school I had
> tea and then back to Hymans finishing at 8 p.m.
> Saturday I would go 6 to 1.30 and 3 to 8, which
> was a weekly total of 42½ hours outside school
> ... After about 2 months my mother ended the
> job as she said I was costing more in shoe
> leather than I got in wages.[62]

He claimed he earned only threepence a week which
seems incredible but the same earnings were reported
by a Preston newspaper seller. However small their
wages, children were proud of their achievement and
acutely aware that every penny counted in their
mothers' budgeting. One girl who worked all day
Saturday in the market earned one shilling and added
'I was keeping the house with that shilling.'[63]
     While the exploitation of these children is
obvious in many cases and cannot be ignored, neither
can the feeling of pride and achievement so frequently expressed. The entry of many boys into a
full-time job in the adult world of work was eased
by their experiences as part-time workers from an
early age. Historians have commented upon the dis-
tancing between parents and children, indeed between
almost all adults and children.[64] But it is also
clear that there was an absence of intergenerational
conflict. One of the reasons for this relative
harmony could be the lack of distinction between the
world of working class childhood and the adult world
of work.

VII

It is clear that the majority of working class
parents (and consequently their children) did not
have a deep attachment to education, or any great
confidence in its advantages. There is some evidence that in the years immediately after the introduction of compulsory state education in 1876, there
was parental opposition to it. In London some
parents regarded compulsory education as a threat to
themselves because it prevented their children working for wages.[65] The long struggle of London attendance officers to raise the attendance rates from
76.7 percent in 1876 to 88.2 percent in 1906 was
fought mostly with the poorest classes.[66] Oral

evidence, while not revealing overt working class hostility to the principle of education, especially for younger children, (although there was some hostility towards individual teachers), certainly reveals a widespread attitude that apart from instilling the 3Rs education had little to offer the working class child.

Education was less important than family needs, and this attitude could affect the working class child's schooling in different ways. Firstly, children, and most especially girls, could be kept at home to help. A Preston woman spoke of her mother, 'She had to stay at home and look after ten children, therefore she could hardly read or write, ... she never went to school because she was just a little drudge.'[67] Mrs A. in Barrow said of her mother's confinements, 'M'father used to go and bring this lady and she used to come every morning just to wash the baby ... I'd stay at home and look after the others, m'dad and look after m'mother.'[68]

Secondly, and not surprisingly, there is little evidence of working class children either taking up the free places in grammar schools or staying on at school a day longer than was legally necessary. (In 1908 only 1.5 percent of fifteen to eighteen year olds were in grammar schools).[69] Grammar schools were rejected because they involved the cost of books and uniform and they implied that pupils would stay on at school until sixteen. From the oral history sample for the period before the First World War there are many examples of children either refusing even to bother taking the scholarship exam to the Grammar or Higher Grade Schools, or if they passed not telling their parents. One Barrow man commented

> I think about 6 got in (to the Grammar School) ... to me it was no good at all because we had no room to study at all. We had no light, we used to have a bit of a candle or a lamp. We didn't light the gas, because we couldn't afford it.
> Did your parents say they wanted you to go or did they not mind?
> They didn't know anything about it. I left school when I was 13 and I went as an errand boy at the Co-op.[70]

In a few cases parents wanted their children to go to the Higher Grade School but the children themselves, imbued with the work ethic, rejected this.

Mrs H. rejected her parent's pleas: 'I wanted to leave school, I wanted to go to work.'[71]

It is difficult to suggest that in the sphere of secondary education girls were treated more unfairly by parents than were boys. In fact the only respondent from the sample from the pre First World War period who enjoyed a grammar school education (and later training as a pupil teacher) was a woman. (The particular mother's determination to get her children to do well led her to open a parlour shop to finance their education and four out of five became teachers).[72]

The third result of working class attitudes to education was that many children left full-time schooling as soon as it was legally possible to do so. The school leaving age was raised to fourteen in 1899, but part-time exemptions were permitted under local bye-laws from the age of eleven for agriculture and from twelve under the Factory Acts, provided *either* a standard of efficiency was reached and a labour exam passed (the system which was used in Barrow and Lancaster), *or* a required number of school attendances had been achieved (the system used in Preston).

A very high percentage of respondents in Preston who finished at school before 1914, left as half-timers to work in the mills at twelve and started full-time work at thirteen. So did thousands of children in the textile areas of Lancashire and Yorkshire where families, despite many criticisms by social reformers, continued to exercise this right until after 1918 when it was abolished. As the editor of the *Preston Guardian* noted in 1911, Preston parents were not in favour of the law abolishing the half-time system.[73] It is clear from the oral evidence that the overriding concern of such parents was to get their children working and earning as soon as possible.

VIII

Not all children were of course half-timers; indeed, the great majority in the country as a whole were not. It is clear from statistics that the local tradition for a child to leave school the day he or she was fourteen was in fact a national trend. Figures demonstrate how very few children remained in school after their fourteenth birthday, the great majority preferring to be out at work.

Those who left school as rapidly as possible showed little or no resentment of the fact, but

Table 1.1: Percentage of age groups in full-time education in England and Wales, 1870 and 1902 [74]

Age	Year	
	1870	1902
10	40	100
14	2	9
17	1	2
19	1	1

simply an acceptance of the financial realities of life and of the paramountcy of their parents' decisions. Familial needs continued to be more important than individualistic concerns. Mr C. was a highly intelligent respondent, with several books to his credit, and I asked him if he would have liked to have stayed at school longer.

> I hadn't any choice in the matter ... there was one occasion when they were wanting an office boy in the Goods Department on the railway where my father worked and if I had applied for it there is no doubt that I would have got it. But it would have meant a drop in wages of about 4s a week and the money was wanted at home so I stayed on at the mill. I don't regret it.
> Why did you choose the mill?
> I didn't choose it. It was simply that I was old enough to go to work. The mill was the usual thing for children to go to. I followed the usual trend. [75]

Mr B. was sent by his father as a half-timer into the mill at twelve.

> When I was 12 my father said to me, 'Thou comes with me on Monday morning and I'll learn you to spin.' There was no dispute, no argument. 'Do as you're told.' I had to go and learn with him to spin. [76]

Mr S. started in the mill full-time at the age of thirteen and earned five shillings a week 'tenting', that is helping and learning from a weaver.

It was 6 to 5.30, five days a week and 6 to
12 on a Saturday.
Why did you choose to go into the mill?
I had no option. In fact when I was 13 the
teacher had asked three of the boys to ask
their parents if they could go in office jobs,
one at a solicitor's office and I was one of
them asked. Of course you would have to go in
your Sunday suit it you were doing that kind
of thing and mother said 'No you will have to
go in the mill'. That were that so I went in
the mill and I was there till 1916.
Would you have liked to have gone into an
office?
Looking back on it, no. I don't think I would.
Did your mother feel that she couldn't afford
the suit ... was that what bothered her?
It was definitely.[77]

IX

Observable throughout the nineteenth century,
amongst those who argued for a curtailment of working class children's participation in the labour
market, was not only a genuine concern for the
children's wellbeing but also a distinct fear that
an early entry into the world of work would lead to
the break up of the family and the growth of an independent and possibly delinquent youth. Charles
Bray, in 1857, wrote of working class girls, 'If
they had cause to be dissatisfied with the conduct
of their parents they would leave them.'[78] In the
same year J.S. Wright wrote, 'The going from home
and earning money at such a tender age has, as might
be expected, the effect of making the child early
independent of its parents.'[79] These fears of
youthful independence have been well documented and
discussed.[80]
    In Edwardian times there was a mass of writing
about the too early independence of working class
children and their loss of childhood innocence and
dependency. E.J. Urwick in 1904 wrote of 'aspects
of man-child in whom the natural instincts of a boy-
hood are almost overwhelmed by a feverish anxiety
to become a man.'[81] Alexander Paterson observed:
'The difference between a child and an adult is
everywhere regarded as one of degree rather than of
kind.'[82] These comments are simply representative
of many others. It is indeed possible to discover
examples of youthful independence in the sample; the

ten year old girl who against her father's wishes
left school and went to work full-time in 1893, the
twelve year old who had just started work and who
demanded (and received) the same share of meat and
fish as her parents, the boy who did not want to
work in the mill and so sabotaged his loom. Some
children, when once in work, began to criticise
their fathers' (but hardly ever their mothers') behaviour. There was more open flouting of certain
parental rules, notably those about the times for
coming in at night.

But individual examples of independent behaviour in certain circumstances, should not be
taken as indications of a generally independent
working class youth. Indeed, in view of their early
conditioning about the importance of obeying parents
and of making their contribution to the family's
well being, it would be unusual to find much real
independence, still less youthful rebellion. Young
workers may have earned a wage but this did *not* make
them financially independent. There was an old
tradition in Lancaster of all the family's wage
earners giving their wages, unspent, to mother, who
then decided how the income should be spent. Mr F.
spoke for virtually all the respondents, 'I can
always remember that my father always handed his
wage over and so did the rest of the family. I
never brought home my envelope opened. I brought
my children up the same way and they handed their
wages over.'[83] Young workers were given pocket
money at the rate of a penny in the shilling depending on the family's meanness/generosity. Even in
the days of very low prices it was difficult to be
independent on a few pence a week. In the sample
there are no cases of a young worker refusing to
hand over his/her wages.

At the workplace the young worker was likely to
find him or herself either working for a member of
the family or for someone well known to the family.
This person regarded him or herself as acting *in loco
parentis* and was regarded as such by the young
worker. This had the advantage of encouraging their
relatively good treatment, but obviously inhibited
their independence. Mr G. went to work in 1915,
which is just out of the period covered by this book,
but his evidence demonstrates the long survival of a
custom first commented on by observers in the 1820s.
Neil Smelser quoted from them, 'It is fathers or
friends who work in factories and they all have a
common interest in checking immorality among the
younger assistants both boys and girls.'[84]

Presumably immorality could cover all kinds of un-
acceptable behaviour. Mr G. said, about the woman
who taught him weaving as a twelve year old, 'Well
it was my aunt. Then when I went full-time I worked
for two and the second one was a cousin of mine.
She was much older than I was ... Then I moved up
and I went with my father into the warehouse.'[85]
There are no examples either of unmarried young
workers leaving home to set up house independently,
except in some special cases. 'Few children desert-
ed their families, kin loyalty remained strong.'[86]
The exceptions were young girls who went away to be
living-in domestic servants, and young men who
joined the armed services or who went to do farm
service. In none of these cases would the young
person be described as having an independent existence and these absent children still contributed to
the family budget. In Barrow there were a large
number of young men who were migrants and who were
not living with their families: these, however,
tended to be older men in their twenties who, having
served an apprenticeship, were forced to move to
find a suitable skilled job.
Two girls in the Preston sample, who had very
difficult home circumstances, married very young,
but the average age of women at marriage was 25-26
years, which suggests that the great majority of
young people were living at home for a long period
after leaving school.[87] Even marriage did not
necessarily bring complete independence. Many young
couples were forced to live with in-laws for some
time as they had been unable to save much money for
a house of their own before marriage. Once married
they were not expected to hand over all their wages,
but to pay a set amount for board and lodging and
save the rest!
For the unmarried young person at home, there
was little moral independence, despite the flouting
of some rules already mentioned. The majority continued to live by their parents' rules and standards
which had by now become internalised as their own.
They accepted a significant degree of parental interference in their personal lives and many were
undoubtedly influenced in their choice of marriage
partner by their parents. The most extreme example
of this kind of interference discovered in the
sample was that of the grandmother of a Preston respondent.

> She was a real old battle-axe. She brought up
> 7 children, six daughters and one son, my

father. Her husband died when they were all
children ... My grandmother forbade her daughters to get married. Apparently she had had
such a very bad time herself bringing up a
family and also she had terrible trouble in
childbirth and she decided that her daughters
were not going to suffer as she had done and
she absolutely forbade her daughters to have
boyfriends or contemplate getting married. It
was alright for m'dad, no problem for him. On
the whole the maternal diktact was observed ...
one kicked over the traces, left home and got
married and she was the black sheep of the
family ... her name had not to be mentioned.[88]

And yet despite this lack of personal independence
and personal autonomy, working class youth were not
like their middle and upper class counterparts. They
were not shielded from the adult world. They were
forced to leave childhood behind, as contemporaries
observed, in their desperate hurry to become men and
women. But they were not adults in the full sense
of the word, they were adults only in their earning
power. It was poverty which so dominated the lives
of working class families.
    Finally, it is only if the deep abiding bond
between the working class child and his family is
understood, that the position of the young people in
a wider society can be understood. On one hand the
lessons of obedience, of conforming to the norms of
respectability and of understanding the family's
poverty tended to produce a conforming and conformist adult, frightened of being different, of being
socially ostracised, frightened of being too radical
at work in case of victimisation and the consequent
loss of wages and possibly a job. But on the other
hand working class children or young people were not
entirely conformist and conforming. If they believed that their family's standards, whether moral or
physical, were being directly threatened then they
could and did act. Schools' moral standards were
accepted as long as they reinforced those of the
home. If they did not they could be challenged,
usually by the parent and child acting together;
protests were made about unfair or excessive punishments (when compared to those prevailing in the
family). Later at work, the family's interests were
very important. This usually meant conforming
closely to the rules of the workplace and being
deferential to those in authority. But occasionally
a worker stood up for him or herself because he or

she felt their family to be threatened; Mrs H. stood up, for example, to a bullying tackler who was being difficult about repairing her loom, 'My mother couldn't afford to have my loom stopped ... It was urgent with my family at home that we had those looms going.'[89]

The working class child and youth in the late Victorian and Edwardian period was wholly part of the working class family. The bonds tying young and old together would only weaken with the decline of poverty and the weakening of the strong traditional *mores* which ruled working class life, and neither of these processes are observable until well after 1914.

NOTES

1. James Walvin, *A Child's World: A Social History of English Childhood 1800-1914* (Harmondsworth, 1982), pp.12-13. This is one of the few books which attempts a history of English childhood. It is a stimulating book but there are points of difference between Walvin's interpretation and my own. Some of these are indicated in the text and footnotes. There is a dearth of published material on working class childhood and this makes comparisons between areas rather difficult. For this reason it is not easy to say whether or not my own empirical evidence is applicable to a wider area. References are made to work on other areas where possible. I. Pinchbeck and M. Hewitt, *Children in English Society*, II, *From the Eighteenth Century to the Children's Act, 1948* (London, 1973) is a fascinating account of children's lives, particularly as they appear in official documents. It complements this chapter which is essentially about the view the working class had of themselves and their lives.

2. University of Lancaster, Oral History Collection, S.S.R.C. funded projects, Elizabeth Roberts, 'The Quality of Life in Two Lancashire Towns 1890-1930', (1974-6); 'Working class social life in Preston 1890-1940', (1978-81) (hereafter E.R.). In a short chapter there is not the opportunity to develop an analysis of the use of oral material by historians. A comprehensive and useful survey of the achievements and possibilities of oral

history can be found in Paul Thompson, *The Voice of the Past: Oral History* (Oxford, 1978).

3. Helen Bosanquet, a member of the Charity Organisation Society, based her book on the case study notes made by members of the society when visiting working class London families.

4. Philip McCann (ed.), *Popular Education and Socialisation in the Nineteenth Century* (London, 1977), p.xi.

5. Stephen Humphries, *Hooligans or Rebels; An Oral History of Working-class Childhood and Youth (1889-1939)* (Oxford, 1981), p.61. This is essential reading for anyone interested in working class childhoods. Again there are differences of interpretation and analysis between Humphries' work and my own, notably on the question of how far working class children were involved in stealing (see below). However, we would both argue that working class children and their parents were aware of a serious cultural clash between their values and those of the middle classes.

6. M. Pember Reeves, *Round about a Pound a Week* (1913; repr. London, 1979); *Family Budgets, Being the Income and Expenses of Twenty-Eight British Households 1891-4* (London, 1896); D.N. Paton, J.C. Dunlop and E. Inglis, *A Study of the Diet of the Labouring Classes in Edinburgh* (Edinburgh, 1902); J. Oliver, 'The Diet of Toil', *The Lancet,* June 29, 1895.

7. Charles Booth, *Life and Labour of the People of London* (London, 1889); also E.P. Hennock, 'Poverty and Social Theory in England: the experience of the 1880's', *Social History,* 1, 1976.

8. B. Seebohm Rowntree, *Poverty: a Study of Town Life* (London, 1902), p.296.

9. Elizabeth Roberts, 'Working-class standards of living in Barrow and Lancaster 1890-1914', *Economic History Review,* xxx(2), 1977; Elizabeth Roberts, 'Working-class standards of living in three Lancashire Towns 1890-1914', *International Review of Social History,* xxvii(1), 1982.

10. Hugh McLeod, 'New Perspectives on Victorian Working-class Religion', (Unpublished History Workshop Paper, Sheffield, 1982); Robert Moore, *Pitmen, Preachers and Politics: The effects of Methodism in a Durham mining community* (Cambridge, 1974).

11. Standish Meacham, *A Life Apart: The English Working Class 1890-1914* (London, 1977), pp.26-9. This is essential reading and one of the best books on working class life in this period.

12. E.P. Thompson, *The Making of The English*

Working Class (Harmondsworth, 1968), pp.392-3.

13. Humphries, *Hooligans*, p.31; Walvin, *Child's World*, pp.183-5.

14. Walvin, *Child's World*, p.47.

15. M.L. Kohn, 'Social Class and Parental - Child relationship', in M. Anderson (ed.), *Sociology of the Family: Selected Readings* (Harmondsworth, 1971), pp.323-37.

16. Alexander Paterson, *Across the Bridge or Life by the South London Riverside* (London, 1911), p.16. This is one of several contemporary books written about the social conditions and problems of the Edwardian working class. Paterson's book is about working class men, women and children in south London. Books concentrating on the lives of boys and young men in London include R. Bray, *The Town Child* (London, 1907); R. Bray, *Boy Labour and Apprenticeship* (London, 1911); E.J. Urwick (ed.), *Studies of Boy Life in Our Cities* (London, 1904). A. Freeman, *Boy Life & Labour: The Manufacture of Inefficiency* (London, 1914), while drawing his evidence from Birmingham, displays the same concern about the welfare, education and job opportunities for working class youths as do the other writers.

17. John R. Gillis, *Youth and History: Tradition and Change in European Age Relations, 1770-Present* (London, 1974), p.120. This is a stimulating account of both working class and middle class youth and is again essential reading.

18. Meacham, *Life Apart*, p.160.

19. E.R., Mrs W.2.B., p.19. B.1889, father a shipwright, mother ran a fish and chip shop (with children's help). 15 children, 10 grew up.

20. E.R., Mr S.I.P., p.35. B.1900, father a horseman, mother in domestic service before and after marriage. 4 children.

21. E.R., Mr T.I.P. B.1897, father a soldier, then a docker. Mother a winder. 17 children born, 13 survived.

22. Robert Roberts, *The Classic Slum: Salford Life in the First Quarter of the Century* (Harmondsworth, 1973), p.45.

23. Paul Thompson, *The Edwardians: The Remaking of British Society* (London, 1975), p.60. This book uses as one of its sources interviews carried out with some 400 respondents throughout Great Britain. There are interesting and illuminating sections relating to Edwardian childhoods. Thea Thompson was also involved with this research project and describes parts of it in her book, *Edwardian Childhoods* (London, 1981), a collection of

memories of childhood in the respondens' own words.
       24. Paul Thompson, 'The War with Adults',
Oral History, 5(2), p.3.
       25. Board of Education, *Annual Report for 1910
of the Chief Medical Officer*, PP.1911.
       26. E.R., Mrs W.4.P., pp.43-4. B.1900, father
a bricklayer, mother went out cleaning. 10 children,
8 survived.
       27. E.R., Mrs W.I.P., p.37. B.1899, father a
stoker in the gasworks, mother dead and respondent
brought up by grandmother. 9 children, 8 survived.
       28. E.R., Mrs M.6.P., p.31. B. 1904, father a
docker, mother a weaver. 5 children, 4 survived.
Some historians have expressed scepticism about this
lack of knowledge on sexual matters in working class
children and young people. Given the overwhelming
oral evidence indicating ignorance, it is impossible
for me to do other than report it. It is possible
that in country areas, ignorance was not so widespread or profound: Arabella in T. Hardy, *June the
Obscure* could be mentioned in this context!
       29. E.R., Mrs G.1.B., p.3. B.1888, father a
fitter and turner. Mother no occupation outside
home. 16 children, 11 survived.
       30. Walvin, *Child's World*, p.135.
       31. E.R., Mrs M.3.P., p.45. B.1898, father a
docks' checker, mother a cleaner. 7 children, 3
survived.
       32. Carol Dyhouse, *Girls Growing up in Late
Victorian and Edwardian England* (London, 1982), ch.
iv. This book is principally concerned with middle
class girls, but does have some analysis of working
class girls' lives. It is very useful for comparisons between the different class approaches to the
education of girls.
       33. E.R., Mrs S.4.L., p.46. B.1896, father a
gravedigger, mother a washer woman. 9 children.
       34. E.R., Mrs M.3.L., p.17. B.1917, father a
fitter, mother died. 8 children.
       35. For a very thorough examination of ille-
gitimacy, see P. Laslett, R. Smith and K. Osterveen
(eds.), *Bastardy and its comparative history*
(Cambridge, 1980).
       36. E.R., Mr T.3.P., p.48. B.1886, father a
labourer, mother took in washing. 7 children, 4
survived.
       37. Roberts, *Slum*, p.57.
       38. Humphries, *Hooligans*, p.151.
       38. Humphries, *Hooligans*, p.151.
       40. E.R., Mr T.2.P., p.64. B.1908, father a
slasher's labourer, mother a weaver. 7 children, 5

survived.
    41. Walvin, *Child's World*, ch. 2.
    42. Meacham, *Life Apart*, p.199.
    43. E.R., Mrs G.I.B., p.9.
    44. E.R., Miss T.2.B., p.20. B.1888, father
a manager of the corn-mill, mother a cook after
being widowed. 13 children (including 8 step
sisters).
    45. E.R., Mrs S.3.P. in C.3.P., p.42. B.1892,
father a carder, mother a weaver. 8 children, 6
survived.
    46. E.R., Mr B.4.P., p.9. B.1896, father a
beatler (in the bleach works), mother a fowl dres-
ser. 10 children.
    47. E.R., Mrs P.I.L., p.105. B.1898, father a
foreman in the linoleum works, mother a housewife.
5 children, 1 died.
    48. E.R., Mrs P.2.P., p.49. B.1907, father a
sketching master in mill, mother a shopkeeper. 6
children, 4 survived.
    49. E.R., Mrs A.3.B., p.28. B.1892, father a
caretaker and boilerman, mother a washerwoman. 9
children, 7 survived.
    50. Patricia Branca, *Silent Sisterhood: Middle
Class Women in the Victorian Home* (London, 1978)
contains a description of the development of working
class attitudes to motherhood in ch. iv.
    51. Bosanquet, *The Family*, p.305.
    52. E.R., Mrs G.I.B., p.6.
    53. Pinchbeck and Hewitt, *Children*, II, p.368.
    54. Rowntree, *Poverty*, p.60.
    55. Bray, *Boy Labour*.
    56. Nettie Adler, 'Child Employer and Juvenile
Delinquency', in G.F. Tuckwell (ed.), *Women in
Industry* (London, 1908), p.132.
    57. Meacham, *Life Apart*, p.175.
    58. The Lancaster Schools' Medical Officer of
Health reported in 1911 that 260 boys and 24 girls
out of a total of 8,097 children were employed out
of school hours.
    59. Roberts, *Slum*, p.157.
    60. E.R., Mr M.I.B. B.1892, father a railway
labourer, mother a housewife. 12 children, 10 survived.
    61. E.R., Mr H.3.L., pp.1-2. B.1904, father a
blacksmith, later handyman, mother a weaver. 4
children.
    62. E.R., Mr I.I.L., p.2. B.1902, father a
fireman, mother a housewife. 3 children.
    63. E.R., Mrs A.2.B., p.6. B.1904, father a
boilermaker's holder-up, mother a domestic servant.

4 children.

    64. Meacham, *Life Apart*, pp.158-60.

    65. Gillis, *Youth*, pp.65-6.

    66. David Rubinstein, *School Attendance in London 1870-1904* (Hull, 1969), p.112, and ch.vii.

    67. E.R., Mrs C.3.P., pp.1, 4. B.1897, father unknown (Mrs C. was illegitimate), mother a weaver. 1 child.

    68. E.R., Mrs A.3.B., p.4.

    69. G.A.N. Lowndes, *The Silent Social Revolution* (Oxford, 1937), pp.78-90 and A.M. Halsey (ed.), *Trends in British Society since 1900* (London, 1972), p.163.

    70. E.R., Mr M.I.B., p.15.

    71. E.R., Mrs H.2.B., p.140. B.1885, father a carter, mother took in lodgers. 4 children.

    72. E.R., Mrs M.3.B., *passim*. B.1886, father a shipwright, mother a small shopkeeper. 10 children, 5 survived.

    73. *Preston Guardian*, June 4, 1910: see also Meacham, *Life Apart*, pp.172-3, and Harold Silver, 'Ideology and the factory child: attitudes to half-time education', in McCann (ed.), *Popular Education*.

    74. D.C. Marsh, *The Changing Social Structure in England and Wales, 1871-1961* (London, 1965), p.218.

    75. E.R., Mr C.I.P. pp.30-31. B.1884, father a railway worker (labourer to foreman), mother a weaver before marriage. 6 children, 4 survived.

    76. E.R., Mr B.8.P., p.2. B.1896, father a mule spinner, mother died. 6 children.

    77. E.R., Mr S.I.P., pp.13-14.

    78. Charles Bray, 'The Industrial Employment of Women', *Transactions of the National Association for the Promotion of Social Sciences*, 1857.

    79. J.S. Wright, 'Employment of women in the factories in Birmingham', *Transactions of the National Association for the Promotion of Social Sciences*, 1857.

    80. Victorian fear and anxieties about the independence of working class youth are examined and documented in, *inter alia*, Gillis, *Youth*; Frank Musgrove, *Youth and the Social Order* (London, 1964); Meacham, *Life Apart*.

    81. Urwick, (ed.), *Boy Life*, p.xii.

    82. Paterson, *Bridges*, p.38.

    83. E.R., Mr F.I.P., p.48. B.1906, father a poultry dresser, mother a washerwoman. 5 children.

    84. N.J. Smelser, *Social Change in the Industrial Revolution: An Application of Theory to the Lancashire Cotton Industry 1770-1840* (London, 1959),

p.190.

85. E.R., Mr G.I.P., p.2. B.1903, father had a variety of jobs in the mill, mother a weaver. 8 children, 6 survived.

86. Gillis, *Youth*, p.10.

87. These figures were calculated according to a formula given and used by J. Hajnal, 'Age at Marriage and Proportions Marrying', *Population Studies*, 7, 1953, pp.111-36.

88. E.R., Mr S.4.P., p.17. B.1915, father a pattern maker, mother a housewife. 2 children, 1 survived.

89. E.R., Mr H.I.P., p.9. B.1911, father and mother pub keepers. 15 children, 10 survived.

Chapter Two

HEALTH

F.B. Smith

I

Ten years ago an essay on 'Health' would have been
inconspicuously absent from a collection such as
this.   Traditional medical history presented as a
narrow inventory of great men and their deeds had
little to offer the student of the thoughts and
doings of the people or, indeed, their rulers.
Similarly, historians of sanitary reform had concentrated upon embattled heroes such as Edwin
Chadwick, and preoccupied themselves with legislative forms and administrative stratagems.   Their
studies proceeded upon the assumption that enact-
ments and orders worked in the manner in which they
were intended: the particular impacts of these
changes upon groups and localities over time remained generally unexplored.
     The traditions of celebratory medical inter-
vention and sanitary progress were plausibly joined
in the work of G. Talbot Griffith and M.C. Buer,
who published books in 1926 that were to remain
influential for fifty years.[1] They were deeply
impressed by the successes of British preventive
medicine, therapeutics and surgery during the Great
War, and by the triumphs of sanitary improvement
that had preceded it.   They retrojected those
successes back into the earlier nineteenth century,
heedless of chronology, and invoked medical prowess,
the growth of the voluntary hospitals and sanitary
reform to explain the fourfold increase of population since the Industrial Revolution. We now know,
thanks to the critical work of Professor Thomas
McKeown, that this interpretation is largely base-
less, although it retains its Old Believers among
economic historians, historical demographers, and
medical antiquarians. In fact, the doctors were

powerless to cure illness or specifically prevent disease, except in the case of smallpox. The hospitals had too few beds, about 12,000 in 1861,[2] to make much difference to the containment of infectious disease. From what we know of the hospitals before the implementation of antisepsis and asepsis in the 1880s, they did their patients little good. Similarly, sanitary improvement in the shape of domestic provision of safe water and milk to a majority of town populations, efficient disposal of sewage from all areas of the towns, the control, through bye-laws, of damp and access to air and sunlight in dwellings, and the protection of foodstuffs against contamination, did not become widely effective until the 1880s. The chronology of these developments precludes their having had any sizeable effect upon the increase of population in the century after 1760.

The doctors' contribution came in a different form. Many of them were in the vanguard of the local and central campaigns for better sanitary services. The true medical heroes of the nineteenth century are the medical officers of health and the numerous local general practitioners who courageously goaded local authorities into raising the rates and enforcing new sanitary bye-laws and standards. Their story has yet to be written.

Recently, historians have begun to weigh the life chances of individuals, families and occupational sets by analysing variations in morbidity and mortality through time, and by attempting to reconstruct lay and professional notions of health and ill-health, the pursuit of the first and the acceptance and management of the latter. It follows that the new history declares a new range of priorities, for historians at least: a concern with endemic, chronic illnesses and the relegation of epidemics.[3] This makes the historians' job harder: evidence about chronic illness is much more diverse, obscure and patchy than the relatively abundant, chronologically and aetiologically circumscribed, evidence for epidemics, replete with bizarre anecdotes. Nonetheless the inescapable priority is that during every twenty four months in the later nineteenth century more infants died from diarrhoeal infections than the whole mortality, about 140,000, from the four great cholera outbreaks which hitherto have preoccupied historians. (They have been really only preoccupied with the first, and not the worst one, of 1831-2 and this for its supposed impact upon the national political crisis and not as a mortality and morbidity crisis in itself).

It is odd that historians have been slow to explore such a controlling element in human experience as everyday health and ill-health, particularly when a distinguished line of investigators of current problems in community health, including Dr William Farr, Sir Arthur Newsholme, Dr G.C.M. McGonigle and Richard Titmuss had long furnished an agenda and a method.[4] The historians' slowness to ask fresh questions is sad testimony to the staying power of received ideas.

II

The years between 1880 and 1914 are the crucial ones in the great transition from the age-old pattern of mass morbidity and mortality occasioned by infectious diseases, poor nutrition and heavy labour, to the contemporary assemblage of functional disorders, viral disease and bodily decay associated with old age. Above all, this period covers the decisive fall in infant mortality and the emergence of the present dispensation, entirely novel, so far as we know, in the history of the world, under which death occurs preponderantly in later adult life. These changes represent the greatest improvement in life chances in British history, but historians have paid small attention to them. Marxists have consistently obscured the issue because diminished mortality rates and increased longevity among all classes under nineteenth century industrial capitalism fundamentally challenge assertions about the inevitable *verelendung* of the working classes. Right wing historians also distort the problem because they attribute the improvements, without showing how, to the providence of the market, whilst evading mention of public intervention and redistribution as necessary and beneficent mechanisms.

The putative causes of this transition are complicated and vary in their results by sex, class, age and locality. One leading cause is improvement of the environment. Its association with the dramatic reduction in mortality from typhus and typhoid fevers, for example, seems indisputable. Typhus is transmitted through body lice among people with low resistance resulting from poor nutrition and shelter. In the 1860s the London Fever Hospital is said to have admitted 2,000 cases a year.[5] By 1880 the incidence had fallen to 530 reported deaths in England and Wales and by 1914, with four deaths, it had ceased to be endemic in Great Britain.[6] Ireland, which was said to supply many of the victims in Britain, also showed an improvement over the same period from 934 deaths to 45.[7] The clearing of rat infested rookeries and dank, unsewered courts that proceeded in fits and starts from the mid 1870s must have done much to remove the condition under which the lice could flourish. The dislodgement of typhus represents a major amelioration in the life chances of the poor because the disease killed them at a rate of about one in four and left survivors debilitated and open to other life threatening infections. Well fed and sheltered victims, from what we know of contemporary cases, must have come through with less damage.[8]

The important point about the removal of damp and delapidated housing is that local authorities and private entrepreneurs were guided in their decisions to clear 'overcrowded' areas by the local mortality statistics. In this way relatively small outlays of money upon very small areas (although the numbers of people forced to shift without help with rehousing ran into tens of thousands) yielded great reductions in endemic, infectious diseases.[9]

The containment of typhoid fever depended upon the wider provision of safe domestic water and milk supplies and the change to more thorough systems of sewage and waste removal. Typhoid is conveyed in water, milk and food contaminated by the faeces and urine of patients and carriers. Its incidence declined as mains water supply developed and bye-laws governing the handling of milk and food were elaborated and enforced. These services in turn underpinned the increasingly familiar usage of personal cleanliness through washing with soap (although this change in behaviour is likely to have affected the incidence of contagious typhus and dysentery more nearly than water-borne typhoid). Soap consumption in the United Kingdom doubled from eight pounds per head in 1861 to 15.4 pounds in 1891, and declined slightly to reach about fifteen pounds per head in 1907, after which consumption levelled out. France, by contrast, was reported to consume one third less soap per head in 1881. The French continued to rely on perfume while the healthier English must have smelt of coarse soap.[10] Typhoid mortality in England and Wales declined dramatically. By 1906-10 it was down to 70 per million and represented 1,900 deaths over the four years, or a saving of over 4,000 lives per year as against 1875.[11] The crucial importance of effective sewage disposal and drainage systems is demonstrated by the typhoid mortality

Table 2.1: Typhoid mortality in England and Wales, 1875-1910

Years	Rate per million
1875	370
1881-5	210
1896-1900	110
1906-10	70

rates before and after reconstruction schemes: at Merthyr Tydfil, for instance, the rate fell from 215 per million to 86 per million and at Ely the rate was halved from 104 per million to 45 per million. This repulse of the disease, as with other infectious diseases during this period, was achieved without any useful development in therapeutics.

The general reduction of the typhoid rate proceeded despite the persistence of widespread 'overcrowding', meaning, according to the official definition, the occupation of a single dwelling unit by more than one family. In the Black Country over one fifth of the urban population was 'overcrowded'; on Tyneside it was one third. Overall, the number of persons per dwelling in England and Wales was reduced only very slowly and remained at 5.05 in 1911.[13] Nonetheless, it seems probable that the fabric of the housing of the people improved: put very simply, new houses were being built at a faster rate than the rate of increase of the population of Great Britain.[14] This new housing, subject to local bye-laws about access to sunlight, water and sewage services, and precautions against dampness, as a component in the general enlargement of opportunities for domestic cleanliness, must be invoked when one considers the decline in mortality of typhoid fever and the other infectious diseases. Drier housing and sunlight were the important contributions, rather than the reduction of 'overcrowding' which so preoccupied contemporaries and which engendered misguided campaigns for 'slum clearance' in this century.

The scarlet fever mortality rate in England and Wales among children under ten, the most vulnerable group, ran at 210 per million in 1871. It dropped to 140 per million in 1881, that is 17,400 deaths a year, to level out in the mid 1890s at 35 per

million, or about 4,000 deaths a year, a horrifying
number, but still representing a huge saving of
young life.[15] Epidemiologists are agreed in attri-
buting the reduction to a decrease in virulence of
the causative agent, the haemolytic streptococcus.
Certainly this huge diminution in the death rate was
achieved before effective therapeutic procedures
were devised, although this is true of almost all
the major killers discussed in this chapter. I am
inclined to add to the epidemiologists' interpretation of this decline an emphasis upon legally
imposed standards of cleanliness in dairies and milk
marketing which contributed to reducing prior and
cross infections. This began to become effective in
the 1880s.

As with other infections, whether airborne as
scarlet fever usually is, or conveyed by milk and
food, scarlet fever mortality had its worst incidence and lingered longest in the Black Country and
the Durham and Welsh coalfields.[16] Yet in terms of
wages these were among the more affluent parts of
working class England and Wales (although less so
in the Black Country where miners' wages were lower
than elsewhere) especially during this period. Presumably coalminers' families were at least as well
sheltered as the families of less skilled and poorer
workers, and, of course, warmer, and because they
paid relatively lower rents, a larger share of their
wages was available for food.[17] In these instances,
poverty was not the prime determinant of ill health
and death. We do not know enough about these places
to say why this was so. Mining villages were dis-
tinctively male dominated and rough in everyday
behaviour and sports. The infant and child death
rates in the Welsh valleys suggest that religious
adherence did little to lift the value set on life.
There is a seeming paradox between the high male
cohesiveness in the workplace, trade union branch
and club, much celebrated by novelists and historians, and the seeming unconcern with municipal
improvement and sanitary services, which only A.J.
Cronin among the writers, has depicted. Perhaps the
dramatic dangerousness of mining induced a dull
stoicism which kept expectations low and reduced the
value placed on individual lives, especially those
of non earning women and children (although mining
was absolutely less dangerous, and fast becoming
ever safer in terms of lethal accidents, than the
work of slaters and roof tilers, lead workers,
bridgemen and dock labourers, and seamen, whose
accident death rate was a terrible 75 percent

higher).[18]

Whooping cough also declined steadily through
the period from a reported peak of about 1,450 per
million in England and Wales in the late 1860s.
Again the decline accelerated in the mid 1890s when
the mortality rate fell from about 1,200 per million
in 1890 to 1,000 per million in 1900, to continue
down to about 680 per million in 1910. This represents a reduction from over 13,000 deaths a year in
1880 to 8,700 in 1905.

Scotland always had a higher reported mortality
rate for whooping cough than England and Wales, and
the transition to a lower rate came later, between
1906 and 1910. Particularly in the Scottish cities,
it outlasted scarlet fever and typhoid to emerge,
with measles, to which it was often the sequel, as a
major killer of young children. Even in 1914 there
were over 1,300 deaths. By contrast, the Irish rate
was reportedly always about half the British rates,
but like the Scottish rate, the transition to a new,
low level still half that of the British, did not
come until 1907. Forty percent of the deaths in the
United Kingdom occurred at under twelve months and
95 percent at under five years.[19] Whooping cough
was not a notifiable disease and the reported rates,
especially when we recall that other infections such
as measles were often also involved, are probably
seriously under-registered throughout the period.
It is a distressing disease which parents and
doctors are impotent to alleviate. The sources of
its decline still baffle epidemiologists. Like the
other infections, its diminution began before its
causative organism, *bordetella pertussis*, was identified in 1906, although morbidity from the disease,
as with diphtheria, remained high into the 1940s.
Whooping cough is spread by droplet infection and we
know that it was most common among children sleeping
in crowded dwellings (indeed, recent findings suggest that it is seven times more common in crowded
families).[20] 'Overcrowding' does seem to be the
crucial element here, although the decline in case
mortality during the twentieth century remains to be
explained.

Measles and the secondary infections and
sequelae it brought with it remained a serious
threat much longer into the twentieth century. Its
death rate for England and Wales ran at between
1,200 and 1,000 per million until 1910 and remained
close to that level until 1914, when a dramatic fall
set in to reach 350 per million in 1930. Before
1914 this rate meant over 9,300 deaths a year in

England and Wales in bad years such as 1900, and over 800 deaths in Scotland, equalling 470 per million, compared with 360 in Ireland, where the rate was 143 per million.[21] Compulsory school attendance for tens of thousands of children and their return to mix daily with tens of thousands of younger siblings at home enlarged and concentrated the pool of susceptibles. But that does not explain the rapid fall in mortality rates after 1914 and the significantly lower mortality throughout the period in Ireland.

Here, as elsewhere in British - meaning southern English - history, Ireland provides checks and clues. Between 1891 and 1911 the proportion of the Irish population under fourteen was in step with that of the English and Welsh, while Ireland and Scotland had similar total numbers and proportions under fourteen. Irish wages were lower, 'overcrowding' in Dublin and Belfast was widespread, and charity, in a generally poorer economy, was probably more austere. The diet of the Irish working classes was probably more monotonous than that of their English counterparts, yet its bases in milk, potatoes and bacon probably made it more sustaining. I shall return to this point later. We know that among malnourished children in contemporary poor countries measles and its associated secondary infections is still a life threatening illness with a case mortality rate of 25 percent.[22]

However, if proportionately more Irish children had sufficient resistance to live through measles and diphtheria attacks they paid for it in other ways. The published data on Ireland are sparse and difficult to interpret, but one set of figures, at least, suggests that in 1891 Irish children under fifteen years were reported as 'deaf and dumb' at 0.0457 per million - that is, 700 children, or double the rate for England and Wales and slightly higher than for Scotland. On the other hand, Ireland had a rate of about 30 percent fewer children reported as 'blind' than did England and Wales and about twenty percent fewer than Scotland, although Ireland unhappily made up the difference at up to six times the rates for Great Britain among older age groups.[23] This disproportion must have been aggravated by higher emigration rates among the Irish able-bodied. But throughout the Kingdom the health levels of poor and working class children were low. In Glasgow in 1903-4 40 percent of board school children were reported as suffering from 'defective hearing', while sixteen percent of ele-

mentary school children in London in 1909 and
another sixteen percent in Manchester and Birmingham
in 1912-13 were reported to have various forms of
severe respiratory impairment. Twenty years earlier
about eleven percent of London elementary school
children were reported to exhibit 'deviations from
the normal nerve state' and a further eleven percent
showed 'bodily defects'.[24] At present our understanding of the causes, manifestations and outcomes
of these chronic conditions is rudimentary. Simple
ascriptions of mortality or morbidity to 'measles'
or 'scarlet fever' hide the crucial interplay of
cross infections (let alone wrong diagnosis) and the
importance of predisposing factors such as poor
nutrition, coarse nurture and tiredness, and the
little understood or reported debility and sequelae.
This high incidence of physical incompetence among
the working classes and poor retarded their learning, their acquisition of work skills, their prowess
in sport and their capacity to enjoy life. During
this period, as during the preceding centuries,
endemic ill-health must have played a fundamental
part in keeping the poor in their place.

In Great Britain the largest gain in life
during this period, among young adults at least,
came from the retreat of pulmonary tuberculosis. In
1870 the rate for England and Wales was reported at
about 2,410 per million living, in 1880 it had
fallen to 1,869, and in 1892 it plunged to 1,634 per
million and thereafter diminished at a more gradual
rate. Scotland had always reported a slightly
higher rate, from a bad peak in 1870 of 3,900 per
million until the decisive downturn in 1909.

Table 2.2: Pulmonary tuberculosis mortality in
Scotland 1870-1910

Year	Rate per million
1870	3,900
1880	3,000
1890	2,600
1900	2,300
1909	2,000
1910	1,700

In England and Wales this advance represented a
saving by 1910 of over 70,000 lives a year on the

rates for 1851-60.[25]

The decline in the incidence of all forms of tuberculosis, although much accelerated in our period, continued a trend that had probably begun with the first growth of the industrial economy in the later eighteenth century. The causes of this decline remain a mystery. There were no effective therapies or isolation procedures in the nineteenth century and the system of dispensary attendance and sanatoria residence, the therapeutic results of which are also arguable, developed fully only after the World War.

Morbidity from pulmonary tuberculosis probably also declined through the century and again at an accelerating rate during our period as the chances for continual exposure to active cases and repeated infection from droplets and dust diminished. But post mortem and later x-ray discoveries of healed lesions showed that there was still a lot of tuberculosis about and that mass infection was still the norm.[26] Improved nutrition and shelter and reduced hours of labour and exhaustion among the working population must have increased their resistance. The incidence of all forms of tuberculosis among infants under twelve months fell much more slowly than among other age groups, until the transition in 1906. Here the important contribution seems to be the spread during these years of effective pasteurisation of milk. But our knowledge of the extent of mortality and morbidity of all forms of tuberculosis remains very inexact. Mortality was undoubtedly under-reported, among infants particularly, and we can only draw up crude estimates of adult morbidity for a short time around 1900 from a few dispensary enrolment records based on insecure diagnosis of segments of the general population of Great Britain. Nonetheless those segments represent the lower middle classes, working classes and the poor, and therefore contain a cross section of the classes most at risk. These reports suggest a figure of about 30,000 active cases in Scotland and about 270,000 in England and Wales.[27] Appalling though they are, these estimates must be understatements; yet they also indicate that Britain had the lowest tuberculosis morbidity and mortality rates in Europe. The important point is that this advance represents an enormous lessening in misery among all classes, and among the working classes and poor especially. Members of artisan families died from reported pulmonary tuberculosis in Birmingham, Manchester, London, Aberdeen and Dublin at about twice the rate

of members of professional families. And those who
died in 'bad areas' died at a third higher rate
again than the artisans. The disease hit hardest at
the fifteen to 45 age group, those at the height of
their working lives.[28] The long periods of impaired
earning ability, and then the two and a half to five
years of increasing debility before death, especially when it occurred among bread winners, often
brought destitution. The reduction of tuberculosis
mortality and probably morbidity in our period not
only reduced misery but it greatly stabilised income
among all classes, among the working classes in
particular. It must, moreover, have issued in a
considerable augmentation to the national wealth.

The exception to this happy picture is once
again, Ireland. There, the mortality rate from pulmonary tuberculosis actually rose through the
period, a pitiable distinction in Western Europe
which Ireland shares with Norway. This change, from
a rate of 2,600 per million in 1870, to 2,900 per
million in 1880 and no real fall until 1906, when
the rate, at 2,800 per million was still higher than
Scotland's and remained so through the present century, is as yet unexplored. I shall be writing
about these questions elsewhere and have not the
space to pursue them here, but three points need to
be made. The first is that the Irish rates are,
like those for other diseases, inflated by the emigration of the young able-bodied, although we must
remember that Great Britain also lost many similar
people. Nonetheless, if tuberculosis is spread in
an environment of poor nutrition, poor shelter, and
overcrowding leading to poor resistance and repeated
reinfection of susceptibles, then Ireland represents
a fossil phase of the health history of the United
Kingdom from which England and Scotland and, to a
lesser extent, Wales, had emerged. Moreover, pulmonary tuberculosis rates were over twice as bad
among the huddled poor in Belfast and Dublin as in
the thinly populated west.[29]

Ireland, by contrast, maintained a lower infant general mortality rate than Great Britain
throughout the years to 1914, as table 2.3 shows.
The decisive fall in Scotland and England and Wales
occurred around 1902, from peaks of 137 per thousand
in 1897 in Scotland and 163 per thousand in 1899 in
England and Wales.[30] I have discussed this changed
pattern elsewhere and cannot rehearse the details
here.[31] But the contrast between Ireland and Great
Britain is too striking to be passed over. We need
to explore variations in the practice of breast

Table 2.3: Infant mortality rates per 1,000 births
in the United Kingdom, 1870-1914

Years	Ireland	Scotland	England and Wales
1870-80	95	123	150
1881-90	95	120	143
1891-1900	105	124	153
1901-1905	93	120	138
1906-12	92	112	116
1913-14	90	109	103

feeding. Good evidence about infant nurture in
Ireland is not easy to find but we have numerous in-
direct remarks by informed observers which suggest
that breast feeding was customary among mothers of
all social ranks, except in protestant Belfast.
Other observers noted that breast feeding seemed to
be more common in Scotland than in England and
Wales.[32] We also have inferential claims that
breast feeding in England was least common and
practicable in small manufacturing and textile towns.
These might well be true because the claims were
made by informed observers, but ultimately they are
derived tautologically from the mortality rates for
such places, which were up to 100 percent above the
urban average.[33] Beyond this, we know that ille-
gitimates, wherever they were born, had a 100 percent worse chance of survival than legitimates and
that the rates within towns varied by up to 300
percent between babies born in wealthy suburbs and
those born to tenement dwellers.[34] But this important, neglected subject needs detailed, critical
and comparative investigation.
    Illnesses conveyed by contaminated cows' milk,
condensed milk and water, and other foods handled
by members of families in which diarrhoeal infections
were endemic, seconded by house flies nourished on
the horse manure of the roads and stables, culmin-
ated every summer in mass infant deaths. Particularly hot summers as in 1893, 1895, 1899, 1904, 1906
and 1908 saw the infant mortality graphs mimic the
temperature charts. In cool 1907, for example,
there were 17,283 deaths at all ages (but over-
whelmingly infants) reported from diarrhoeal

diseases in England and Wales; in hot 1908, 26,879.
Nonetheless the decisive decline which began in 1902
in all three nations of the Kingdom occurred mainly
among victims attributed to 'marasmus, atrophy and
debility' and not among reported diarrhoea cases,
where the rates remained roughly constant, or among
infants dying of 'prematurity and congenital
defects', where indeed the rates increased.[35] If
'marasmus' and 'atrophy' are indices of neglect,
their diminution should indicate better mothering
and nurture, and this improvement was possible when
the age of the women at marriage rose, when the
spaces between pregnancies became longer, and when
the size of the completed family was reduced. 1901-2
in England and Wales and 1903-4 in Scotland appear
to be the culminating years in that long advance of
artificial, effective contraception founded upon
time honoured natural methods and supplemented by
continued high abortion rates which we can perceive
among professional middle class families in 1851 and
which were adopted among the working classes gradually after 1876, the peak year in nineteenth century
fertility rates. The interplay of economic
forces and private motives in this transition is intricate and largely irrecoverable, but the survival
of more children within the family, the advent of
compulsory school attendance after 1880 and the restrictions on child employment impelled the working
classes to join the middle and upper classes in the
process of inescapable transfer of intergenerational
wealth, with the result that their children, like
those of their betters before them, were rendered
both more expensive and the bearers of their parents'
enlarged ambitions in an era of rising real wages.
There has been much speculation about the ideological changes which made possible or at least accompanied this demographic transition, and 'seculari-
sation', 'urbanisation' and 'industrialisation' have
all been invoked.[36] I have elsewhere proposed
secularism, in the sense of loss of belief in a
providential order, as a contributing factor and do
not wish to argue that proposition here.[37] But I
want to suggest that attention should now turn from
the middle classes' and artisans' changes in the
1850s and 1860s to the much larger change among the
less skilled working classes in the first decade of
this century, and that greater weight be given to
the factor which demographers observe in contemporary societies adopting artificial contraception: the
simple, rational appraisal among marriage partners
of their immediate family interests and prospects.

Only among mining families did the number of births remain at the old high rates: and only in mining places did the infant mortality rates linger at the 1870s rates, and, indeed, increase in the Welsh mining valleys. Carmarthenshire, for instance, reported a rise of eighteen percent between 1876 and 1908.

Table 2.4: Births per 1,000 women aged 15-44 in the United Kingdom, 1876-1909

Year	England and Wales	Scotland	Ireland
1876	156.7	153.9	119.4
1886	140.4	142.2	103.1
1896	121.9	127.9	100.1
1901	114.5	122.1	96.2
1904	112.7	118.6	100.9
1906	109.2	115.8	102.0
1909	103.5	112.7	103.4

As the table shows, the birthrate in Ireland fell earlier than in Great Britain and remained steady at about the rate the English and Welsh finally reached in 1909. This was in part the outcome of an older population structure and the likely higher age at marriage of Irish women (we have at present inadequate data on this) although the age of women at marriage during this period also rose in England and Wales. I have found no contemporary suggestion that artificial contraception had much to do with it. It seems reasonable to propose that the probable higher incidence of breast feeding in Ireland which sustained the consistently lower infant death rate was itself facilitated by and, indeed, by reducing conceptions contributed to, the smaller size of the completed family. Throughout the United Kingdom the transition occurred before the widespread provision of infant milk depots, health visitors' schemes, and mothercraft centres. Indeed, many of the medical and philanthropic activists in these centres enjoined pro-natalism and thereby retarded the cause they ostensibly espoused. They lost in cloudy, eugenic beliefs the simple lesson of the mining towns that more lives saved and enhanced among a smaller crop of babies would quickly produce a more competent population.

III

The long run of rising real wages enabled people in Great Britain to substantially change their diet, in part for better, but often for worse. Consumption of salt for cooking and condiment in 1887 was said to be about 40 pounds per head per year. The price had fallen to twelve shillings per ton from sixteen shillings in 1860 and domestic consumption had already doubled during that period. By 1889 the 40 pounds level had risen to a reported 62 pounds per head and in 1897 (the data are patchy) to 72 pounds or a scarcely credible average one and a half pounds per week (the figures very likely include some of the salt used in food processing, but this does not affect my argument about the general shape of the increase in domestic consumption). Consumption in France and Germany ran at under half these astonishing figures, which are also 300 percent greater than the currently recorded highest per capita intake, in northern Japan, the 'apoplexy country'. British consumption stabilised at around the 1897 figure, until about 1904 when it began slowly to fall.[39]

Sugar consumption shows a like pattern. In 1870 it was reported at 47 pounds (both refined and unrefined) per head per year in the United Kingdom, in 1880 at 65 pounds (both refined and unrefined), 1890 at 71 pounds, 1900 at 85 pounds (refined and unrefined) and in 1905, at 70 pounds (refined only). Consumption per head in the United Kingdom was reported to be twice that of the next highest European domestic consumer, Denmark, and two thirds higher than that of France.[40] The 1880s and 1890s are the take-off years for mass produced jam and jelly crystals, and milk chocolates made from sugar, cocoa and condensed milk, together with cocoa based drinks made from sugar, flour and starch, and sweets confected from sugar, water, gelatine and artificial colours and flavourings.[41] Sauces, relishes and essences based on salt, sugar, spices, starches and artificial colours and flavourings also emerged as mass consumption items often about 1880. This surge in consumption of sugar and salt as condiments may be related to the decline in the consumption of alcoholic beverages from the mid 1870s, which permitted the expenditure of a larger share of family

income on less socially deleterious sources of
calories and appetisers. (Changes in the basis of
excise calculations and its levels also affected the
price of beer and generally led to reduced alcoholic
strength).

The new sauces helped make palatable the meat
which the people were consuming in gradually increasing quantities as its price decreased. Imports
of meat and butter at declared value doubled between
1875 and 1895 and by 1905 had risen again by one
third. The London wholesale price of 'inferior
quality' meat fell from 4¾d per pound in 1880 to
3¾d in 1900, while consumption per head per year
in the United Kingdom rose from 109 pounds in 1880
to 122 pounds in 1892 to 132 pounds in 1900.42 The
meat was cooked on the new gas and coal stoves which
became popular after the price of coal (London 'best
coal' landed figures) fell by one third between 1874
and 1884, and thereafter to 1912 generally remained
close to the 1884 figure of 16s 6d per ton.43 Working class domestic cookery undoubtedly incorporated
a wider range of comestibles and condiments,
although this is not to assume that the food was
greatly improved, as Mr Polly's dyspepsia attests.

This was also the age of new, mass consumption
patterns of tobacco. In 1880 the population of the
United Kingdom smoked 1.4 pounds per head per year.
Thereafter consumption jumped as follows:

Table 2.5: Tobacco consumption in the United
Kingdom, 1890-1910

Year	Pounds per head
1890	1.55
1900	1.95
1905	1.97
1910	2.00

The penny-per-five cigarette was introduced in 1888
and rapidly captured the market: in 1891 85 million
out of the 126 million cigarettes purchased were
penny ones. In 1910, after the method of measurement changed, 30 million pounds of cigarettes were
sold, in 1914 50 millions.44

The increased survival rates of susceptibles
who formerly would have been lost in infancy or
childhood, coupled with the new diet, produced a new

pattern of disease and disability that has persisted
to the present, where coronary disease, cardiac
disease, cancer and hypertension comprise the four
leading reported causes of death. The two emerging
threats were cancer and heart disease. In England
and Wales between 1851 and 1880 reported male cancer
deaths increased by 62 percent to reach 315 per
million, while female rates rose by 43 percent to
662 per million. The fastest increase occurred at
age 35 and above, at 59 percent. The reported cancers were still the well known ones, observable
from the exterior of the body: in females, cancers
of the breast and cervix; in males, cancers of the
bladder, stomach, lip and mouth and rectum. Consonant with the new eating habits probably, and new
diagnostic methods, the greatest increase showed
subsequently in intestinal cancers in both sexes:
males - 16.6 per million in 1868 to 185.5 per
million in 1910, to 294.6 per million in 1915;
females - 33.4 per million in 1868, to 124 per
million in 1910, to 368 per million in 1915. Already
in the 1890s deaths attributed to cancer had risen
above 20,000 a year in England and Wales.[45] The
cancer rates for Ireland, again probably related to
the delay in mortality changes and a slower transition from the old diet based on potatoes, milk and
bacon, did not begin to rise until 1877 and even
thereafter continued at below the British rates
throughout the period.[46] Significantly, in view of
the tremendous increase in tobacco consumption, the
reported incidence of lung cancers in England and
Wales rose from 5.5 per million at all ages over 35
in 1868, to 18.4 per million in 1888, to 29.3 per
million in 1901-10 to 36.4 (the civilian rate) in
1915. The rates among males were double those for
females. Next to intestinal cancers, prostate and
lung cancers among both sexes showed the fastest
increase in reported cancers through the period.[47]
     Reported deaths from diabetes and renal dis-
eases, which develop most commonly in people over
40 who are also obese, jumped by 100 percent for
males 45-65 between 1870 and 1910, when the rate
reached 415 per million, and rose by 400 percent for
males over 65, to reach 731 per million. The great
acceleration in the rate occurred in the mid 1890s.
The rise among females was even more catastrophic:
for women 45-65, from 37 per million in 1870 to 129
per million in 1910, a rise of 348 percent; and for
women over 65, from 62 per million to 574 per
million, a rise of 925 percent.[48] In Ireland the
rise in these diseases began later and proceeded at

a slower rate, from 81 per million in 1908 to 92 per million in 1914.[49] As with cancer, one might have expected that the older structure of the Irish population and the removal of many of the hardiest, presumably, by emigration, would have brought the figures nearer to the British ones. But that is not the case and we are compelled to emphasise the importance of nutrition in these contrasts, coupled with the lesser pollution of Ireland relative to Great Britain with its numerous developing chemical industries.

High blood pressure, arterial disease, coronary disease and cerebrovascular disease again show an appalling rise, at least for England and Wales. The Registrar-Generals' figures are derived from widely varying criteria over time and are probably greatly understated. Nonetheless the English and Irish figures are all we have in a usable form but they do provide some idea of the dimensions of change: the figures are inflated by the decline in infant mortality, but not to the extent that the trend is falsified.

Table 2.6: Deaths from 'Heart diseases etc.' in England and Wales and Ireland, 1903-14

| Year | Per million deaths at all ages | |
	England and Wales	Ireland
1903	403	NA
1906	450	189
1909	481	206
1912	579	176
1914	636	181

Table 2.7: Deaths from 'Cerebral Haemorrhage, etc.' in England and Wales, 1903-13 [50]

Year	Per million deaths at all ages
1903	403
1905	434
1907	477
1909	506
1911	513
1913	563

(The Scottish data were reckoned upon a different basis and barely acceptable figures for comparative purposes could not be produced without a vast amount of calculation).

These figures, taken with those for diabetes and cancer, suggest that between 1880 and 1914 the United Kingdom, led by England and Wales, experienced a revolution in diet and disease patterns very similar to that which has been happening during the last decade in, for instance, Papua New Guinea and western Samoa, associated with greatly augmented intake of refined carbohydrates and decreased exercise.[51]

Two other diseases emerged as killers and disablers during this period, although they have no demonstrable link with dietary changes and altered ways of life. The first is influenza which apparently mutated in about 1890 and suddenly became virulent, after 50 years of relative mildness. In 1890-92 110,000 deaths in England and Wales were attributed directly to it, principally among infants and persons over 55. It must also have helped to lift the death rates reported among sufferers of pulmonary tuberculosis, pneumonia and whooping cough.[52] Waxing and waning, influenza was to remain a threat to life, a debilitating precursor to other infections, a source of mental depression, and a major cause of lost work time to the present. Among the working classes especially it must also have inflicted recurring shortfalls in family income: it was a malady which did not carry compensation. Poliomyelitis was first reported as a killer and crippler of children between five and ten in 1911, when there were 206 deaths in England and Wales.[53] Its occasional epidemics were to remain as a dreadful threat until the advent of Salk vaccine in the mid 1950s.

Possibly because greater numbers of mentally handicapped children were surviving and adult insane persons were living longer, and certainly because institutions to receive them had been erected and extended in the 1880s, the number of persons certified as of 'unsound mind' in England and Wales rose to its highest ever rates, around 3,500 per million, between 1894 and 1904. By 1914 the rate was at 3,710 per million, which meant about 138,000 human beings. Between the late 1890s and 1914 there was a huge rise in admissions to the newly capacious asylums. Hitherto only half the known persons of unsound mind had been institutionalised but after 1900 the proportion ran at about two thirds.[54]

The anxieties among the ruling and professional classes about the mentally incompetent extended to the physically incompetent too. As more chronically weak children survived, so these classes saw the need to investigate the incidence of poor eyesight and hearing, head lice, body sores, adenoids, infected tonsils, and anaemia and to treat these conditions by inventing new categories, inspections, compulsory washings and dabbing with ointments and frequent surgery. The Idiots Act was passed in 1886, the Lunacy Act in 1890, the first Royal Commission on the Deaf and Dumb reported in 1893, and an Education Act for Defective Children was carried in 1899. The misnamed Interdepartmental Committee on Physical Deterioration sat through 1904. The rejection rates of volunteers for the Boer War and the ravages of typhoid fever among the troops in South Africa helped fuel the reformers' anxieties and enlarged their demands that taxation be spent on promoting health among mothers, infants and school children.[55] But the drive to create these health promoting activities and institutions for the chronically sick predated the Boer War disillusionments by over a decade as the dates of the legislation listed above indicate. School health inspections, school meals, national insurance support for consumptives, the elements which comprise the emerging social service state, were the outcome of the great health transition and developed in essentially similar ways after the transition in other European countries, North America and Australia. The redistribution entailed in the social service state did help to increase resistance and thereby eradicate rickets and reduce the incidence of tuberculosis through the 1920s and 1930s. Other illnesses associated with prolonged deprivation also gradually disappeared during the 1920s as living standards rose: tertiary syphilis, gout, strangulated hernias, displaced uteruses were all less frequently reported.[56] But, as more susceptibles lived longer, rheumatism and other slow-acting degenerative diseases became more common.

Nonetheless, the generation raised during the transition, which reached manhood in 1914, was the biggest and most vigorous that the United Kingdom had ever seen, as were their fellows in Western Europe, Australasia and North America. Officers and private soldiers in the armies of the Great War incarnated the twin ideals of health that sanitarians had promoted since at least the 1860s. As Charles Kingsley had preached in 1872, the higher order of health approximated to that exhibited in statues of classical Greek athletes. This higher order was the exemplar for the classes emerging from the flourishing public schools. They were to be the bearers of social duty and high national aspiration. Through disciplined games, restraint in eating, drinking and carnal pleasures, and bodily cleanliness they had to ascend to that 'chaste healthfulness' which ensured from compliance with the 'laws of nature which are the voice of God.' The classes' sinewy, strong bodies, seconding quick and honourable minds, would produce that 'tender grandeur' which would retain for them their moral authority among the democracy. Health was a state of political grace, won from within, embodied in male musculature and female *tournure*. The masses were directed to a different ideal. They were to be made 'large, strong, ruddy, cheerful, active, clear-headed for their work'. They were to eschew drunkenness and care better for their offspring and dwellings.[57]

By 1914 these ideals had in large part been achieved. Only fit and dedicated men could have endured, indeed maintained, the terrible war that engulfed them. Weaker men from weaker nations in eastern and southern Europe and the African and Indian colonies dropped out first. Their stronger comrades, newly emancipated from the hazards of typhus, cholera and scarlet fever, were preserved for decimation at the Somme and the Marne. Their younger siblings and the women who survived them, and their children in turn, were to enjoy increasing life expectancies (and expectations from life) in ever growing proportions through the twentieth century. Over half the female cohort born in Great Britain in 1891-1900 could expect to live to 50 years of age; the cohort of 1901-10, to 52; the cohort of 1920-22, to almost 60; that of 1950-52, to 71; that of 1970-72, to 73. Their male contemporaries began in 1891-1900 with almost two years less life expectancy, at around 48½ years, and thereafter higher incidences among them of cigarette smoking, war casualties, traffic and industrial accidents retarded the male rate of increase, so that it did not reach 67 until the 1970-72 cohort, a life expectancy truncated by six years as compared with the female level.[58] Since then, the spread of cigarette smoking among young women, together with other self-inflicted risks, has tended to narrow the gap.

This transformation in life expectancies has issued an intricate set of alterations in life

chances which historians have barely begun to
explore. Among them are extensions in the span of
active working lives; increases in production made
possible by stronger, healthier (and more experienced - if set in their ways) workers; the steadily
growing numbers of people retired or widowed, liable
to the physical and social disabilities attendant
upon ageing; and the belated social and official
condonation of birth control. These changes have
profoundly affected family life, patterns of work
and trade union activity, distributions within the
domestic and national economies and public expectations and values. Beyond these, there are many
other important but less obvious outcomes worth
investigation: one is the probable increase in
attention and income which parents and grandparents
in all classes devote to children in smaller
families; another is the possibly very considerable
redistributional effects of wives outliving their
husbands in a society which pays pensions and levies
relatively low duties on transfers of marital property at death; a third set derives from the altered
patterns of death and disease that came in with the
transition - for instance, a changed emphasis upon
individual responsibility for maintaining a healthy
body or at least keeping a seedy organism going,
co-existent, paradoxically, with public underwriting
of advice and treatment; or, another instance, the
redirection towards cancer of the old public and
private fears about infectious diseases and tuberculosis; and, one final example, the changed management of illnesses which proceed episodically or
chronically, by contrast with the traditional ones
which were lingering, largely beyond palliation, and
which were charged with dramatic climacterics.
   One fundamentally important element in the
distribution of life chances remained, it seems,
little affected by the transition. The huge differentials in morbidity and mortality rates between
classes I and V that prevailed in 1880 continued in
much the same ratios through to the 1920s, the 1950s
and to the present. While the prospects of the
majority of infants, mothers and middle aged men and
women in all five classes have improved enormously
upon the chances of their ancestors, the grim fact
endures that despite decades of social engineering
and expensive medical intervention people in class
V experience higher morbidity and mortality rates
than people in the other classes. The patterns of
illness, and of disability and of causes of death
have changed, but the inequalities persist: death

rates still bear an inverse relationship to income
levels.

NOTES

1.   G. Talbot Griffith, *Population Problems in
the Age of Malthus* (London, 1926); M.C. Buer,
*Health, Wealth and Population in the Early Days of
the Industrial Revolution* (London, 1926).
2.   Thomas McKeown, *The Modern Rise of Population* (London, 1976); John Woodward, *To Do The Sick
No Harm* (London, 1974), p.36.
3.   F.B. Smith, *The People's Health 1830-1910*
(London, 1979); Anthony S. Wohl, *Endangered Lives*
(London, 1983); J.M. Winter, 'The decline of mortality in Britain 1870-1950', and D.J.Oddy, 'The health
of the people', in Theo Barker and Michael Drake
(eds.), *Population and Society in Britain 1850-1910*
(London, 1982), pp.100-140.
4.   William Farr, *Vital Statistics* (London,
1885); Arthur Newsholme, *The Last Thirty Years in
Public Health* (London, 1936); G.C.M. McGonigle and
J. Kirby, *Poverty And Public Health* (London, 1936);
Richard Titmuss, *Birth, Poverty and Wealth* (London,
1943); Richard Titmuss, *Problems of Social Policy*
(London, 1950; new ed. 1976).
5.   R. Thorne, *The Progress of Preventive
Medicine during the Victorian Era* (London, 1888),
p.17.
6.   *53rd Annual Report, Registrar-General for
England*, PP 1890-91, vol.xxiii, p.xlviii; *77th
Report for England and Wales*, PP 1916, vol.v, p.36.
7.   *42nd Report ... for England; 23rd Report
... for Scotland*, PP 1881, vol.xxvii, pp.lxxix,
civ,xxxiv, *51st Report ... for Ireland*, PP 1914,
vol.ix, p.135.
8.   *Lancet*, Jan. 7, 1882, p.31; George Rosen,
'Historical trends and future prospects in public
health', in Gordon McLachlan and Thomas McKeown
(eds.), *Medical History and Medical Care* (London,
1971), pp.63-4.
9.   Wohl, *Endangered Lives*, pp.313-8.
10. Michael G. Mulhall, *The Dictionary of
Statistics* (London, 1892), p.542; Charles Wilson,
The History of Unilever (London, 1954), I, p.115.
11. John Tatham, *Supplement to 65th Report ...
for England and Wales, part I*, PP 1905, vol.xviii,

pp.lxxx-lxxxi; *76th Report ... for England and Wales*, PP 1914-16, vol.ix, pp.35-8.

12. Smith, *People's Health*, p.245.

13. Wohl, *Endangered Lives*, p.327; Anthony S. Wohl, *The Eternal Slum* (London, 1977), p.xv.

14. John Burnett, *A Social History of Housing 1815-1870* (Newton Abbott, 1978), pp.139-40.

15. Thomas McKeown and C.R. Lowe, *An Introduction to Social Medicine* (Oxford, 1968), p.12.

16. Smith, *People's Health*, p.137.

17. A.L. Bowley, *Wages And Income in the United Kingdon since 1860* (Cambridge, 1937), p.8.

18. *58th Report ... for England*, PP 1897, vol. xxi, pp.iv, xxvii, lxii, lxxvii; *Supplement to 65th Report ... for England and Wales*, Part II, PP 1905, vol.xviii, pp.xxviii, xcvi, clxxvii.CF John Benson, *British Coalminers in the Nineteenth Century: A Social History* (Dublin, 1980).

19. *71st Report ... for England and Wales* and *45th Report ... for Ireland*, PP 1909, vol.xi, pp.21, xl; *44th Report ... for Ireland*, PP 1908, vol.xi, pp.xvi, xl; *60th Report ... for Scotland*, PP 1914-16, vol.xi, pp.xxiv-xxv.

20. McKeown and Lowe, *Social Medicine*, p.186.

21. *37th Report ... for Ireland*, PP 1901, vol. xv, p.10; *47th Report ... Ireland*, PP 1911, vol.xi, pp.xvi-xvii, pp.138-9.

22. Alan D. Berg, *The Nutrition Factor: its role in national development* (Washington, 1973), p.4.

23. Appendix ix to *Royal Commission on the Financial Relations between Great Britain and Ireland*, PP 1896, vol.xxxiii, p.210. I am indebted to Professor Oliver MacDonagh for this unlikely source for these otherwise elusive figures.

24. *Lancet*, July 17, 1909, p.168; Smith, *People's Health*, p.183; Helen Bosanquet, *Social work in London 1869-1912* (1914; repr. Brighton, 1973), p.198.

25. *51st Report ... for Ireland*, PP 1914-16, vol.ix.pp.xxv, xxxviii; *British Medical Journal*, February 20, 1926, p.322; April 28, 1928, pp.703-4.

26, Marc Daniels *et. al.*, *Tuberculosis in Young Adults* (London, 1948), pp.168-9.

27. Arthur Latham and C.H. Garland, *The Conquest of Consumption* (London, 1910), pp.159-60.

28. Tatham, *Supplement to 65th Report ... for England and Wales*, part I, PP 1905, vol.xviii, p.xx; Tatham, *Appendix to Royal Commission Report on Tuberculosis*, PP 1898, vol.xllx, p.359; *51st Report ... for Ireland*, PP 1914-16, vol.ix, pp.xxv,

xxxviii; J. Stewart in Anon. (ed.), *Prevention of
Destitution* (London, 1911), pp.473-4; John Robertson
Housing and the Public Health (London, 1919),
pp.14-15.

29. *Supplement to 32nd Report ... for Ireland,*
PP 1904, vol.xiv, p.36; *British Medical Journal,*
July 2, 1887, p.23; James Craig, *Consumption in
Ireland* (Dublin, 1900), pp.5-11.

30. *51st Report ... for Ireland,* PP 1914-16,
vol.ix, pp.v-ix, xxxvii-xxxviii.

31. Smith, *People's Health,* pp.122-7.

32. Sir C.A. Cameron to *Royal Commission on
Tuberculosis,* PP 1898, vol.xlix Q. 2,730, 2,868;
Lancet, April 26, 1884, p.775; June 20, 1885,
p.1,144.

33. *Lancet,* June 17, 1882, p.1,005; November
24, 1894, p.1,241; August 23, 1902, p.524; B.L.
Hutchens, 'Note on the Mortality of Young Children',
Journal of the Royal Statistical Society, lxxi, 1908,
pp.174-8.

34. *74th Report ... for England and Wales,* PP
1912-13, vol xiii, p.xxxviii; Smith, *People's
Health,* pp.126-7

35. *74th Report ... for England and Wales,* PP
1912-13, vol.xiii, p.xxxiv; T.H.C. Stevenson,
Supplement to 80th Report ... for England and Wales,
PP 1919, vol.x, pp.xlii-xliii.

36. J.A. Banks, *Victorian Values, Secularism
and the Size of Families* (London, 1981); Richard
Allen Soloway, *Birth Control and the Population
Question in England, 1877-1930* (Chapel Hill, 1982).

37. F.B. Smith, 'The Atheist Mission', in R.
Robson (ed.), *Ideas and Institutions of Victorian
Britain* (London, 1967), pp.219-20.

38. *71st Report ... for England and Wales,* PP
1909, vol.xi, p.xlii; *74th Report ... for England and
Wales,* PP 1912-13, vol.xiii, p.xxii; Stevenson,
Supplement to 75th Report ... for England and Wales,
PP 1914-16, vol.viii, p.xxviii; see also Robert E.
Kennedy, Jr., *The Irish Emigration, Marriage, and
Fertility* (Berkeley, 1973), pp.173-95.

39. Mulhall, *Dictionary of Statistics,* p.518;
Mines and Quarries: General Report and Statistics,
PP 1900, vol.cii, pp.249-5; 1906, vol cxxxiv,
pp.272-4; Derek Denton, *The Hunger for Salt* (Berlin,
1982), pp.592-3.

40. Mulhall, *Dictionary of Statistics,* p.550;
B.R. Mitchell and Phyllis Deane, *Abstract Of British
Historical Statistics* (Cambridge, 1962), p.357.

41. Iolo Williams, *The Firm of Cadbury 1831-
1931* (London, 1931), pp.81-93, 281.

42. E.W. Hope to *Royal Commission on Tuberculosis*, PP 1898, vol.xlix, Q. 1,163-5; Richard Perren, *The Meat Trade in Britain 1840-1914* (London, 1978), p.3; Mitchell and Deane, *Abstract*, pp.298-9.

43. Mitchell and Deane, *Abstract*, p.476; Alison Ravetz, 'The Victorian Coal Kitchen and its Reformers', *Victorian Studies*, xi(4), 1968.

44. B.W.E. Alford, *W.D. and H.O. Wills* (London, 1973), pp.165-71, 315.

45. *Lancet*, August 8, 1896, p.427; *Medical Chronicle*, 1896, p.322; *63rd Report ... for England*, PP 1901,vol.xv. pp.xxviii-xxix; *72nd Report ... for England*, PP 1911, vol.x, p.cxxvii; *76th Report ... for England and Wales*, PP 1914-16, vol.ix. p.45.

46. *51st Report ... for Ireland*, PP 1914-16, vol.ix, pp.xvi-xviii; *55th Report ... for Ireland*, PP 1919, vol.x, p.xiv.

47. *72nd Report ... for England*, PP 1911, vol. x, p.xci; *80th Report ... for England and Wales*, PP 1919, vol.x, pp.lxxiii-iv.

48. *80th Report ... for England and Wales*, PP 1919, vol.x, p.10; *British Medical Journal*, May 18, 1934, p.1,075.

49. *25th Report ... for Ireland*, PP 1889, vol. xxv, pp.16-17; *55th Report ... for Ireland*, PP 1919, vol.x, p.xiv.

50. *75th Report ... for England and Wales*, PP 1913, vol.xvii, p.lvi; *80th Report ... for England and Wales*, PP 1919, vol.x, pp.xv, 10, 45.I cannot find readily comparable data for Scotland and Ireland.

51. B.K. Armstrong and A.J. McMichael, 'Overnutrition', in N.F. Stanley and R.A. Joske (eds.), *Changing Disease Patterns and Human Behaviour* (London, 1980), p.496.

52. *55th Report ... for England*, PP 1893-4, vol.xxi, p.xvi; *65th Report ... for England and Wales*, PP 1905, vol.xviii, p.lxxxvi.

53. *76th Report ... for England and Wales*, PP 1914-16, vol.ix, p.lxix.

54. Kathleen Jones, *A History of the Mental Health Services* (London, 1972), pp.356-8; Mark Finnane, *Insanity And The Insane In Post-Famine Ireland* (London, 1981), p.233.

55. John E. Gorst, *The Children Of The Nation* (London, 1906), esp. pp.1-14.

56. C.E.S. Fleming in *British Medical Journal*, February 20, 1926, pp.321-2.

57. Charles Kingsley, 'The Science Of Health', and 'The Two Breaths', in his *Sanitary and Social*

Lectures And Essays (London, 1880), pp.42,50; see also Bruce Haley, *The Healthy Body and Victorian Culture* (Cambridge, 1978), esp. ch.5.

58. J.M. Winter, 'Some aspects of the demographic consequences of the First World War in Britain', *Population Studies*, xxx, 1976, pp.539-52; Statistical Office of the United Nations, *United Nations Demographic Year-books* (1957, 1974), pp. 5,701, 1032.

Chapter Three

WORK

John Benson

I

The historical study of work has been unduly
circumscribed. It has been restricted by a definition of work so narrow as to exclude activities
other than those 'directly rewarded in a financial
sense', an exclusion which has resulted, most
strikingly, in the virtual neglect of women's 'non-
market household labour'.[1] Even the study of paid
work - the subject of this chapter - has been restricted by the interests and preoccupations of
those who have undertaken it. Economic, business
and labour historians alike have tended to limit
their attention to skilled, organised workers in the
expanding, mechanised, capital intensive, modern
sectors of the economy - to industries such as coal,
cotton, the railways, engineering and iron and steel
- where growth appeared the most dynamic and/or industrial relations the most bitter. This perspective too is seriously misleading; for so long as the
'economy is thought of in terms of a division
between the "modern industrial system" and an array
of "pre-industrial" "survivals" (always on the point
of extinction, but still miraculously there a
generation later), the effect will always be to
marginalise the latter - to assign one sector disproportionate importance because it points to the
future and to relegate the rest to a rapidly dis-
solving past.'[2] Even historians studying the modern
industrial sectors of the economy, have tended to
view work, not from the work bench or shop floor,
but from the standpoint either of the directors'
board room or of the union head office. Thus in
coalmining - perhaps the most intensively studied of
all industries - a great deal is known about the
institutional structure of work, about trade unions,

conciliation boards and other bargaining organisations, but next to nothing about what minework
actually entailed, about the grinding, dirty, dangerous jobs that were the daily lot to the rank and
file miner.[3]

It is only recently that a new generation of
historians has begun to escape some of these limitations and tried to examine the complex history of
work itself. Dissatisfied with the existing
historiography, scholars such as Patrick Joyce and
Richard Price have attempted to reconstruct the
working experiences of ordinary men and women; to
examine the challenge to which traditional labour
controls were subjected; and to assess the impact
which the resulting struggles had upon the development of class and political consciousness.[4]

Fortunately, much of this revisionist activity
has been directed towards the nineteenth and early
twentieth centuries so that a good deal new is now
known about the structures and processes of work
between 1875 and 1914. Indeed it is even becoming
possible to identify something approaching a new
consensus, a consensus which suggests that during
this period work underwent the most profound
challenge and change. It is argued that there
occurred a marked shift in the occupational structure; that the employers mounted an increasingly
successful attack upon the craft controls of skilled
workers; and that as a result the gap between the
skilled and the unskilled became significantly
reduced.[5] In fact 'one of the most commonly accepted notions in the economic and social history of
late Victorian and Edwardian England is that the
working people were slowly but assuredly being
moulded into a homogeneous working class which enjoyed a common work experience and outlook.'[6] At
last, then, this revisionist activity had begun to
bear fruit; at last the impact of sectoral changes
and new methods of production upon the working lives
of ordinary men and women has begun to find a central place in the historiography of late nineteenth
and early twentieth century Britain.

II

Historians of work have always laid great stress
upon the structural changes which took place in the
late Victorian and Edwardian economy. However un-
observant in other respects, they have never failed
to appreciate the significance of the shift in employment from the primary to the secondary and

tertiary sectors of the economy. Census analysis
confirms that wage-earners were increasingly likely
to find themselves working in mining, manufacturing
or one of the service industries.[7] Historians have
emphasised too the decline in outwork and self-
employment and the corresponding growth of larger,
more capital intensive industries. Thus it is
widely accepted that this period witnessed the final
displacement of outworkers and small, self-employed
producers of all types by the centripetal forces of
urban, industrial development.[8] Census analysis
seems to confirm too the importance of other structural changes long recognised by historians of work:
a reduction in the scale of both child and female
employment and a certain expansion in the job
opportunities open to working class women.[9] Indeed
it is to such structural changes in the economy that
attention is drawn by those who view the period from
1875-1914 as one of dislocation and conflict.

Supporters of the new orthodoxy are able to
point to other signs of change and of the emergence
of a more homogeneous working experience: the level-
ling effects of new legislation,[10] some diminution
of regional wage variations[11] and, most crucially, a
closing of the gap between skilled and unskilled
workers. They argue that skill, whether genuine or
socially constructed, was under sustained and successful attack and that this led to the progressive
deskilling of working class jobs. The skilled
worker, it is claimed, saw his job become increasingly subdivided, more closely supervised and then -
the final indignity - redistributed among his semi-
skilled and unskilled workmates.[12] There is no
doubt that employers in certain leading sectors of
the economy did mount concerted attempts to rationa-
lise their work systems in order to circumvent the
craft controls exercised by skilled workers. From
the 1890s onwards employers in 'modern' industries
facing increasing competition, tried to tighten
their supervision both by the establishment of
elaborate systems of rules and procedures and by
the replacement of internal contractors and piece-
masters, first by directly employed foreman and
later by white collar personnel in central welfare
departments.[13] This closer supervision was often
supplemented by the introduction of new methods of
wage payment, most commonly of course by piecework,
the system which Marx considered most appropriate to
a capitalist economy.[14] The combination of closer
supervision and new systems of payment could be both
stifling and offensive. In 1911 a factory inspector

discovered one firm employing over five hundred women in which each worker had to hand a tally to a male overseer whenever she went to the lavatory. The time spent in the lavatory was recorded and passed to the manager and at the end of the month the worker was fined if it was found that she had spent more than four minutes in the lavatory.[15]

Yet even this was not enough. In their attack on skill and their search for control over the labour process, the employers' most common strategy - and that which has received most attention since - was the introduction, or the speeding up, of machinery. Indeed it is often supposed that such technological innovation led generally to the intensification, division and deskilling of work. 'In virtually every industry', it is said, 'the cumulative effect of technological innovation throughout the nineteenth century resulted in the creation of a more homogeneous labour force.'[16] New technology was introduced to a wide range of jobs: from printing to coalmining, from building to sailmaking, from ironworking to office work.[17] But the industries chosen most often to demonstrate the onset of mechanisation are textiles, metals and engineering. There is a considerable body of evidence to support the view that in these industries at least formal apprenticeship degenerated and the gap between skilled and unskilled workers was narrowed by mechanisation and other managerial innovations, while in the economy as a whole 'pay differentials between occupations of various skills' which had 'peaked between 1851 and 1871, declined subsequently up to World War I.'[18]

Best known perhaps of all the evidence for the narrowing of the gap between skilled and unskilled workers were the developments taking place in industrial relations. It was during this period that trade union membership grew apace: from about half a million in the mid 1870s, to one and a half million in 1892, and over four million in 1914. The proportion of the working population which was unionised increased from just four percent in 1880 to nearly 25 percent in 1914. But it was not just that trade union membership was growing rapidly; even traditional, craft unions were ceasing to be the exclusive preserve of skilled workers. By 1914 a substantial minority of unskilled workers were union members 'and trade unionism had at last ceased to be largely the preserve of a privileged minority.'[19] It was during this period too that in certain, leading sectors of the economy isolated, craft strikes began to give way to industry-wide confrontation and to the establishment of industry-wide systems of collective bargaining. In coalmining the organisation of employers and employed in the central English coalfields led both to the growth of collective bargaining and to the proliferation of large, set-piece battles such as the 1893 Lockout and the 1912 Minimum Wage Strike. In engineering the reorganisation of the Amalgamated Society in 1892 was followed in 1896 by the formation of the Federation of Engineering Employers' Associations and, in the following year, by the national lockout of 1897-8. Even London building saw a marked change in the nature of its industrial disputes. The isolated, craft strikes of the 1890s gave way to industry-wide bargaining and the general building strike of 1914, in which the artisans finally abandoned their struggles for special treatment and joined forces with their unskilled workmates.[20]

The period 1875-1914 is seen then as one in which work underwent profound challenge and change. Despite the iconoclastic views of historians like Eric Hopkins who believe that 'working conditions were improved in the second half of the nineteenth century',[21] the whole weight of recent research suggests that, on the contrary, conditions deteriorated sharply between 1875 and 1914. It is pleasing that recent research has moved work back to where it belongs: at the centre of the historical stage. Work, whether paid or unpaid, visible or invisible, whether it took place in factory, fields or in the home, was always of crucial significance to ordinary people. Work, in the words of Patrick Joyce, 'got under the skin of everyday life'.[22] Indeed according to Richard Price, work was so important that it is the key to labour's political, social and legal history. Political and class consciousness, he goes so far as to argue, can be understood only in terms of the labour process which, in its turn, 'under industrial capitalism can only be understood as a struggle for authority and control'.[23]

III

If struggle and change constitute one major theme in the history of work between 1875 and 1914, then acquiescence and continuity certainly provide the other. For despite the welcome which must be afforded to recent studies of the labour process, too often they have had the effect of diverting attention away from the continuities which formed so marked a feature of much late nineteenth and early twentieth century working life. Continuity, of course, always tends to be overlooked. Yet despite the comments of contemporaries and the observations of historians, most workers did not join trade unions and most remained remarkably little affected either by structural changes in the economy, by new legislation, by decreasing regionalisation, by closer supervision or by the introduction of more advanced mechanisation. More workers than we suppose continued to earn their living in much the same way, in much the same variety of jobs, as their predecessors earlier in the century.

Of course it would be absurd to deny that major structural changes took place in the British economy between 1875 and 1914. Yet it is misleading to overlook the continuing importance of the traditional, small-scale sectors of the economy. At least a seventh of the workforce was always employed in domestic and personal service while in many other parts of the economy - in building, inshore fishing, transport and services for example - increasing demand was met, not by that concentration of ownership and production that was so characteristic of the basic industries, but by the proliferation of any number of small units.[24] Even in the expanding manufacturing sector, large firms were confined to a relatively limited range of processes. Small firms continued to survive: as late as 1913 more than half a million people (nearly eight per cent of all those employed in manufacturing) were to be found in workshops with no more than four or five workers.[25]

It is equally misleading to exaggerate the decline of self-employment. Even in the most mechanised, modern sectors of the economy few families were dependent simply upon the one or two jobs which they described to the census enumerator. Informal work patterns persisted: most families continued to derive at least part of their income from a whole number of different - and easily overlooked - occupations: from begging and petty crime, as well as from self-employment proper and from various kinds of small-scale entrepreneurial activity. Begging is one of the jobs which has been almost completely overlooked. In so far as it has received any attention at all, it has been viewed as a form of crime rather than as a job of work and has been regarded as the last resort of those on the margins of society.[26] This is doubly misleading. For while beggars were never reluctant to parade their physical infirmities and sick children, to tell tales of

tragedy or to exhibit their capacity for violence,
this did not prevent begging from being a form of
work - and often boring, distasteful and ill paid
work at that.[27] Nor can it be maintained that begging was confined to those on the margins of
society. Oral and autobiographical evidence con-
forms that, in the towns at least, beggars were
drawn from the 'great mass of ordinary working people for whom...poverty provided the backdrop against
which they played out their lives.'[28] They took to
begging for food, goods, money or credit when times
were hard and there appeared no obvious alternative.
Arthur Harding remembers that his family turned
first to its immediate relatives in the East End of
London but that his father had no compunction in
'cadging' from complete strangers: 'the people in
charge of the Mission gave him a ticket to go round
the restaurants to see what they would give him in
leavings.'[29] Naturally it is no longer possible, if
indeed it ever was, to quantify the importance of an
informal, casual and quasi-illegal activity such as
begging. Nonetheless, it is clear that begging remained one of the many strategies of poverty: an
expedient which, it is true, allowed a few people to
avoid regular work, but which enabled many more to
eke out a bare existence in times of particular
distress.

Equally persistent and, until recently, almost
equally overlooked was petty crime: the theft of
such things as food and fuel, usually for consumption but sometimes for resale. Like begging, petty
crime tended to be most common among the most dis-
advantaged: the unskilled, the unemployed and one-
parent families. So here again, there seems little
justification for identifying offenders as members
of a distinct criminal class.[30] Every type of local
economy seemed to sustain its own form of crime. On
the coast there survived a deep-rooted tradition of
plundering any wreckage washed in by the sea. In
coalmining districts 'The "picking" of coal from pit
heads and slag heaps was so deeply ingrained...that
it formed part of the daily domestic routine for
many children, who were expected to salvage coal
both before and after school.'[31] In the countryside
there were 'innumerable opportunities for the plun-
der of its rich bounty.' Children pilfered fruit
and vegetables as a matter of course on their way
home from school;[32] and, despite the risks, poaching
proper remained common among the rural working
class, particularly in isolated communities or those
close to the suburbs of large towns.[33] Some chaps

lived by poaching, recalls a Kent labourer, but
everybody used to do a little bit.[34] Despite some
decline during the later years of the nineteenth
century, poaching remained an accepted, everyday
part of rural life.[35] Not that the growing towns
and cities failed to offer their own temptations and
opportunities. Children and adults scavenged from
gutters, markets and rubbish heaps; they stole from
their places of work and from the local shops. An
Edinburgh boy remembers that in the early years of
this century,

> My mother used to send Jimmy or me for a bottle
> of Tizer or a couple of half loaves, a tin of
> milk, something like that you know, well Jimmy
> and me would work out a plan of action and go
> into a shop, to see if we could skim something
> off it, you know. And my mother she'd said get
> two applies, I've seen me coming back with
> four, a pound of tatties, coming back with a
> pack, that's half a stone I think. Things like
> that, see, we used to nab it, steal 'em in the
> shop. Pretty cheap but than people must have
> thought they were nae stealing.[36]

In both countryside and town, on the coast and
around the collieries, such petty crime continued
virtually unabated. All over the country it continued to provide work and income for a large -
though unknown - number of working class families.
    Nor should it be assumed too readily that other,
more conventional forms of self-employment were destroyed by improved communications and the spread of
urban, industrial growth. Indeed recently completed
research suggests that self-employment and petty
entrepreneurial (or 'penny capitalist') activity
survived among working people to an extent which has
never before been recognised.[37] Although it cannot
be proved that such forms of work survived unscathed
into the twentieth century, it can certainly be
shown that they were not destroyed by the centripetal forces of urban and industrial development.
Thus what little statistical evidence there is
suggests that petty entrepreneurial activity remained a widespread and vital component of working class
life well into the twentieth century: between 1890
and 1914 at least forty percent of working class
families engaged in some form of 'penny capitalist'
work.
    Some ten percent of the working population -
chiefly middle aged, skilled men who had managed to

save some money - went into business in the hope of
attaining independence from wage labour; it was part
of their mid-life search for freedom from the restraints of factory and other work disciplines. They
bought fishing boats, obtained smallholdings, started small building firms, began selling in the
streets and, with their wives, opened small corner
shops. But full-time 'penny capitalism' was always
much less common than part-time. Skilled men, reluctant to abandon wage labour completely, went into
business on a part-time basis. Even in engineering
workshops,

> Apprentices were encouraged to make tools, and
> although youths and fully rated men were not so
> encouraged, foremen generally winked at it when
> work was slack... "I haven't a job in the
> place!" many a foreman has said to me. "Go and
> make something for yourself, and be busy when
> the 'old man' come round, I expect there'll be
> a job in tomorrow."
> The material could usually be "scrounged", but
> sometimes we surreptitiously extracted it from
> the stores. The "heads" rarely arrived until
> nine o'clock, so the pre-breakfast period was
> spent on "contracts," "jobs for the king," or
> "foreigners," as such jobs were colloquially
> called...
> "Contracts" were not confined to small tools.
> Sets of fire-irons and dogs, toasting-forks,
> kitchen shovels, and ornaments of novel design
> and ornate handles, brass, copper, bronze, and
> gunmetal candlesticks, photo frames and mantel-
> piece ornaments, door-knockers, model engines
> for the son, were some of the "foreign orders"
> executed in the bosses' time.[38]

However the vast majority of working people turned
to part-time 'penny capitalism', as they did to
begging or petty crime - simply to cope with the
persistent, nagging poverty of underemployment.
More often than not, it was intended to prevent
things getting worse, rather than to make them get
better. Consequently part-time 'penny capitalism',
like petty crime and begging, was typically the resort of women and children, the casually employed
and the unskilled. In Barrow-in-Furness, Lancaster
and Preston between 40 and 42 percent of working
class mothers engaged in some form of part-time
'penny capitalist' activity after marriage; they
took in washing, put up boarders, sold home-made

food and drink, and opened parlour shops.

The persistence of begging, petty crime, penny capitalism and other forms of self-employment makes it necessary to treat with profound scepticism any belief that levels of female and juvenile employment were relatively low during this period. Even according to the census returns a third of women aged ten and above, and a seventh of children aged between ten and fifteen, were working at the beginning of the present century.[39] But any argument based upon the census is bound to conceal the true extent of female and juvenile labour. Not only did the census exclude unpaid, domestic activities; it also underestimated the amount of paid work performed by women and children. The census always tended to underrate the incidence of women's, and particularly of married women's, part-time work. Thus in the course of her detailed oral investigation of turn of the century Barrow, Preston and Lancaster, Elizabeth Roberts discovered that

> The local census figures show that very few married women were in full-time employment outside the home...only four of the respondents' mothers out of 75 earned a full second income for the family. There were, however, 24 others employed on a casual part-time basis. Their occupations are not enumerated on the census returns but their financial contribution to their families could be of considerable significance.[40]

In the same way, the census always tended to underestimate the extent of child labour. Many children began to work for money long before they left school. Girls went baby-minding and helped their mothers with home, as well as with house work; boys ran errands, washed windows, took on milk and paper rounds and worked on the land. An investigation carried out in 1908 revealed that almost a tenth of the country's two million school children worked outside school hours, a figure which, high though it was, excluded half-timers, street traders and no doubt beggars and petty criminals as well.[41] Although such early twentieth century evidence can throw little light upon the alleged decline in the employment of women and children between 1875 and 1914, it does challenge most strongly the view that juvenile and female employment was relatively unusual during this period. It shows that, largely unknown to census enumerators and historians alike, at least a third of adolescent children and a third of their mothers were still engaged in some form of part-time, paid work during the first decade of the present century. In this respect, as in so many others, the historiography of late Victorian and Edwardian work stands in need of substantial modification.

Another aspect of the historiography that requires revision is the suggestion that during this period the working experience of ordinary people became markedly less heterogeneous; that there occurred in particular a significant narrowing of the gap between skilled and unskilled workers. The evidence brought forward by proponents of this view is far less compelling than it at first appears. Contrary to general belief, legislative action did little to stimulate uniformity of working experience. Factory, workshop, mining, children's, trade union and employers' liability legislation all tended to be complicated and/or ambiguous. Enforcement was difficult. Workers were fearful and ignorant of their rights; employers and magistrates were often hostile; government inspectors were hindered both by bureaucratic restraints and by their inadequate numbers. 'The whole system of inquest and inquiry is so rotten and obnoxious', complained one trade union leader, 'that working men are afraid to give evidence for prosecution or compensation.'[42] At the beginning of the period one Black Country inspector claimed to be responsible for 10,000 workshops while as late as 1905 there were just 151 inspectors to supervise a total of 255,000 registered workplaces: an average of more than 1,750 each.[43] The consequences were predictable. The constant evasions of the law, especially by small employers, show once again how undue concentration upon the activities of large firms in leading sectors of the economy can reinforce the beguiling - yet misleading - impression of an increasingly homogeneous workforce.[44]

Nor is there any reason to suppose that the development of a more homogeneous workforce was aided by any marked diminution in regional variation. Nineteenth century industrialisation had produced a number of specialised regional economies; and regional - not to mention intra-regional - diversity remained one of the outstanding characteristics of the late nineteenth and early twentieth century British economy.[45] There remained wide variations in the scale and concentration of production, in degrees of mechanisation, in the

recruitment methods and wage systems adopted, and in
the workers' levels of earnings. Regional wage
differentials remained stubbornly persistent. Farm
labourers in Oxfordshire earned only two thirds as
much as those in County Durham; miners in Somerset
and North Wales brought home no more than three
quarters as much as their colleagues in the Midland,
South Wales and Northumberland and Durham coalfields. Thus it has been found that a recent
attempt 'to elucidate regional economic structures
in Victorian Britain...justifies, and indeed requires, disaggregation at regional level'.[46]

The closer supervision and new methods of payment associated with the doctrines of systematic
management were adopted in only a minority of firms,
in a minority of trades such as textiles, engineering and metalwork. Internal subcontract systems
survived even in textiles and remained common in
parts of ironworking, building and civil engineering, pottery, shipbuilding and coalmining; in 1908
a quarter of the entire labour force in Black
Country coalmining was still working under the hated
'butties'.[47] Even the few industries which adopted
piecework and similar systems of payment, did not do
so comprehensively. As late as 1914, 54 percent of
fitters in the engineering industry and 63 percent
of turners were still not on piece rates. And even
when piece rates were introduced, they were sometimes successfully resisted. In the building
industry, for instance, every union, at one time or
another, fought the introduction of piecework -
indeed this was said to be one of the few issues on
which even Applegarth had been prepared to fight.
Such resistance makes it easy to forget that the
vast majority of workers, on farms and building
sites, in shops, private houses and on the railways,
remained quite unaffected; they continued to be paid
in the same ways as had always been the custom.[48]

It is equally easy to overestimate the extent
to which employers introduced mechanised production
and thus to exaggerate the division and deskilling
of working class jobs. Even in industries such as
textiles and engineering, which were at the forefront of technological change, mechanisation proceeded at a halting pace. The bulk of engineering
work continued to be produced, not in large runs by
unskilled workers on specialised machines, but in
small batches by skilled workers using general
purpose machines. In the textile industry in 1911
there were still fewer than 5,500 fully automatic
Northrup looms out of more than 800,000 in weaving

as a whole.[49]   In other parts of the economy the
spread of mechanisation was slow indeed.   The great
mass of workers, whether skilled or unskilled, remained unaffected in any direct way by the profound
consequences of the consolidation of modern factory
industry.[50]

So although it is undoubtedly possible to point
to signs of an increasingly homogenous workforce,
this would be seriously misleading.   A careful
examination of the available evidence shows that
rather than coming to share a common experience and
outlook, the workforce remained remarkable for its
heterogeneity.   There remained, for example, a wide
gap between male and female workers; a vast gulf
between the unskilled and the skilled, who managed
to retain some considerable control over their working lives.   What is striking is not the growing
homogeneity of work experience, but rather its persistent diversity. Women continued to be subordinate
at the workplace.   They remained confined over-
whelmingly to the same narrow range of low status,
low skill, low paid jobs in textiles, dressmaking
and domestic service.   Although attitudes towards
married women's work were by no means uniform, there
survived an assumption, common to both sexes, that a
woman's work and wages were temporary and/or
supplementary to a man's.[51]   Even where wage rates
were nominally equal, there were all sorts of ways
of depressing women's earnings by unofficial means.
In the North Staffordshire pottery industry, for
example, custom decreed that women were not allowed
to earn more than their male colleagues: female tile
makers were forced to stop work by the men in their
shops if it was found that their dexterity was enabling them to exceed male earnings.[52]

Just as enduring as this sexual division (and
sometimes congruent with it) was the gap between
unskilled and skilled workers.   In his recent,
pioneering study of skill in manual labour, Charles
More concludes that while 'it would be unwise to
make any general comments about changes in the
average level of skill during the nineteenth century
there does seem a *prima facie* case for saying that
the evidence does not support a thesis of unilateral
decline.'[53]   Thus although it is true that in many
of the older crafts there did take place a slow
decline in formal, indentured apprenticeship, this
method of training survived because it continued to
meet the needs of both sides of industry.   At any
time early in the present century there were still
at least 340,000 apprentices in training, largely in

engineering, shipbuilding, printing, building and
woodworking. However in many of the newer industries - papermaking, milling, footwear, clothing,
food manufacturing and the precious metal trades -
skill was acquired, not by formal apprenticeship,
but by migration or by some system of 'following
up'. The years 1875 to 1914 saw, then, an expansion
of work which, if not formally apprenticed, nonetheless definitely continued to demand the acquisition
of skill.[54]

Except for the relatively few workers confronted directly by irresistible technological change,
wage differentials remained sharp and status differences pronounced. Skilled and unskilled workers
were rewarded very differently. Even within the
same trade or occupation wage differentials of 25 to
50 percent were not uncommon. Although there was
some narrowing of the gap over the period, it has
been estimated that in 1913 semi-skilled workers in
coal, cotton, building and engineering were still
earning 12 to 29 percent less - and unskilled
workers 34 to 49 percent less - than their colleagues who could boast a skill.[55] Older, skilled
workers remained reluctant to accept the younger or
less skilled as equals. Coal hewers looked down
upon other miners, train drivers upon their firemen.

> At the turn of the century in Kentish Town
> there existed separate 'drivers'' and 'fire-
> men's' bars in the local public houses, and
> when men lodged away in company hostels,
> drivers and firemen had separate dining tables.
> On these 'lodging turns' it was not unusual for
> drivers to order their firemen to bed, or to
> advise them when they had had enough to
> drink.[56]

It was the skilled workers who were able best to
retain a degree of control over their work. Indeed
one of the great benefits of recent research has
been to draw attention to their tenacious struggles,
to their attempts at informal organisation, sabotage
and various forms of restrictive practice. In
industries as varied as mining and textiles, building and engineering, skilled men proved surprisingly
successful - though not of course without constant
struggle - at resisting the encroachments of the
employers.[57] Coalmining and engineering were two
very different industries. Yet in both skilled men
sought, and managed, to retain a certain amount of
job control. In the old established Northumberland

and Durham coalfield hewers and other workers fought
to preserve cavilling: the

> system of job control which operated for
> hundreds of years...and took the form of a kind
> of lottery to allocate working places. The
> system was evolved of drawing places out of a
> hat along with names of men to work them. This
> lottery gave everyone the same chance of good
> and bad places, and prevented union men and
> agitators being victimized with bad and danger-
> ous work places and 'crawlers' or 'gaffers'
> men' from getting the good places as a reward
> for their collaboration.[58]

Despite the fact that engineering is one of the
occupations selected most often to illustrate the
disastrous consequences of mechanisation, craftsmen
in the industry are also 'justly famed' for their
resistance to the imposition of new job controls.
Well known is the apocryphal story told to James
Hinton:

> There used to be a craftsman in this shop who
> always came to work with a piece of chalk in
> his pocket. When he arrived each morning he
> would at once draw a chalk circle on the floor
> around his machine. If the foreman wanted to
> speak to him he could do so as he wished, as
> long as he stayed outside the circle. But if
> he put one foot across that line, he was a dead
> man.[60]

A London engineer recalls the disruptive impact of
new machinery in the workshop in which he was employed in 1897; but he goes on to explain that,

> Passive resistance and sabotage were practised
> ...We persuaded the man in the tool room to
> allow us in "just to touch this tool up, Jim,"
> and ended by walking in and out at will. Time
> limits, fixed by theoretic charts, were in-
> variably all wrong. When excessive - as they
> sometimes were - we ca'cannied so as not to
> earn too much; if insufficient, we "went slow"
> just the same, and lodged a complaint to the
> foreman, who sent for the rate fixer. When he
> arrived there ensued a wordy war between the
> three, then the rate-fixer timed the job with
> a stop-watch; but it was easy to "swing the
> lead" on an inexperienced clerk by providing

> that the tool would not cut properly. We
> seldom got the increase we demanded - we didn't
> expect to - but we usually got enough to suit
> our purpose.[61]

It is only too easy then to exaggerate the narrowing
of the gap between different parts of the country,
between men and women, between the skilled and the
unskilled. Even in industries such as textiles,
metals and engineering which were affected most in-
tensely by mechanisation and other managerial
innovation, the workforce remained most strikingly
divided.

It is tempting to turn to industrial relations
in search of signs of the supposed increasing homogeneity of working experience. Yet here again the
evidence is less compelling than it appears at first
sight. For while it is true that trade union
membership grew rapidly between 1875 and 1914, the
vast majority of the working population - over 75
percent - were never unionised. Even in the heavy,
capital intensive sectors of the economy where trade
unionism was strongest, membership remained patchy.
Coalmining is a case in point: to judge from the
proliferation of published and unpublished trade
union histories, it would be easy to imagine that
the history of the miners is synonymous with the
history of their unions. But nothing could be
further from the truth. It was not until the 1890s
that half the coalmining labour force became unionised and not until the very end of the century that
the mining unions even began to accept into membership that fifth of the labour force which worked on
the surface. By 1910 the only occupational groups
able to boast union membership equal to even a third
of their workforces were shipbuilding, mining and
quarrying, cotton, printing and national government.[62]

It was not just that trade union membership
generally remained very much a minority activity.
Women and other unskilled workers remained largely
non-unionised. Despite the efforts of such pioneers
as Lady Dilke, Mary Macarthur and Margaret Bondfield,
women were always difficult to organise. Female
trade unionism remained impeded not only by low
wages, domestic burdens, the hostility of the employers and popular prejudices against working
women, but also by the attitudes of union members
themselves. Women often found themselves refused
membership, given an inferior membership grading or
discriminated against in other ways. Although two

thirds of female unionists were members of textile trade unions, here too they continued to be treated as second class citizens. Thus although more than 80 percent of the membership of the Cardroom Workers' Association were women, they were largely excluded from positions as lay officers or as permanent officials. Even when the Kidderminster Power Loom, Carpet Weavers' and Textile Workers' Association finally brought itself to accept women members during the First World War, it ruled that the vote of 25 female members should be equivalent of one man's. The result of all this was, not surprisingly, that in 1914 there were still no more than 358,000 women in trade unions out of a recorded female labour force of over three and a quarter million. Search as one will, there is little sign here of the workforce becoming more homogeneous, little indication of the trade unions helping to heal the workplace divisions between men and women.[63]

Nor can significant signs of an increasingly homogenous workforce be discerned in union attempts to represent the great mass of the workers. The persistence of small work units; the resilience of self-employment, begging and petty crime; low and uncertain wages; employer hostility: all these militated against trade union organisation. So too did ignorance: when Robert Roberts looked back at his Salford childhood in the early years of this century, he concluded that:

> general apathy stemmed not from despair at the unions in chains nor the failure of such political action as there was; it sprang from mass ignorance: the millions did not know and did not want to know. At that time one had to work hard indeed to convince the unskilled labourer of the need for trade unions at all. An individualist, he was simply not interested in easing the common lot, but concerned entirely with improving his own, and that not too vigorously. From what little he understood, the aims of trade unionism seemed quite impracticable and those of socialism utterly unreal.[64]

As late as 1910 trade unionists accounted for fewer than a fifth of workers even in organised industries such as metals, engineering and shipbuilding, building, transport, clothing, woodworking and printing and paper. At the end of the period three quarters of the working population remained un-unionised.

'The attempt of the "new unions" to bring trade unionism to all sections of the working class had largely failed'.[65]

It is also easy to exaggerate the development of industry-wide systems of collective bargaining and the growth of industry-wide strikes and lock-outs. Despite the establishment of well publicised conciliation and arbitration boards and the fact that by 1910 'almost every...well-organized industry, except the railways, had evolved its own system of collective bargaining,' it cannot be concealed that 80 percent of workers were still not covered by such bargaining procedures.[66] pointed out, an unrealistic amount of attention has been directed towards the industry-wide form of industrial bargaining: but he is able to show that in the North Staffordshire pottery industry, for example, many of the so called general agreements covering the whole industry which were reached in 1900 and 1911, were not really worthy of the name. As Phelps-Brown long ago pointed out, relations between employer and employed at the place of work remained remarkably unregulated...four out of five employees made their own bargains'.[67] It is easy, too, to fall into the trap of paying too little attention to small, sectional disputes and too much to industry-wide, set-piece struggles. Not even in the leading sectors of the economy such as coal and cotton, did the growing organisation of employers and employed lead simply and inexorably towards industry-wide confrontation. Indeed this growing organisation also led industrial relations in the opposite direction: towards local initiative, local action and local, often unofficial, disputes. Joseph White's judgement on labour relations in the pre-First World War Lancashire cotton industry has a wider validity.

> Although it was the two trade-wide lock-outs that rivetted the attention of the nation and most subsequent historians, they were not totally representative of the 1910-14 unrest. In scale and content they marked a continuation of the workers' propensity to weave a small, dense pattern of strikes fought over local and immediate issues.[68]

Thus the conduct of industrial relations is no more suggestive of a growing homeogeneity of work experience than the limited progress made by the unions towards organising the vast majority of workers.

The British experience of work remained, as it always had been, striking for its heterogeneity.

IV

Recent research has done an enormous amount to deepen our understanding of late nineteenth and early twentieth century work, not least in directing our attention towards the struggles between employers and employed for control of the labour process. It is no longer possible to view work from the directors' board room or the union head office, unaware apparently of the changes which were taking place at the point of production; no longer possible to overlook the importance of these changes in the lives of ordinary working men and women. Nonetheless, the new approach is not without its dangers. So far it has done little to redress one profound imbalance which exists in the historiography of work: the disproportionate amount of attention which has been directed towards skilled workers in the expanding, capital intensive sectors of the economy. This can still lead to unsound extrapolation from the known, but probably untypical, work experience of the few to the unknown, but probably more diverse and certainly more typical experiences of the many.[69] Thus it is still possible to be misled into overlooking one major theme which is present in the best of the new historiography: the persistence, in even the leading sectors of the economy, of major continuities in workplace organisation, experiences and attitudes.[70] The conclusion, unspectacular and cautious though it is, must surely be that the years from 1875 to 1914 were a period neither of unthreatened stability nor of revolutionary change. It was rather a transitional period in the history of work, one in which acquiescence was probably as common as struggle and continuity almost certainly more common than change.

NOTES

1. Eric Richards, 'Women in the British Economy since about 1700: An Interpretation', *History*, 59 (197), Oct. 1974, p.338. It is extremely difficult to draw precise distinctions between work, occupation and income: see, for example, S.R.Parker

and M.A. Smith, 'Work and Leisure', in R. Dubin (ed.), *Handbook of Work, Organization, and Society* (Chicago,1976), pp.41-2; Peter Worsley, *et. al.*, *Introducing Sociology*(Harmondsworth, 1980), pp.274-7.

2. Editorial Collective in *History Workshop*, 3, 1977, p.2.

3. Charles More, *Skill and the English Working Class, 1870-1914* (London, 1980), preface; John Benson, *British Coalminers in the Nineteenth Century: A Social History* (Dublin, 1980), pp.1-5; M.J.Daunton 'Down the Pit: Work in the Great Northern and South Wales Coalfields, 1870-1914', *Economic History Review*, xxxiv(4), 1981, pp.578-80.

4. Patrick Joyce, *Work, Society and Politics: The culture of the factory in later Victorian England* (London, 1982); Richard Price, *Masters, unions and men: Work control in building and the rise of labour 1830-1914*(Cambridge, 1980); Harry Braverman, *Labor and Monopoly Capital: The Degradation of Work in the Twentieth Century* (New York, 1974).

5. Joyce, *Work*, pp.62-3; E.J. Hobsbawm, 'Custom, Wages and Work-Load in Nineteenth-Century Industry', in Asa Briggs and John Saville (eds.), *Essays in Labour History* (London, 1967), p.345; Standish Meacham, *A Life Apart: The English Working Class 1890-1914* (London, 1977), p.38; Van Gore, 'Rank-and-File Dissent', in Chris Wrigley (ed.), *A History of British Industrial Relations 1875-1914* (Brighton, 1982), p.64; Sylvia Grossman, 'The Radicalization of London Building Workers 1890-1914' (Unpublished Univ. of Toronto Ph. D. Thesis, 1977), pp.319, 323, 333.

6. James A. Schmiechen, 'State Reform and the Local Economy: An Aspect of Industrialization in late Victorian and Edwardian London', *Economic History Review*, xxviii(3), 1975, p.413. See also Grossman, 'Building', p.xv.

7. Phyllis Deane and W.A. Cole, *British Economic Growth 1688-1959: Trends and Structure* (Cambridge, 1969), pp.141-2; Gregory Anderson, 'Some Aspects of the Labour Market in Britain c.1870-1914', in Wrigley (ed.), *Industrial Relations*, pp.9-10; M.W. Kirby, *The British Coalmining Industry 1870-1946: A Political and Economic History* (London, 1977), p.6.

8. Geoffrey Crossick, 'The Emergence of the Lower Middle Class in Britain: A Discussion', in Geoffrey Crossick (ed.), *The Lower Middle Class in Britain 1870-1914* (London, 1977), p.15; Duncan

Bythell, *The Sweated Trades: Outwork in Nineteenth-century Britain* (London, 1978), pp.14-15, 19, 143, 147-8, 151; Joyce, *Work*, pp.74, 136, 159, 340; P.L. Payne, 'The Emergence of the Large-scale Company in Great Britain, 1870-1914', *Economic History Review*, xx(3), 1967, pp.519, 527, 534.

9. E.H. Hunt, *British Labour History 1815-1914* (London, 1981), pp.8-10, 15-18, 21-3; Meacham, *Life Apart*, p.103; Bythell, *Sweated Trades*, p.148; Craig Littler, 'Deskilling and changing structures of control', in Stephen Wood (ed.), *The Degradation of Work?: Skill, deskilling and the labour process* (London, 1982), p.137; B.L. Hutchins, *Women in Modern Industry* (London, 1915), pp.84-8; Barbara Drake, *Women in the Engineering Trades: A Problem, a Solution, and some Criticisms...* (London, 1917),p.8.

10. Eric Hopkins, *A Social History of the English Working class 1815-1945* (London, 1979), pp. 104-5; A.E. Musson, 'Industrial Motive Power in the United Kingdom, 1800-70', *Economic History Review*, xxix(3), 1976, p.435.

11. E.H. Hunt, *Regional Wage Variations in Britain 1850-1914* (Oxford, 1973), p.358; Hunt, *Labour History*, p.102.

12. The classic statement is of course Braverman, *Labor*. See also Cunningham, *infra*; R.J. Morris, 'Whatever happened to the British working class, 1750-1850?', *Bulletin of the Society for the Study of Labour History*, 41, 1980, pp.14-15; Grossman, 'Building'; Richard Price, 'The Labour Process and Labour History', *Social History Society Newsletter*, 6(1), Spring 1981; Joseph Melling, 'British Employers and the Human Factor in Industry: the ideology of welfare management in Britain, c. 1880-1930', *Social History Society Newsletter*, 6(1), Spring 1981; Stephen A. Marglin, 'What do bosses do? The origins and functions of hierarchy in capitalist production', in A. Gorz (ed.), *The Division of Labour* (Hassocks, 1976).

13. Littler, 'Deskilling', pp.133-5, 137; W.R. Garside and H.F. Gospel, 'Employers and Managers: Their Organizational Structure and Changing Industrial Strategies', in Wrigley (ed.), *Industrial Relations*, pp.100-103.

14. W.R. Watson, *Machines and Men: An Autobiography of an Itinerant Mechanic* (London, 1935), pp.94-7; Richard Price, 'Rethinking Labour History: The Importance of Work', in James E. Cronin and Jonathen Schneer (eds.), *Social Conflict and the Political Order in Modern Britain* (London, 1982), p.201; Joyce, *Work*, p.100; Grossman, 'Building',

pp.38, 317-8; Roger Penn, 'Skilled manual workers in the labour process, 1856-1964', in Wood (ed.), *Degradation*, pp.93-5.

15. Meacham, *Life Apart*, p.110. See also Watson, *Machines*, pp.90-91.

16. Grossman, 'Building', p.xv. Also Mark G. Hirsch, 'The Federation of Sailmakers of Great Britain and Ireland, 1889-1922; A Craft Union in Crisis' (Unpublished Univ. of Warwick M.A. Thesis, 1976), p.69; Meacham, *Life Apart*, pp.25, 134-5, 140, 143; H.F. Moorhouse, 'The Marxist theory of the labour aristocracy', *Social History*, 3(1), 1978, p.68.

17. Benson, *Coalminers*; Joyce, *Work*, p.52; Grossman, 'Building', pp.xiii, xvii, 15, 86-93, 105-6, 315-19, 333; Jonathan Zeitlin, 'Craft Control and the division of labour: engineers and compositors in Britain 1890-1930', *Cambridge Journal of Economics*, 3, 1979. For textiles, see Joyce, *Work*, pp.xiv, xviii, 3, 50, 67, 73-4, 77, 166-7, 226; Joseph L. White, 'Lancashire Cotton Textiles', in Wrigley (ed.), *Industrial Relations*, pp.211, 213. For metals and engineering, see Penn, 'Skilled manual workers', pp.92-3; Hirsch, 'Sailmakers', p.70; Watson, *Machines*, pp.12-13, 214; James Hinton, *The First Shop Stewards' Movement* (London, 1973), pp.58-9; Drake, *Women*, pp.8-9; Garside and Gospel, 'Employers', p.109; Price, 'Rethinking', p.192.

18. Jeffrey G. Williamson, 'Earnings Inequality in Nineteenth-Century Britain', *Journal of Economic History*, xl(3), 1980, p.465. Also R. Halstead, 'The Stress of Competition from the Workman's Point of View', *The Economic Review*, 4, Jan. 1894, pp.54-6; Meacham, *Life Apart*, pp. 141-2, 179; Grossman, 'Building', pp.xvi-xvii; Watson, *Machines*, p.32; Charles More, 'Skill and the survival of apprenticeship', in Wood (ed.), *Degradation*, p.110; More, *Skill*.

19. Hunt, *Labour History*, p.302. Also pp.296, 301, 305; Henry Pelling, *A History of British Trade Unionism* (Harmondworth, 1963), p.95; Benson, *Coalminers*, pp.196-7; Drake, *Women*, p.10; K.D. Brown (ed.), *Essays in Anti-Labour History: Responses to the Rise of Labour in Britain* (London, 1974), pp. 4-5; James Hinton, *Labour and Socialism: A History of the British Labour Movement 1867-1974* (Brighton, 1983), p.24.

20. John Benson, 'Coalmining', in Wrigley (ed.), *Industrial Relations*, pp.200-204; Pelling, *Trade Unionism*, pp.112-13; Penn, 'Skilled manual workers', p.93; Grossman, 'Building', pp.314-7, 320; Joyce,

Work, p.64.

21. Hopkins, *Social History*, p.106. Also
Hobsbawm, 'Custom', p.114; Meacham, *Life Apart*, pp.
129-31; Patrick Joyce, 'The Culture of the Craft and
the Culture of the Factory in 19th Century England',
Social History Society Newsletter, 6(1), 1981.

22. Joyce, *Work*, p.97.

23. Price, 'Rethinking', p.197. Also Price,
'Labour Process', p.2; Grossman, 'Building', p.333.

24. Raphael Samuel, 'The Workshop of the World:
Steam Power and Hand Technology in mid-Victorian
Britain', *History Workshop*, 3, 1977; Editorial
Collective, 'Work'; Deane and Cole, *Economic Growth*,
p.142.

25. Payne, 'Large-scale Company', p.520; John
Benson, *The Penny Capitalists: A Study of Nineteenth-
Century Working-Class Entrepreneurs* (Dublin, 1983),
pp.41-9; Deane and Cole, *Economic Growth*, p.143;
Littler, 'Deskilling', p.132.

26. J.J. Tobias, *Crime and Industrial Society
in the 19th Century* (London, 1967), pp.73-7. Several
of the contributors to this volume, and a number of
those to whom I read an earlier version of this
chapter, disagree with my view that begging was a
form of work.

27. David Jones, *Crime, Protest, Community and
Police in Nineteenth-Century Britain* (London, 1982),
pp.199-200; Tobias, *Crime*, pp.76-7; Robert Roberts,
*The Classic Slum: Salford Life in the First Quarter
of the Century* (Manchester, 1971), p.150; W.H.
Davies, *The Autobiography of a Super-Tramp* (London,
1924), pp.203, 206, 213, 249-50.

28. Colin Bundy and Dermot Healy, 'Aspects of
Urban Poverty', *Oral History*, 6(1), 1978, p.79.

29. Raphael Samuel, *East End Underworld:
Chapters in the Life of Arthur Harding* (London,
1981), pp.23-4, 29-30.

30. Jones, *Crime*, ch.1, pp.126, 135.

31. Stephen Humphries, 'Steal to Survive: The
Social Crime of Working Class Children 1890-1940',
Oral History, 9(1), 1981, p.27. Also p.29; Benson,
Penny Capitalists, pp.9-10.

32. Humphries, 'Steal', p.28.

33. Jones, *Crime*, pp.66-7, 69, 75-6; Humphries,
'Steal', pp.28-9

34. University of Kent, Oral History Collection,
Michael Winstanley, 'Life in Kent before 1914', G2,
H. Gambrill, pp.161-2. Also B8, P.H. Barnes, p.36;
B10, J.H. Barwick, p.46.

35. Jones, *Crime*, pp.62, 67, 84.

36. Humphries, 'Steal', p.30. Also Bundy and

Healy, 'Urban Poverty', pp.86, 92; Benson,*Penny Capitalists*, pp.96, 99-100; Raphael Samuel, 'Industrial Crime in the 19th Century', *Bulletin of the Society for the Study of Labour History*, 25, 1972.

37. The following section is based upon by book, *Penny Capitalists*.

38. Watson, *Machines*, p.22.

39. Richards, 'Women', p.352; Meacham, *Life Apart*, p.95.

40. Elizabeth Roberts, 'Working-Class Standards of Living in Barrow and Lancaster, 1890-1914', *Economic History Review*, xxx(2), 1977, p.311. See also E. Bridge, 'Women's Employment: Problems of Research', *Bulletin of the Society for the Study of Labour History*, 26, 1973; *Select Committee of the House of Lords on Sweating System*, PP 1889, 3rd Report, Q.19,701, R. Juggins.

41. Meacham, *Life Apart*, pp.100, 175-6; Hunt, *Labour History*, p.9; Bythell, *Sweated Trades*, pp. 144, 159, 166, 172; Schmiechen, 'State Reform'; D.H. Morgan, *Harvesters and Harvesting 1840-1900: A Study of the Rural Proletariat* (London, 1982), pp. 58-73.

42. University of Bristol, Wills Memorial Library, Forest of Dean Miners' Association, E.A. Rymer, *To the President and Members of the Trades Union Congress Aberdeen*, Sept. 5, 1884.

43. Hopkins, *Social History*, pp.104-5; Meacham, *Life Apart*, p.243, n.60; John Benson, 'The Compensation of English Coal Miners and their Dependants for Industrial Accidents, 1860-1897' (Unpublished Univ. of Leeds Ph. D. Thesis, 1974); Hutchins, *Women*, p.184; Sir Andrew Bryan, *The Evolution of Health and Safety in Mines* (London, 1975), pp.90-91; Roy MacLeod, 'Social Policy and the "Floating Population": The Administration of the Canal Boats Acts 1877-1899', *Past and Present*, 35, 1966, pp.123, 131.

44. Joyce, *Work*, pp.69-70; Hopkins, *Social History*, pp.104-5; Lowell J. Satre, 'After the Match Girls' Strike: Bryant and May in the 1890s', *Victorian Studies*, 26(1), 1982. The smallest employers were often excluded from the legislation.

45. C.H. Lee, *Regional economic growth in the United Kingdom since the 1880s* (Maidenhead, 1971), pp.19-20; C.H. Lee, 'Regional Growth and Structural Change in Victorian Britain', *Economic History Review*, xxiv(3), 1981, pp.451-2.

46. Lee, 'Regional Growth', pp.439, 451. Also Hunt, *Regional*, pp.1, 61-6; Joyce, *Work*, pp.77, 100, 166-7, 225; Benson, *Miners*, p.78.

47. Littler, 'Deskilling', pp.124-5, 128, 133, 138; Garside and Gospel, 'Employers', p.102; Grossman, 'Building', p.39; Benson, *Miners*, p.72; Richard Whipp, 'Some Aspects of Work, Home and Trade Unionism in the British Pottery Industry 1900-1920' (Paper read at Anglo-Dutch Labour History Conference, Maastricht, 1982), p.4.

48. Penn, 'Manual workers', pp.94-5; Price, 'Rethinking', p.201; Grossman, 'Building', pp.38,80.

49. More, *Skill*, p.27; Joyce, *Work*, p.54.

50. Joyce, *Work*, pp.312-3, 341; Grossman, 'Building', pp.88, 331; Whipp, 'Pottery', p.2.

51. Hunt, *Labour History*, pp.98, 101, 106; More, *Skill*, pp.229-30.

52. Whipp, 'Pottery', p.7. Also Joyce, *Work*, pp.112-3.

53. More, *Skill*, p.184.

54. More, *Skill*, pp.64, 164, 181, 228, 231; Meacham, *Life Apart*, pp.179-80; Eric Hopkins, 'Were the Webbs wrong about apprenticeship in the Black Country?' *West Midland Studies*, 6, 1973.

55. J.W.F. Rowe, *Wages in Practice and Theory* (London, 1928), p.49; Grossman, 'Building', pp.5, 315; Williamson, 'Inequality'.

56. Frank McKenna, 'Victorian Railway Workers', *History Workshop*, 1, 1976, p.42. Also Benson, 'Coalmining', p.193.

57. Price, 'Rethinking', pp.185-8, 192-8; Price, 'Labour Process'. For building, see Grossman, 'Building', p.42; Price, *Masters*. For textiles, see Joyce, *Work*, p.96; White, 'Cotton Textiles', pp.214-6; William Lazonick, 'Industrial relations and technical change: the case of the self-acting mule', *Cambridge Journal of Economics*, 3, 1979, pp.231-62.

58. Dave Douglass, 'The Durham pitman', in Raphael Samuel (ed.), *Miners, Quarrymen and Salt-Workers* (London, 1977), p.312. See also Mike Holbrook-Jones, *Supremacy and Subordination of Labour: The Hierarchy of Work in the Early Labour Movement* (London, 1982), pp.114-9.

59. Hinton, *Shop Stewards*, pp.56-100; Price, 'Rethinking', p.193.

60. Hinton, *Shop Stewards*, p.96.

61. Watson, *Machines*, p.92. Also 12-13, 214.

62. Benson, *Miners*, pp.189, 196, 199; H.A. Clegg, A. Fox and A.F. Thompson, *A History of British Trade Unions since 1889* (Oxford, 1964), pp. 467-9.

63, Richards, 'Women', p.353; Whipp, 'Pottery', p.22; Norbert C. Soldon, *Women in British Trade Unions 1874-1976* (Dublin, 1978), p.63; Sheila

Lewenhak, *Women and Trade Unions: An Outline History of Women in the British Trade Union Movement* (London, 1977), pp.92-3; Angela John, *By the Sweat of Their Brow: Women Workers at Victorian Coal Mines* (London, 1980), p.163, n.80; Sheila Lewenhak, 'Women at Work: Sub-contracting, Craft Unionism and Women in England, with Special Reference to the West Midlands, 1750-1914', in Anthony Wright and Richard Shackleton (eds.), *Worlds of Labour: Essays in Birmingham Labour History* (Birmingham, 1983), pp.11-13.

    64. Roberts, *Classic Slum*, p.90.

    65. Clegg, Fox and Thompson, *Trade Unions*, p.487. Also pp.456, 468.

    66. Clegg, Fox and Thompson, *Trade Unions*, p.47. Also Joyce, *Work*, pp.63-4, 68.

    67. Whipp, 'Pottery', pp.18-19.

    68. White, 'Cotton', p.225. Also 225-7; Benson, 'Coalmining', pp.203-5.

    69. For a similar argument applied to an earlier period, see Eric Hopkins, 'Working Hours and Conditions during the Industrial Revolution: A Re-Appraisal', *Economic History Review*, xxxv(1), 1982.

    70. For example, Samuel, 'Workshop'; Joyce, *Work*, p.225; D. Bythell, *The Handloom Weavers: A Study in the English Cotton Industry during the Industrial Revolution* (Cambridge, 1969).

Chapter Four

STRIKES

M.J. Haynes

I

On July 14th 1900, 36 men in a Willenhall iron
foundry walked out. Casting iron was an unpleasant
job at the best of times but the price of graphite
had risen and their employer reintroduced clay
crucibles worsening, as they saw it, their conditions. For the men this had been the last straw.
As they came blinking out into the daylight no doubt
their feelings were mixed. Could we listen to their
conversations as they walked out of the yard we
would hear bitterness, anger and resentment that
they had been forced to strike but we would also
catch a certain elation that the habits and routines
of years past had suddenly been thrown off. Perhaps
this elation would affect us too though through it
we might also catch a tinge of fear that when it was
over some of them, perhaps all of them, would not
walk through these gates again. On the 26th of
August it was all over and the men had lost. Work,
our report says tersely, 'resumed by most workpeople
on employer's terms.' And so our strike passes into
obscurity. We only know of it because the statis-
ticians at the Board of Trade listed its bare
details.[1] A year later we would not even have
these, for the task of trying to cover all strikes
overwhelmed the civil servants and they abandoned
it. Then it would only have been what it has since
become for historians - a statistic; one amongst the
648 strikes recorded in 1900, one amongst the 19,000
strikes recorded by the Board of Trade in the years
1888 - 1914. Even in 1900 the 36 men made up only
an infinitesimal proportion of the total number of
strikers and strike days. In the terms set by the
late E.H. Carr our Willenhall iron casters' strike is
not an 'historical fact'.

And yet it is just in its very banality that it lays claim to our attention because for the iron casters themselves it was a fact, just as was every one of the strike days recorded by the state and the many more that did not creep into the statistics. Moreover, if the evidence of oral history is any guide, it was a 'fact' that would still figure in their memories in later years. For those few weeks they had not only challenged their employer, they had challenged themselves and even if, at the end of the day, the experience chastened them and reinforced old attitudes, historians still have the task of disentangling the meaning of this and thousands of similar actions in the context of working class life in our period.

Yet for some historians such actions are not a problem. Strikes, writes one, were 'blind protests' which might be garnished by socialists 'with the jargon of class warfare' but which in reality were little more than responses to changing economic conditions.[2] There is a condescension in the words themselves that mark out these views as those of a conservative historian. But from the left too, albeit by a different route, we find the same conclusion. Thus strikes were largely 'sectional' and 'economistic', detached from the 'wider arena of working class experience' which created a class culture 'to a significant degree autonomous of ... immediate workplace connections.'[3]

It is in no small part due to these attitudes that we actually know so little about strikes. Strike statistics are endlessly quoted, often with insufficient appreciation of their limitations; some of the biggest strikes are well discussed and occasionally a smaller strike in a particular factory such as that at the Manningham Mills in Bradford in 1890 enters into the wider stream of history - in this case because it led, in part, to the founding of the Independent Labour Party. But generally we still know relatively little and when it comes to the strikers themselves the gaps are even greater. Writing thirty years ago in a now classic study, K.G.J.C. Knowles spoke of 'rank-and-file attitudes and opinions as surely one of the most important aspects of strikes and the one about which least is known.' Today little has changed even for such an important wave of militancy as that before the First World War. Here a recent historian, Bob Holton, notes that the analysis of consciousness and behaviour is still 'extremely thin ... superficial', with the actions and motives of the participants 'rather obscure.'[4]

But, as both Knowles and Holton in their
different ways have been concerned to show, it is
not so easy to marginalise strikes. The work
relationship does not dominate every pore of our
existence but it is the central fact of life: 'non-
work clearly compensates for work alienation, at
least to some extent, yet does not remove the experience of the latter.'[5] Indeed we can go further;
without work as the point of reference the concept
of class itself becomes meaningless except as an
arbitrary descriptive classification. Of course the
work situation is ambiguous, the very fact of work
requires the worker to submit to an unequal situation. But to the extent that workers try collectively to control that relationship it also breeds
and directs resistance. It is just because of this
basic type of ambiguity that the consciousness of
class is so volatile - continually changing and
oscillating, being built up only to be broken down
again through time. Strikes are a crucial part of
this process for even when they take the most sectional of forms they still involve a significant
heightening of the basic ambiguities of class. In
these terms an examination of strikes is not only an
important part of understanding the experience of
many members of the working class but it also opens
up the contradictions in the wider issue of working
class 'subordination' in late Victorian and Edwardian England.

II

Strikes have a history almost as long as paid work
itself but it has only been with the development of
capitalism and more particularly industrial capitalism that they have become, in James Cronin's words,
'the dominant mode of social protest.' For this to
occur a number of conditions are necessary; obviously there must be a working class organised in industries where a strike potential exists; equally
the political and legal framework must not directly
repress strikes though it may continue to hamper
them. Both these conditions were present in Britain
from the mid 1820s but strikes did not immediately
become the distinctive form of working class protest. For this a less obvious condition was necessary - workers had to learn what have been called,
perhaps misleadingly, 'the rules of the game' in the
sense of accepting the inevitability of the development of industrial capitalism and seeking to change

it by working within it and attempting to move beyond it. On this basis Cronin argues that it was
only in the 1870s that 'the strike truely came into
its own as a form of collective organisation....'
Other forms of protest such as the food riot lingered on but now as a subordinate rather than a major
vehicle of protest.[6]

Cronin's view that we can date the dominance of
the strike weapon from the beginning of our period
has broad support from those like Peter Stearns who
see in the changing dimensions of strikes an index
of the 'modernisation' of the working class and its
attitudes.[7] There is a danger, however, that what
we see in the 1870s is not the strike itself 'coming
into its own' but the perception of it and we know
from our own experience that the 'popular' perception of industrial conflict is often at one remove
from its reality. Individual strikes had achieved
prominence and notoriety before but it seems that it
was only in the late 1860s and early 1870s that with
the 'Sheffield Outrages' and the subsequent Royal
Commission and legislation that 'strikes' as a whole
became the focus of attention. By the 1880s individuals were making the first attempts to chart the
changing level of strike activity and taking their
analysis back to around 1870. Their pressure on the
government to take over this task was rewarded in
1888 when the Board of Trade was given responsibility for the collection of strike data.[8]

Two related elements were involved here.
Firstly, there was the development of a definition,
or we should say competing definitions, of a 'strike
problem' related to the development of a modern industrial society. George Bevan, who made the first
attempt to count the strikes of the 1870s, spoke of
them as being 'a very grave disease in the body
social' and claimed, though his own evidence hardly
supported it, that in the 1870s they were an
'epidemic ... which has unfortunately become chronic,
and seems, if anything to grow in intensity', only
to have them a few pages later as a 'terrible cancer
in the midst of our industrial body.' This overblown but commonplace definition of 'a strike
problem' was not shared by everyone - one of his
critics argued that far from his evidence showing
the 'industrial body' at death's door, strikes were
'more of a "measly", than of a "cancerous" description.'[9] The second element was a related belief
that strikes arose in large part out of inadequate
information on both sides and that to define 'the
problem' was therefore to go some way to solving it.

Both these elements were brought together by John Burnett, the first Labour Correspondent of the Board of Trade, in introducing the first *Annual Report of Strikes and Lockouts for 1888*,

> In Great Britain, especially, as the foremost producing nation of the world, labour quarrels have been more frequent, on a larger scale, and more pertinaciously fought out, than elsewhere ... In no way, perhaps, can more be done to effect reform ... than by the collection and publication from time to time of correct information ...

On this basis he hoped that strikes would less and less become 'the only arbiters in the struggle of employer and employed.'[10]

Because of this it is only in the 1870s that strikes began to emerge from their statistical dark age. But as more light is thrown on the period before 1870 we may well find that they had become the 'dominant mode of social conflict' long before. This is certainly suggested by Richard Price's pioneering attempt to tabulate masons' strikes on the basis of union records for the period 1836-1896. In these terms what may be important about the 1870s is both a new perception about strikes and an attempt to create the embryo of an industrial relations system to regulate them.[11]

Nevertheless, if this hypothesis is correct it only serves to reinforce the need to study strikes as the distinctive form of working class protest throughout the period 1875-1914. But it also shows the danger in the way in which our view of strikes is affected by the contemporary perception of them - especially when that perception is hidden in apparently cold statistics. Since we will lean heavily on statistics here and especially those collected by the Board of Trade after 1888, it behoves us to be clear at the outset about their limitations.

'Strike statistics', writes a recent commentator, 'are incomplete and therefore a "sample" of the entire "population" of strikes that actually occur'.[12] This incompleteness arises from three sources. In the first place the criteria for inclusion are deliberately restrictive. In the period 1888-96 an unsuccessful attempt was made to count all known strikes but this involved the Board of Trade in what seemed to be a disproportionate amount of time and effort chasing information on the smallest strikes. In 1897 therefore the fundamental restriction was introduced which remains today. To be counted, a strike must involve at least ten workers and last at least a day unless, in either case, more than one hundred working days were lost. The Board of Trade then recalculated its main series back to 1893 on this basis. A consistent but restrictive set of aggregate statistics therefore exists from 1893 and all the lesser series are consistent from 1897.

Incompleteness arises secondly because the coverage of the statistics is limited. There is no obligation to report strikes and therefore only those can be counted that come to the state's attention. In the period before 1914 the main method of collection of information depended upon a network of labour correspondents throughout the country reporting strikes and the Board of Trade then requesting information from employers and trade unions. Although the Board of Trade frequently expressed its confidence in this method there is no doubt that it was less than adequate, though whether it was any worse than modern methods is not clear.

But incompleteness also arises for a third and more complex reason. The process of defining a strike as a strike is itself a social one. Strikes are part of a whole series of sanctions that workers can impose on their employers. The evidence suggests that workers have a relatively clear idea when a strike becomes a strike. However it is employers who have the real power of definition by choosing whether or not to withhold pay or take more extreme measures. This definition by employers has been termed 'strategic' in the sense that they must decide whether to overcome the issue by negotiation or confrontation. Obviously employers' strategy and consequent strike definition will vary from workplace to workplace but it may also vary between workgroups within the same workplace. Generally the consequence is that employers will think that they experience more strikes than workers themselves will recognise.[13] But the social process of strike definition can also operate the other way and lead employers to deny the existence of a strike. This was perhaps more common before 1914 than today when the widespread use of subcontracting might lead employers to substitute one group of workers for another. The substituted workers might well feel that they had effectively been locked out but, wrote Llewellyn Smith, the Labour Commissioner at the Board of Trade; in these circumstances 'it is not uncommon for an employer to deny the existence of a trade dispute, although the men formerly in his employ may be actually drawing "strike pay" from their unions and "picketing" his works to prevent their places being filled.'[14] This process of social definition of the strike is not therefore just semantic. Today it is known to produce enormous differences in employer, union and state estimates of the number of strikes and this was no less true before 1914. In 1895, for example, it was claimed by the Oldham Master Spinners Association that 158 disputes had taken place in their district alone whereas the Board of Trade recorded just fifteen disputes in the entire spinning section of the cotton industry.[15]

III

Bearing these limitations in mind we can now proceed to look at the aggregate record of strikes on the basis of the data collected by the Board of Trade. Table 4.1 sets out the annual averages of the three basic series of strike statistics and the two averages that can be derived from them. We follow the conventional practice in presenting a separate series for coalmining since it is often argued that this industry is uniquely strike-prone and can therefore distort any national series.

The first point that arises relates to this issue of the role of coalmining in the overall profile of disputes. When Table 4.1 is examined in conjunction with Table 4.2 it is immediately apparent that the historical dominance of coalmining disputes has been a limited one. In the period 1893-1914 coalmining accounted for only one fifth of all recorded disputes. The industry was still 'strike-prone' but to a much lesser degree than later. It did, however, have over half the total number of strikers so that coalmining strikes were obviously larger than those in the rest of the economy. There were two reasons for this. In the first place the size of colliery units was much larger than those in the rest of the economy. Of 1,784 colliery businesses surveyed by Chapman and Ashton on the basis of *Rylands' Directory* for 1912, 458 (26 percent) employed less than 100 men; 552 (31 percent) employed between 100 and 499; 393 (22 percent) between 500 and 999; and 381 (21 percent) over 1,000.[16] But secondly, the number of strikers was inflated by the major disputes of 1893 and 1912 and large scale regional disputes such as those in 1892 in Durham, 1894 in Scotland and 1898 and 1910

Table 4.1: Strikes in Great Britain and Northern Ireland recorded by the Official Statistics, 1893-1914 [17]

Annual Averages of	No. of strikes	No. of strikers 000's	Total striker days 000's	Strikers per strike	Strike days per striker
(a) Non-coalmining					
1893-95	563	138	3,405	258	25
1896-98	686	126	6,479	181	48
1899-1901	525	107	2,363	201	24
1902-04	261	49	1,005	186	21
1905-07	387	95	1,694	243	19
1908-10	263	151	4,806	548	28
1911-14	875	451	7,521	562	21
(b) Coalmining					
1893-95	180	267	11,810	1,680	33
1896-98	130	98	4,813	798	34
1899-1901	133	74	877	548	11
1902-04	125	104	1,403	756	15
1905-07	84	57	817	690	16
1908-10	181	217	2,973	1,138	14
1911-14	160	430	10,161	2,826	16

Table 4.2: Share of Coalmining in Total Disputes, 1893-1976

	% Strikes	% Strikers	% Strike Days
1893-1914	21	52	56
1915-1924	17	47	52
1925-1944 *	41	52	34
1945-1964	63	26	18
1965-1976	12	8	20

* excludes 1926

in South Wales. When we turn to strike days the
high pre 1914 percentage is accounted for almost entirely by the weighting of these major strikes. In
fact in other years in this period coalmining
strikes appear to have been significantly shorter on
average than those in the rest of the economy. The
place of coalmining in the overall strike profile
therefore was the reverse of what it was to be later
- relatively numerous but smaller strikes. Since
the mid 1960s, by contrast, as Table 4.2 shows,
there has been a partial return to the pre 1914
pattern of relatively fewer strikes (proportionately
and absolutely) but more major disputes.

If we turn to the rest of the economy the value
of separating out the coal industry becomes apparent. By later standards the numbers of strikes
were quite high. It was only with the upturn of
strike activity in the 1960s that strike levels began to run consistently above the pre 1914 levels.
This suggests that real levels of striking were
considerably higher before 1914 than later. This is
because strike frequency depends, amongst other
things, on the share of the labour force in industries where strikes are likely. Clearly the structure of the pre 1914 economy was much less conducive
to striking than it would be later. Similarly,
strike frequency is also related to the degree of
trade union organisation but before 1914 trade union
density was much lower than later - approximately
six percent in 1892, thirteen percent in 1900,
fifteen percent in 1910 and 23 percent in 1914. But
even these figures give an exaggerated impression of
the real density since they are inflated by the
large number of miners in unions - in 1892 they made
up one seventh of all trade unionists, in 1900 a
sixth and in 1910 a quarter.

The series for the number of strikers and
strikers per strike are lower than after 1914 as one
would expect since these reflect both the size of
the work unit and the degree of interdependence of
both business and worker organisations. But it is
interesting, if not unpredictable, that there is a
slight tendency for the size of strike to increase
before 1914. It is when we turn to the series for
strike days and especially strike days per striker
that we see one of the sharpest differences with the
later experience. Strikes were simply much longer
in our period.

It is tempting to ascribe this difference to
the greater bitterness of industrial relations in
our period and in a sense this is obviously so.[18]

97

The problem is that a comparison of any two strikes soon reveals that concepts like 'bitterness' or 'intransigence' are too indiscriminate to be of much analytical value. For example, in 1893 in the south east Lancashire cotton strike that led to the Brooklands agreement, nearly 50,000 workers were on strike for five months. Such a long conflict could only have been sustained with considerable 'resolve', 'bitterness' and 'intransigence'. But in the same year in the Hull docks a strike of some 7,500 dockers and 2,500 workers in associated trades lasted only six weeks before the workers were forced back 'practically on the masters' own terms.'[19] Yet 'resolve', 'bitterness' and 'intransigence' were no less apparent in this shorter dispute - indeed it could be argued that they were more apparent. The introduction of well paid blacklegs led to violence and arson attacks. Extra police were brought into the town from Leeds, Nottingham and Lancashire, mounted police came from London and finally mounted troops were introduced. As one perhaps still excited contemporary put it after the dispute had ended

> a sort of panic seized the town, and many respectable citizens became walking arsenals. The gun-shops were cleared of their stock over and over again. Life preservers, knuckle-dusters, and batons were at a premium. The weapons of the dockers were not of such an elaborate description but consisted of such things as came ready to hand.[20]

To understand the differences between the length and character of these disputes therefore it is necessary to have a much sharper focus. They were distinguished by such factors as previous history, the character of the workers' organisations, the size of funds, the degree of preparation, the forms of organisation of the strikes themselves, the extent of wider links both locally and nationally, the nature of the employers' strategies both generally towards unions (in Hull they aimed to destroy their power) and specifically in dealing with the dispute (the use of blacklegs was deliberately avoided by the cotton masters in their dispute). No doubt this list could be extended without much effort but it is sufficient to illustrate a point that applies to the whole experience of strikes, from their causes to process to results and aftermath - namely their complexity. Unfortunately this has too often been ignored in discussions of strikes but as Alvin

Gouldner noted many years ago now 'a "strike" is a social phenomenon of enormous complexity which, in its totality, is never susceptible to complete description, let alone complete explanation.'[21]

The statistics suggest then that strikes were a major form of conflict in our period in which workers, from engineers to music hall artists, showed themselves to be both tenacious and resilient in spite of having in many respects a weaker position than their modern counterparts. It would, of course, be interesting to supplement these domestic statistics with international ones. Unfortunately the difficulties of comparison are all but insurmountable. In the first place even where statistics exist they vary too much in their criteria. This problem invalidates, for example, the attempt of Peter Stearns to compare strike frequency in different industries internationally.[22] The only possible comparisons that can be made are in terms of strike days since these are least sensitive to differences in criteria and coverage. But these will also be subject to the confusing effects of different levels of development, union organisation, government policy etc. The first of these can to some extent be overcome by using strike days per 1,000 workers as the standard measure but the interpretation of any differences is still ambiguous because of other influences which cannot so easily be held constant. However one thing is clear - the comparisons that can be made do not show that the United Kingdom had a significantly lower level of strike days than other countries.[23] To this extent, without enabling us to make precise comparisons, the statistics help to cast doubt upon the assumption implicit in much recent social history that militancy was greater elsewhere.

If we turn now to look more closely at our period itself certain broad trends stand out from Table 4.1. The best accepted indicator of fluctuations in the level of strike activity is the number of strikes. This shows that strikes tend to cluster or come in 'waves'.[24] The first of these that can be clearly identified came in the early 1870s before any reliable attempt was made to collect statistics. The second took place in 1888-91 coinciding with the first official attempts to collect strike data. Unfortunately because of classification differences the statistics are not comparable with latter ones so they are not given here.[25] Our series begins, therefore with the downturn that followed the 1888-91 strike wave. In the

1890s the number of strikes gradually declined. As
the number of strikers fell so did the average size
of strikes. Strike days were high because workers'
resistance involved major set-piece confrontations.
The average length of strikes also increased as the
balance of forces swung to the employers. This
downturn continued into the 1900s when some contemporaries could begin to anticipate elements of the
famous Ross and Hartmann 'withering away of the
strike' thesis of the 1950s.[26] The number of
strikes continued to fall and the lack of national
disputes rapidly brought down the numbers of strikers and strike days. The size and length of
strikes now both fell.

Then in 1911-14 our statistics document the
dramatic upturn of the pre war strike wave although
the combativity of workers was prefigured in the increase in the numbers of strikers and the increase
in strike days per striker in the period 1908-10.
In 1911, however, the number of strikes rose dramatically and this was sustained, with variations,
right through to the beginning of August 1914.
Strikers and strike days rose as well. The average
size of strikes also increased significantly.
Strike days per striker however now tended to fall
somewhat, reflecting the way in which gains were
more easily won in these years.

The general contours of this type of strike
wave have been analysed by Cronin. Briefly he has
shown how they played a 'pivotal' role. During
them, strikes broadened to involve new groups of
workers, new demands were put forward, new tactics
developed. Organisationally they led to a spreading
of trade union organisation and a revamping of union
structures.[27] The strike wave thus involves a
breakdown of existing 'norms' and a heightened consciousness of what is possible on the part of
workers and insofar as it is possible to speak of
the 'forward march' or 'rise of labour' the strike
wave tends to concentrate this in relatively short
periods of qualitative transformation whose gains
have subsequently to be defended.

IV

How then are we to explain these variations in the
level of strike frequency? Recent critiques of the
analysis of strike dynamics have focussed on two
problems which clearly also exist in the historical
discussion of strikes. The first is a tendency to
see strike activity as a mechanical response to the

various structural factors which condition industrial and broader social relations, so implicitly
marginalising 'the perceptions, intentions and
strategies of the men and women involved'. The
second problem has been that in discussing these
structural factors economists, sociologists, psycho-
logists etc. have been afflicted by a 'disciplinary
parochialism' to the further detriment of a full
understanding of the social complexity of strike
activity.[28]

The three most common approaches have been what
we can call the economic, the social and the organisational. Economists have stressed how, once workers have learnt 'the rules of the game', strike
levels will depend upon the interaction of worker
expectations and economic conditions. Strikes will
be more frequent in years when unemployment is low
and wages are rising. The social approach, by contrast, stresses the role of social disorganisation
in strike causation. This may occur at a general
level through 'industrialisation' or 'modernisation'
or at the level of the workplace through the introduction of new work processes, work conditions etc.
Clearly both these approaches point to important
dimensions of strike action but they have not proved
convincing explanations in themselves whether taken
singly or together. This has led to a stress on
the third approach which emphasises the role of
working class organisation. While economic and
social forces are broad in their impact, not all
those affected actually strike. This is because
striking is a form of collective action and it
therefore depends upon the organisational capacity
and 'resources' of particular groups of workers and
these are not uniformly distributed. Applying this
approach to strikes in Britain in the period 1892 to
1938 Bean and Peel have claimed that 'a dominant
role in strike activity appears to have been played
by organisational factors and especially the activity and recruiting campaigns of trade unions ...'[29]
However, while this approach adds a further dimension, it does not resolve the problem of strike
dynamics as can be seen if we consider that the
number of workers who strike is always fewer than
those organised into trade unions. Even if we allow
for an admittedly unequal distribution of resources
amongst organised workers, the problem is still not
solved; rather we have the makings of a dangerously
tautological argument where we know that organisational factors produce strikes because strikes only
occur where sufficient organisational and resource

elements are present. Why is it then that these approaches have proved insufficient?

The obvious reason is the problem of 'parochialism'. The three approaches are all partial but this though true is too simple. Even if we try to mould them together we still encounter two major difficulties: firstly, they can each be criticised for the weakness of their theoretical foundations; and secondly, they ignore a crucial dimension present in all strikes which at certain decisive points acts to transform the nature of strike activity itself. We will deal relatively briefly with the first difficulty before looking at the second in more detail.

The problem with both the social and organisational approaches is that both are underdeveloped. Edwards has recently examined at some length the difficulties with the former and the reader must be referred to his valuable discussion but his central point, that the social approach is 'inchoate', can be extended to the organisational approach too.[30] For example, is the decisive factor trade union organisation and if so where does this leave the argument that unions moderate strike levels? Perhaps the key is to be found more in informal work group solidarity so that formal organisational measures are significant only when they are underpinned by this? As yet we simply do not know. The same criticism cannot be levelled at the economic approach - here we encounter an overblown theory vitiated by the questionable nature of some of its underlying assumptions. This is most notoriously the case with that tradition which implies that strikes are irrational given that market forces set determinate wage levels or so reduce the area of indeterminacy as to make one wonder what all the fuss is about.[31] Strikes then appear only as a result of inadequate information on both sides or more wildly still as bouts of collective irrationality when the emotions run free.

Obviously there are complex issues here and we can do no more than alert historians to the hidden dangers. The fact that they have tended to use elements of these approaches in a less than rigorous fashion does not remove this problem.[32] For example, many historians have stressed the way in which unemployment affected strike activity in our period. But granted that it was an important factor we still need to know how it operated. Did low unemployment reduce the costs of moving elsewhere for workers and therefore make them more militant - but why not move

in the first place? Did it, as Pelling has suggested, reduce the supply of potential blacklegs - but
then how serious a factor was this?[33] Did it increase the costs of strikes to employers? But then
was unemployment ever that low in the period and did
not buoyant demand make it easier, at least to some
extent, to hold out against a strike? These questions are not meant to dismiss the importance of
unemployment as a factor but to show that its role
is much more complex than has often been assumed.

Unfortunately these theoretical problems have
tended to spill over into weak testing of the different approaches. The social approach is intrinsi-
cally difficult to test at an aggregate level though
some attempts have been made to relate strike activity statistically to indices of modernisation.[34]
The economic and organisational approaches, however,
have been more often used with what their supporters
would claim is some success. That statistical tests
show them to be important factors should not sur-
prise us given that any adequate account of strike
dynamics must take account of them. What is surprising has been the readiness to claim superiority
on the basis of the tests. The problem here is that
it is difficult to ensure that the variables against
which strikes are regressed are truly independent.
Two examples will suffice - if strikes and trade
union power influence wage levels, then inadequate
testing will make strikes appear as a function of
changing wage levels. Equally if strikes influence
union organisation, then similarly inadequate testing will make them appear as a function of changing
union organisation.[35]

In fact there is good reason to think that this
problem has seriously affected econometric studies
of strike series. One of the reasons for this is
that while it is possible to get uncorrected monthly
strike data, this is not available before 1945 for
most other variables.[36] Thus if we take Bean and
Peel's study as an example, workers may well have
struck and then joined trade unions (there are many
individual instances of this happening). But if we
then relate the annual level of strikes to the
changing annual level of union membership we will
obviously find a strong relationship and (in the
absence of the proper statistical checks) on this
basis draw possibly the wrong causal connection.

But even if we apply these approaches properly
a more important problem still remains. This is the
fact that there is always a residual element of
strike action that econometric studies cannot

satisfactorily explain and over time this grows. The value of James Cronin's recent work is that it has focussed on just this point (although it must be recognised that his statistical work is open to much the same sort of criticism as that made above). What he has successfully shown is the way in which the parameters of strike activity can suddenly shift over time so that any strike equation has only a limited life. The reason for this is precisely the wave like character of strikes which leads them to develop explosively in certain periods transforming the character of strike variables as they do so.

To understand how this happens we need to add a fourth element to our understanding of strikes. This missing dimension, which has recently received some attention in industrial relations literature and which we will stress here, is the consciousness of the workers themselves. For a strike to occur the ideas of workers must first change and this transformation will be maintained and perhaps developed as long as the strike lasts. In placing so much weight on this neglected aspect of strike activity there is a danger that we will bend the stick too far. But our intention is not to produce an articulated theory of strikes which 'dialectically' relates structure and consciousness. Rather we want to demonstrate the importance of consciousness in analysing strike dynamics and link this to some wider issues in the analysis of changing class consciousness.

IV

The problem with the previous structural approaches to strikes is that they 'are concerned with the conditions under which strikes are likely to occur rather than with whether they will actually occur'.[37] Strikes are important but relatively exceptional events and there is nothing automatic in the way they develop. Workers collectively need to convince themselves that no alternative exists and when they do strike it is seen by them as a distinctive form of action. One aspect of this is the way that the outbreak of a strike involves a visible sign from the workers that they are engaging in a qualitatively different form of collective action. This could be a strike ballot but in its absence the mass meeting, the collective walkout or march on the employer's office or other forms familiar from accounts of individual strikes can act as this signal that the situation has changed.

It is only because we stand outside of the workplace when we look at strikes that the latter forms of action appear as 'spontaneous'. Once we penetrate behind the factory gate a different perspective comes into view. It then appears that, in the words of one workers' leader at a mass meeting that followed an unplanned walkout at a Welsh slate quarry, 'the storm has been coming for some time'. The precipitant in this case was a dispute between a worker and an undermanager that boiled over. But it had been preceded by growing disagreements during which the attitude of the workers had begun to change. As the argument developed a crowd gathered and when the man 'was sent home they walked out too bringing the rest of the mine with them'.[38]

It would have been fascinating to have watched this process of strike mobilisation developing. Unfortunately it is only the outbreak of the strike that usually alerts us to the changes that have been taking place. The few inside accounts that we do have of strikes, however, show that they need a qualitative break in workers' ideas for them to occur. The determining influence here seems to be the work group. Within it individuals play a key leadership role in taking up issues and winning the rest of the group over to support for strike action but it is as a collective group that action is finally undertaken. In this sense the development of a strike is a political process involving arguments about objectives and the types of action that will achieve them. Opposition may have to be overcome to any form of action or, more usually, to the strike as a particular tactic.[39]

This opening up of workers' attitudes and perceptions continues to a greater or lesser extent during the strike itself. To see why, it is necessary to understand how a strike changes the position of workers for its duration. Strikes increase the cohesion of the strikers themselves through emphasising their mutual interdependence; strikes increase reliance on fellow workers; they focus opposition on the employer and in some cases on community leadership and the state; they enable workers to participate in running something for themselves and the experience of the strikers clashes directly with the dominant ideas in society and their own past assumptions.

Clearly the degree to which each of these elements is present will vary from strike to strike. A short 'token' strike will have much less impact than a major and prolonged dispute. For example the token strike may only focus opposition on a particular 'bad' employer and therefore offer only a limited

challenge to ideas of social harmony whereas 'it is
not much use to preach the doctrine of the solidarity of the interests of capital and labour as an in-
tegral part of a single national unit in the middle
of a bitter industrial war'.[40] But there will also
be variation within the different categories of
strikes. For example, we need to view the series of
short lightening strikes which took place in various
hotels in 1913 (and which incidentally were too brief
to get into the government statistics) very differently from token action in a strongly organised
workplace.[41]

        This lack of homogeneity means that every strike
needs to be understood in its own terms. But it has
also been suggested that the differences between
strikes are so great that it may not be helpful to
define them as the same type of action. It is this
thought that appears to lie behind Patrick Joyce's
analysis of class relations in the Lancashire cotton
industry in later Victorian England. For Joyce the
working class experience in this industry was characterised by 'dependence' on the factory and 'deference' to the factory owner. Class feeling was 'con-
tained and eroded' by 'the development in Lancashire
of a modern system of industrial relations'. In this
'climate' a 'groundswell of local disputation' often
led to brief one day strikes (or less) which had an
'almost ritual quality' and which were largely
'domestic and ceremonial affairs'.[42]

        This is not the place to deal with Joyce's
overall thesis but his analysis of this type of
strike as 'almost ritualized' is important because
it expresses a widespread attitude amongst historians
as well as echoing the strand of analysis that
dominated the examination of strikes in the 1950s
and 1960s. The problems with it are many. In the
first place the idea that strikes occur within an
institutionalised framework reflects more the experience of employers and union officials. From the
workers' point of view strikes have meaning more in
terms of work as they experience it than an abstract
'system' into which they may only be partially inte-
grated.[43] Unfortunately the labour process and the
various shopfloor practices that developed to deal
with it are conspicuously absent both from this type
of analysis in general and from Joyce's in particular. What then happens is that a line is drawn
between this 'groundswell of disputation' and the
big disputes that did periodically break out in
cotton and other industries rather than an attempt
being made to understand the links between them.[44]

Strikes do involve both ritual and ceremony (which must be understood) but it is doubtful if they are ever simply 'rituals'. The potential costs are hardly ever so low if only in terms of the possible dismissal of 'the leaders'.[45] But perhaps the most important point and the element that links all strikes is that they are exceptional events. If their meaning is so limited, we are entitled to ask why they did not occur more often and more widely. The fact that they are exceptional suggests that we cannot properly dismiss all of the elements we have identified even in the smallest disputes.

But if the degree to which the different elements are present varies between strikes so it will also vary over time in the same strike. One important consequence of this is the way in which a strike demands change. As Bean has emphasised 'because a strike is a dynamic phenomenon the emphasis accorded to particular issues can alter during its course'.[46] In most major strikes this internal dynamic tends to operate in two directions. One is to increase militancy and broaden demands, perhaps bringing to the surface issues that were latent when the strike originally began. This is particularly important given that wage issues were given as the 'principal causes' of disputes in 62 percent of strikes between 1893 and 1914. This does not necessarily imply limited objectives; we have to recognise that 'since wages stand for more than can be bought with them, wage strikes tend to be symbolic of wider grievances'. But the internal dynamic of the strike can also involve a wearing down of enthusiasm preparing the way for a return to work. Too often historians have seen this simply as a response to distress. This underpinned many defeats when workers were forced back but 'to understand the progress of a dispute toward peace the changing subjective attitudes and beliefs of the parties are a key element to be understood.'[47]

An obvious problem in understanding these issues is that we have few accounts of strikes written from the inside with an eye to these issues but this does not mean that no evidence is available. Both the character of the strike itself and the behaviour of workers as well as the overall pattern of strike activity are clues to the nature of strike action. If we look afresh at questions like the size of support for strikes, the nature of strike meetings, picketing, the language of the strike, forms of mutual aid and so on there is sufficient evidence to allow us to map out, sometimes directly,

sometimes indirectly, the way in which consciousness
changed over time.

The character of the strike organisation is
particularly important since a strike which involves
little participation is likely to result in boredom
and quickly dissipate support. This raises the problem of the control both of the strike committee by
the workers and of the negotiations undertaken by
the strike committee. The tensions involved here
reflect the significant 'unofficial' element in most
strikes. In the first place the process of calling
a strike is usually unofficial; 'although most
strikes are controlled by trade unions, cases are
comparatively rare in this country in which the central committee of a trade union takes the initiative
and directs its members to cease work.'48 In fact
although the majority of strikes were later made
formally or tacitly official in our period there
were a significant core which were never approved.
This runs counter to the general view which tends to
see unofficial strikes as being more a feature of
the period after 1910. But this does not accord with
evidence collected by the Board of Trade in the
early 1890s. This seems to show that roughly a
quarter of the strikes it investigated had not been
approved for various reasons. Table 4.3 presents
the data for 1895 when it is also possible to calcu-
late the average size of these strikes which interestingly turn out to be quite large in contemporary
terms.

But the 'unofficial' nature of strike action
extends also into its running: 'when a strike has
been authorised by the executive the conduct of it
is frequently entrusted to a "strike committee"
appointed ad hoc...' There are a number of reasons
for this. Strikes would often involve more than one
union and they therefore needed a leadership which
would overcome to some extent the sectionalism of
union organisation. In our period too, many strikes
involved significant numbers of non unionists who
also needed to be represented. In the slate dispute
we noted earlier, out of the 486 workers in the
quarry only 125 were in the union and only 75 of
them were paid up. The running of the strike therefore fell to a 24 man strike committee elected at a
mass meeting following the walkout. But even where
union organisation was strong it was common for
strikes to be run outside of the usual union structure. A good example of this was the role of 'lockout' committees in the 1897 engineering dispute.
Here and in similar instances the fact that the

Table 4.3: Trade Union Attitudes to Strikes, 1895 [49]

	% surveyed strikes	average strikers per strike
Approved strikes	72	114
Not approved	12	238
Disapproved	1	144
Not ordered	5	100
Not ordered but approved	3	275
Not consulted	2	191
No union	2	384
Chiefly non union	3	883

strike breaks the routine of industrial relations was reflected also in a break in the routine framework of the organisation of workers.[50]

The responsibility of strike committees could vary widely. Three issues were crucial to the running of a strike. One was finance; normally in local strikes in organised industries strike pay was paid centrally by the union, ten to fifteen shillings a week being a widely quoted figure for an adult male although a large dispute would quickly exhaust funds.[51] Strike committee funds had therefore to be collected by the strikers themselves and they were used not only to provide for additional help to strikers or strike pay itself where there was no strong union but also, on some occasions, to pay the return fares of imported blacklegs. Collecting money was not only important to materially support the strike; it also served as both a focus of activity for the strikers themselves and as a means of gaining support. The typical balance sheet below of a strike gives some idea both of the nature of support and the importance attached to getting it. Collectors travelled all over the north of England and support came for these strikers from all over the country and abroad.

The second issue that had to be faced in all but the briefest strikes was escalation. In general the more complete the strike the greater its chance of success. But a strike committee had to consider three issues. Employers appear often to have resorted to 'sympathy lock-outs' to pressure and divide strikers. Equally if the strike committee

Table 4.4: The Manningham Mills Strike Balance Sheet[52]

Income	£	s.	d.
Collections in boxes	7,348	19	5½
Trade societies	1,386	9	1½
Co-operative societies	81	5	0½
Private Subscribers and friends	194	3	10
Bradford Trades Council Fund	1,152	14	0½
Collections in chapels and churches	25	1	4
Collections in clubs	24	13	10½
Concerts and football matches	54	11	5
Income from soup kitchen	70	6	5
Emigration fund	49	15	0
Miscellaneous	719	3	6½
Total	£11,107	3	1d
Expenditure			
Relief	8,300	10	11
Food and lodgings for collectors	1,200	0	0
Railway fares	884	12	1½
Printing and rent	172	10	4
Emigration	161	16	8
Bands	91	11	7½
Soup Kitchen	70	6	5
Wages to committee	40	16	0
Miscellaneous	174	19	0
Total	£11,097	3	1d

itself escalated the strike, it could seriously increase its financial burdens. Fear of this sometimes led to what with hindsight appears a tactical error - instead of trying to spread a strike from the outset this was often left to a last desperate action which itself could then contribute to defeat.[53] But the third problem was that any escalation had itself to be argued for. Here sectional considerations often intervened. Craft based strikers tended to rely upon their own strength and only reluctantly involve other groups. But sectionalism also meant that other groups were reluctant to respond when asked and many strikes came to grief because of lack of support from small but strategi-

cally situated groups. The solution that was central to the arguments of the syndicalists before
1914 was both to amalgamate unions and in strikes to
link demands between groups so as to generalise
the issues involved.

The other decisive issue for the strike committee was its role in negotiations. Here the tension
with the official trade union organisation was most
apparent and conflict was commonplace. Unfortunately
we still lack a detailed analysis of the development
of the trade union bureaucracy so that it is difficult to generalise but it seems clear that the power
of strike committees where organisation already
existed was related to the degree of shopfloor power
before the strike broke out. The degree of formalisation of collective bargaining was also important
and the fact that it tended still to be local before
1914 gave strike committees potentially more power
over the strike.

'Seizing the sense of the action' is therefore
complex but an important part of understanding any
strike and its potential.[54] Of course the potential
might not be realised. Some strikes; though surprisingly few, were turned to frankly reactionary
ends - notoriously against alien workers. Others
were directed against other groups of workers over
such issues as demarcation. Just how many is difficult to say because they were classified by the
Board of Trade in the 'statistical ragbag category'
of 'employment of particular classes of persons'.
Between 1893 and 1914 this accounted for fourteen
percent of all disputes and only some seven percent
of all strikers. But because this category groups
together six different causes, even this vastly
overstates the significance of these disputes. Moreover they tended to be heavily concentrated in
particular sectors, especially shipbuilding.[55] It
was most common for strikes to remain trapped within
the sectional framework of existing union organisation. Sectionalism of this kind is usually associated with craft unions but critics of 'new unionism'
have argued that it was no less present there. Bean,
for example, in an analysis of 'new' unionist strikes
in the Liverpool docks in 1890 has claimed that they
were 'torn by factional considerations and concern
for self-interest.' There is probably much justification in this in the sense both that sectionalism
is to an extent implicit in union organisation itself and that the fragmented nature of British
industrial relations intensified it.[56] But this
argument misses the point.

Even the most sectional disputes have a rationality in terms of the defence of an existing situation against 'encroachments'. Here it is important to recognise that sectionalism is based upon a group strength which operates both against the employer and often union officials to the advantage of the workers themselves. The difficulty is that when that strength is challenged opposition is directed at other workers. Nevertheless strike action, particularly in major disputes, can still act to open up the perspectives of even the most sectional of groups. In the 1897 engineering dispute, for example, the polarisation was so intense (even the normally sane Alfred Marshall declared 'I want these people beaten at all cost') that the engineers were finally forced to look for wider support, though it proved too late to save them. But this end was not inevitable; because they were based upon an underlying strength and continuity of shopfloor organisation, these groups could also be the basis for a rapid radicalisation such as the engineers were themselves to experience in the First World War.[57] It is also important to recognise that the predominance of sectional considerations depends upon the overall character of strike activity, an issue to which we must now turn.

VI

The degree to which ideas change not only varies within and between strikes; it also varies over time. To see why, we need to decompose the changes in consciousness themselves. Necessarily this will be schematic because ideas do not change in accord with neat categories but it is nevertheless useful to make the attempt. Michael Mann has helpfully distinguished between four aspects of class consciousness: class identity - the definition of oneself as working class; class opposition - the perception of employers and their agents as enduring class opponents; class totality - making both identity and opposition the central defining feature of one's total situation; and class alternative - the conception of an alternative form of social organisation. If the radicalisation in strikes were simply cumulative, an escalation would take place through the four elements. But we know that class totality and, even more, class alternative views amongst large groups of workers have been relatively rare. One reason for this is that the capacity of strikes to generate radicalisation fluctuates with the level of strike activity. To see how this operated we will contrast the strike pattern in the 1890s and 1900s with that in the strike wave of 1910-14.[58]

Strikes fought in the 1890s and early 1900s were primarily defensive, undertaken when the balance of forces was swinging against the workers. In the 1890s the extent of this swing was uneven as a relative domestic boom sustained strikes in some sectors, particularly building which recorded a fifth of all officially recorded disputes between 1893 and 1901 (an average of 157 a year). The tail off in strikes became more general in the 1900s when, for instance, building strikes constituted only six percent of all disputes between 1902-10 (averaging only 27 per annum). At the same time the downturn was also complemented by the well known legal moves against strikes and unions.

In this context disputes could result in considerable polarisation but in the absence of any attempt to link them they tended to take place in relative isolation from one another. This served to limit and mark the ideas that workers developed through strike action. To go on strike workers had to have a degree of confidence that they could win but the overall situation was clearly against them. One hostile contemporary misusing the strike statistics calculated that the odds were 150 : 100 against winning strikes; 'this fact should be an argument against strikes, in the eyes of workpeople, especially when they bear in mind that the cost to them, to their families, and to their trade organisations is relatively greater, than the cost to employers'. But this attitude also spread to many socialist leaders who considered that the strike weapon was increasingly being made outmoded by the power of capital.[59]

The inevitable result was to narrow strike perspectives and make it difficult to generalise any local militancy that did arise. The defensive nature of strikes in these years is reflected in their concern with workers' 'dignity'. Under the pressure of competition, technological changes and new work practices were forced through in a number of industries. Once, however, workers' confidence was bolstered, perhaps by a local economic upturn and fuller order books, they could strike to push back the tide. But to win they had to rely more upon their own strength, upon what Ben Tillett called 'funds and sectional combination'. Obviously this tended to benefit craft unionism and those new

unions that could adopt craft practices. Indeed behind these there was a consolidation of trade unionism in these years. Although workers were regularly
defeated, apparently comprehensively in some instances, they were able to keep informal shopfloor organisation surprisingly intact and push some employers into a 'stalemate' position.[60]

In Mann's terms strikes generally led to an
oscillation between class identity and opposition.
Only in localised instances (mainly in the great
'labour wars' of the 1890s) can we detect consciousness going beyond this. This limited radicalisation
can also be related to the distribution of strikes
between industries. As we have seen, one of the conditioning factors that affects strike activity is the
availability of 'resources' to workers allowing them
to strike. What distinguishes a 'strike-prone' industry is the capacity of its workers to sustain a
higher level of striking in these downturns. But
within a generally unfavourable climate this unequal
distribution of resources between workers is likely
to be more harshly felt and therefore class opposition and unity reduced as it is perceived that only
some groups have access to strikes as a weapon.

However, an upturn in militancy and a strike wave
such as that of 1910-14 changes the context and the
character of strike activity. In this period the balance of forces swung in favour of the workers and
strikes of this period became more offensive and less
isolated. The central feature of a strike wave is
the way in which strike action is generalised reinforcing both class identity and opposition and creating the basis for a move to class totality and perhaps beyond. It is this aspect of changing ideas
that gives strike waves what Knowles called 'a certain momentum' within and between industries.[61]

A measure of the difference in context is given
by the changing proportion of strikers in the labour
force which is given in Table 4.5 on the basis of the
Board of Trade's calculations. Throughout the period
a minority of workers went on strike but the size and
distribution of that minority could change quite
dramatically and the extent of the 'labour unrest'
comes out fully. In particular, even allowing for
those who went on strike more than once in these
years it would seem that between a fifth and a quarter of the labour force went on an officially recorded strike at some point.

Here it is possible to talk of an 'explosion of
consciousness' taking place. To Tom Mann, rushing
from strike to strike, it seemed as if workers were

Table 4.5: Percentage of the Working Population Involved in Disputes, by Trade, 1893-1913 62

	Build-ing	Coal mining	Other Mining	M/E/S*	Textile	Clothing	Other	All Trades**
1893	1.9	74.7	2.4	2.7	3.6	1.9	0.7	7.5
1894	1.6	31.2	0.9	2.5	3.2	1.0	0.5	3.8
1895	1.1	11.9	1.6	4.0	5.2	8.6	0.2	3.0
1896	3.6	8.9	4.9	4.0	2.7	0.7	0.3	2.2
1897	1.6	7.0	1.0	7.8	3.1	1.2	0.6	2.6
1898	1.7	25.2	1.6	1.7	2.1	0.6	0.2	2.8
1899	3.1	6.3	1.3	1.6	5.1	0.4	0.4	2.0
1900	1.9	9.1	3.3	1.5	2.0	0.4	0.1	2.0
1901	0.9	13.7	3.3	1.6	1.4	0.7	0.3	1.9
1902	0.5	25.5	1.0	1.1	1.4	0.4	0.2	2.7
1903	0.3	7.2	2.5	2.2	0.8	0.4	0.1	1.2
1904	0.8	5.4	1.1	0.9	1.1	0.2	0.1	0.9
1905	0.6	4.8	3.1	0.9	1.3	0.5	0.2	0.9
1906	0.1	9.4	1.6	2.9	6.3	1.3	0.1	2.1
1907	0.1	5.4	1.9	1.3	3.9	1.7	0.3	1.4
1908	0.3	8.9	0.7	4.0	11.0	0.7	0.2	2.8
1909	0.1	26.5	1.8	0.7	0.6	0.4	0.1	2.8
1910	0.1	28.6	1.2	3.7	10.7	0.6	0.5	4.9
1911	0.3	13.0	1.2	5.9	17.8	1.3	9.8	9.0
1912	0.6	93.2	0.8	4.6	4.5	4.2	3.6	13.4
1913	4.4	18.6	8.7	8.3	6.7	2.0	2.5	5.6

*   Metal, engineering and shipbuilding
**   Excludes agricultural labourers and seamen.

being moved by 'a psychic wave', but the spirit of militancy had a real tangibility. Class identity and class opposition now reinforced one another and flowed into class totality as new possibilities were opened up on a broader front. At times the actions of workers instinctively pushed beyond this. Holton has spoken of the development of 'proto-syndicalism' - 'forms of social action which lie between vague revolt and clear cut revolutionary action' - as being characteristic of some strikes in these years. Capitalist relations and state power were confronted by apparently 'spontaneous' actions which upon closer investigation reveal a much more clearly articulated set of goals even if not a full consciousness of a class alternative.[63]

Within this militancy it was possible to challenge some of the former limitations of the labour movement. Previously backward groups of workers leapt to the fore, a process in evidence in the transport strikes but which was also reflected in the higher visibility of women strikers. Sectional issues did not disappear but they became easier to resolve as it became possible to generalise arguments and link strike demands. One reflection of this, at first sight paradoxical, is that there were actually few strikes which were principally sympathy actions - between 1911-13 the Board of Trade recorded only 37 involving 25,733 workers. But this did not mean that there was little sympathetic action; rather workers who were encouraged to strike by the militancy of their colleagues were making their own demands felt as well.

Here informal links were often as important as formal ones. They particularly benefited workers who had not been on strike before. One indication of this is the way that strike duration changed. The fall noted in table 4.1 was not distributed evenly across all strikes as an emphasis on broad structural determinants might lead us to expect. It was in the smallest disputes that the fall was the most dramatic; for example, in 1908-10 strikes involving less than 25 workers averaged 24.1 days but in 1911-13 they averaged only 10.4 days. Similarly, those involving less than 100 workers averaged respectively 23.8 days and 12.9 days in the two periods. Since workers were winning more gains in these years it is unlikely that this can be explained by small, unsuccessful strikes though even a new willingness to strike and risk being defeated would be an important sign. What seems more important was the growing confidence of the workers themselves and a related loss of confidence by employers. This affected strike duration in other ways too. Between 1905-9 39 percent of strikes lasted less than a week and 71 percent less than a month but in the strike wave 46 percent were settled within a week and 80 percent within a month. At the other end of the scale 4.7 percent of strikes lasted more than 20 weeks in 1905-9 but only 2.45 percent in 1910-13.

The related loss of confidence by employers can be seen in the way that in key industries like shipping and the railways opposition to unions which had lasted for decades was overthrown. But evidence of this also exists in the records of the results of strikes collected by the Board of Trade. These are perhaps best understood as a measure of what was believed to be happening rather than as an objective index of actual results but even in this more limited sense they are revealing. Forchheimer, in what remains the only serious study of this aspect of strikes, noted that employers' victories and compromises seemed to move closely with the economic cycle. Suggesting that 'compromises' should be understood as a disguised category for workers' victories, he then argued that employers were more willing to make concessions in prosperous years.[64] This argument contains an important truth but it misses the fact that there is an even closer relationship between the number of strikes and the proportion of employers' victories - the more strikes, proportionally the fewer victories they claimed, suggesting once again that the analysis of strikes has to focus on more than structural factors and must examine the hopes and fears of those involved.

VII

So far we have concentrated on the internal nature of strike dynamics. It remains now to look at some of the wider ramifications of strikes. If our emphasis on the importance of consciousness is correct, then we would expect increases in strike frequency to be reflected in, and interact with, a developing class consciousness spreading beyond those directly and indirectly involved. Correspondingly downturns in strike activity would have the opposite effects. But in spite of the importance of these links, their precise form has not been investigated and all we can do here is to focus on some of the possibilities.

One interesting aspect to consider is whether individualised responses to alienation and exploitation such as suicide, drunkenness, crime, etc. might

be related to strike levels. Suicide can serve as
an illustration of the possible mechanism. Opponents
of strikes often spoke of their dire effects on all
involved. In the 1912 London dock strike, for
example, it was claimed that several blacklegs had
been driven to commit suicide by hostility and resentment at work and in the community.[65] But the
more likely effect of strikes would seem to be that
by creating a more optimistic and collective climate
for change they actually diminished suicide. Obviously these effects would be felt most by those
directly and indirectly involved. Hence there is
more than propaganda in the frequent reports of the
way in which 'good order' was maintained during
major strikes. But the ramifications could spread
beyond those immediately affected. If we follow
Durkheim's classic analysis then we could see
strikes as a method of social integration along
class lines in which unity is forged against a
common enemy (on both sides!) so creating a new
meaning in some people's lives. Following this hypothesis, Stack has recently claimed that there is
an inverse relationship,internationally between
strikes and suicide.[66] Problems with the British
statistics may well preclude an investigation to see
if this holds historically but the hypothesis is not
inconsistent with what we know already. Anderson,
for example, has argued that 'expanding industrial
towns ... often seemed places of hope and better-
ment' to workers and so had lower suicide rates but
it is at least possible that this 'hope of better-
ment' involved a collective dimension too.[67]

At a broader level, strikes had an important
impact on the character of the working class community. Strikers were obviously drawn from the
working class community and this itself gave their
struggles a wider dimension. But beyond this the
need for support and solidarity meant that they
often took their strikes directly into the community.
Here the evidence of strike funds can be helpful.
During strikes middle and lower middle class support
was often forthcoming, though the extent of support
in the 1889 London dock strike when strikers were
'helped by subscriptions from the City, cheered on
by stock brokers' was quite untypical.[68] It is
important, however, to examine the terms of this
support. Often it was an expression of concern for
wives and children which involved opposition to the
strike itself; fear could equally be a motivating
factor. Open support for strikes and strikers was
also forthcoming as their cases gained wider

sympathy but this was less widespread and sometimes
dependent on the strikers acting within narrow
limits. The evidence of strike funds (implying a
degree of support for the strike itself) is that
support came largely from the working class itself,
either through trade unions or community collections.
Generating support here often involved considerable
enterprise beyond simple collections - from concerts to football matches, to the hiring of brass
bands and the setting up of tours by working class
choirs.

The interaction of strikes and the working
class community obviously depended upon the nature
of the community itself. It was easier to build
links where it was well established and institution-
ally strong than in cities like London and Birmingham where there was considerable industrial and
social fragmentation.[69] It has been argued that in
these places individuals 'were often unable to
articulate any real grievances that they might have
felt' leaving it open to conservative and nation-
alist propaganda to give some direction to their
discontents. But the 'labour unrest' after 1910, at
least in the case of Birmingham, produced ' a positive growth of a class-conscious solidarity' in
which, interestingly, skilled engineers played an
important role in coming to the aid of the unskilled
and unorganised.[70] Indeed, even the sharpest sec-
tarian divisions could be challenged by strike
action. In 1907 in Belfast a major transport strike
became 'the first strike in the history of modern
Ireland in which the workers forgot their party
divisions and combined ... against the employers.'
In a long dispute the strikers maintained an impressive unity against attempts to divide them on
religious lines, although the defeat of the strike
paved the way for a reinforcement of these divisions. But the potential of strikes to force a
unity across the religious divide (because, as one
protestant strike leader put it, 'men of both faiths
... were determined to stand together against the
common enemy, the employer') was again to be demonstrated in Liverpool in 1911 and Dublin in 1913.[71]

In a number of instances strikes also came to
serve as the focal point of community resentment.
The Manningham Mills strike, for example, in Bradford in 1890 had much community support but when the
town leadership was seen to be siding with the employer it multiplied. 'Riots' took place and attendance at meetings rose at one point from a few
thousand to an estimated 60,000 as the issues

involved broadened beyond the strike itself.[72]   In agriculturally based Norfolk 'rural war' in the 1870s played an important part in challenging the power of the village troika of squire, parson and farmer, and then again before 1914 strikes led to a shift away from the predominance of liberalism.[73] Then alongside these relatively localised examples we have to set the bigger disputes that produced large scale community conflict, particularly those of the 'labour unrest' such as the well documented cases of Tonypandy in 1910, Hull and Liverpool in 1911 and Belfast in 1913.   Indeed, the analysis of community unrest could probably be pursued much more widely than this.   In the West Midlands, for example, 'the prairie fire strikes' of 1913 were preceded by disputes over rents that landlords labelled 'the tenants' war'.[74]

Strikes that 'boiled over' in this way were one of the factors that involved the state in industrial affairs.   The common view of industrial relations as a voluntarist system in which the state played a minimal role is misleading.   Voluntarism, like 'laissez-faire', had to be created and then maintained.   Both required much behind the scenes manipulation particularly from the innovative Board of Trade.[75]   Different degrees of voluntarism also existed and it has been argued that the fragmentation of the industrial and union structure in Britain made necessary a greater degree of state intervention than in other voluntarist systems.[76] The 1893 miners' lock-out was a turning point in open ministerial intervention.   But the pattern was really consolidated by the strikes before 1914. Ministerial intervention gave strikes an overtly political dimension which Asquith was not alone in fearing would lead to 'the degradation of government' if it was seen to fail.[77]

It was as a 'public order' issue though that strikes made the state most visible, contributing a neglected but important element to the tradition of working class hostility to the police, army and state itself.   Strikes were immediately dealt with in these terms by the local police force aided where necessary by neighbouring forces.   The Metropolitan Police then acted as a national backup for beleaguered local forces.   But troops were also used in any emergency.   In 1908 a Royal Commission investigating their use found that they had been involved 24 times since 1870.   They had opened fire twice, first in the 'Featherstone Massacre' of 1893 when they had killed two and injured a dozen.   This was the first

time for half a century that troops had opened fire
on civilians at home. Then again in Belfast in 1907
troops opened fire (parts of the police force were
near to mutiny), killing three and wounding more in
the midst of transport strikes. But if firing was
relatively rare, what General Macready called 'a
little gentle persuasion with the bayonet' was more
common. It was the 'labour unrest' however, that
fully revealed the problems of control that strikes
could pose for the state. The Royal Commission had
considered that it was inappropriate to use troops
in civil strife and recommended a wider use of the
Metropolitan Police.[78] Churchill initially tried to
honour this commitment but troops were soon in use
in South Wales in 1910; in Cardiff and Liverpool in
1911 when they were joined by a cruiser; and then
in August 1911 in the transport strikes, when almost
every home based unit was mobilised, troops were de-
ployed in over 30 towns. Two people were killed in
Liverpool and a further two in Llanelli in Wales.
This widespread deployment was not an aberration
nor can it be explained as a Churchillian foible.
Although there were internal debates about the
extent of deployment, it had widespread support
within government. Rather it reflected the way in
which a major industrial dispute could polarise
issues on a much wider scale and the difficulties
that governments had in dealing with them. In a
modern industrial society strikes have always been
the biggest and most important challenges to government and the state.[79]

But perhaps the most important link that needs
to be made is that between strikes and the development and consequent character of the labour movement.
The existence of a significant level of workplace
conflict and strikes before 1914 suggests that working class attitudes were far more nuanced and less
committed to the existing system than has often been
allowed. And in major disputes, especially in
strike waves, that ambiguity could be opened up on a
considerable scale. But the fact still remains that
relatively little of the political potential created
by this type of action was channelled into support
for socialist politics. Instead the break between
industrial and political life became an institutionalised part of the labour movement.

Because of the radicalisation they involved,
workplace conflict and strikes could act as a bridge
to socialist politics. But strikes cannot last in-
definitely and any radicalisation has to be given a
firmer foundation and built upon if the potential is

to develop. Equally an intervention by socialists in strikes could have been significant both in tactical terms, generalising the experience of different groups and in giving them legitimacy and support. Yet much of the history of socialism is marked by indifference and often outright hostility to these issues.

Socialists were eager to use strikes as a general propaganda weapon; 'to be a trade unionist and fight for your class during a strike and to be a Tory or a Liberal and fight against your class at an election is a folly' declared Robert Blatchford in his *Merrie England* and many socialists would have echoed this, but the point was more often than not simply propaganda. When troops fired on workers in Belfast in 1907 Blatchford condemned attacks on 'the ordinary Tommy'![80] Strikes themselves were often deprecated as a working class weapon both for their ineffectiveness and their inappropriateness. For the Social Democratic Federation they were a 'malign obsession'; in the midst of the 'labour-unrest' Hyndman asked, 'can anything be imagined, more harmful, more in the widest sense of the word, unsocial then a strike ...? I have never yet advocated a strike ... I have never known ... a successful strike.'[81] In the ILP and Labour Party the strength of the trade union link did mean that some national support was forthcoming but it was relatively luke-warm and disappeared at the first sign of union opposition to strikes or violence. Moreover the background of support when it was forthcoming was a scepticism about the value of strikes almost as deep as Hyndman's.[82] These attitudes persisted despite the fact that as individuals many socialists were heavily involved in strikes and supporting them, a contradiction which deserves more investigation.[83]

The roots of this indifference and hostility lay partly in the ridigity of socialist theory (especially in the case of the SDF), but more deeply in the commitment to parliamentary reform and particularly in the ILP - Labour Party nexus, the relationship with the trade union establishment which, after the defeat of the arguments of Tom Mann and others in the ILP in the early 1890s, involved a tacit recognition of the limits of intervention by socialists in union affairs. But beneath these important considerations there was another element too - this was a deep hostility to working class attitudes and actions that many socialists shared. Workers were to be educated into socialism but they would not find their own way there. This attitude had deep roots, some of which can be traced to the set of ideas that made up what Yeo has called 'the religion of socialism' which developed in the 1880s and early 1890s.[84] It was later well captured by Robert Tressell whose book *The Ragged Trousered Philanthropists* both shows the revulsion against workers, at the same time as its continuing uncritical popularity attests to how widespread these attitudes were.

> As he thought of his child's future there sprung up within him a feeling of hatred and fury against the majority of his fellow work-men. They were the enemy. Those who not only quietly submitted like so many cattle to the existing state of things, but defended it, and ridiculed any suggestion to alter it ... (and on for the rest of the page and in various forms throughout the book) ... No wonder the rich despised them and looked upon them as dirt. They were despicable. They were dirt. They admitted it and gloried in it.[85]

Tressell's workers do not strike; their small attempts to get back at their employer are deprecated; there is no argument for them to join a trade union even though we learn towards the end of the book that the hero is a trade unionist himself. Instead socialism is simply an abstract utopia and in the end it is not the workers who offer any hope of it but a member of the middle class with money. Thus strike action and working class resistance at work more generally stood at a tangent to left wing politics before the First World War. Occasionally individuals questioned this but it was not until the development of syndicalism that however haltingly, ambiguously and ultimately inadequately, a break with this was made and politics began to be put back into work - where it has always been.[86]

Nevertheless, even if strikes and militancy stood at a tangent to the development of socialist politics, they still affected it by creating the context in which particular developments were possible. It is a commonplace, for instance, that the development of the Labour Representation Committee was a product of industrial defeat in the 1890s. But it is less often recognised that these defeats, through the dampening effects they had on militancy, made possible the form of alliance where socialism was doubly subordinated to the binds of Hardie's 'Labour Alliance' with the trade union bureaucracy and the 'Labour-Liberal Alliance'. Equally when the upturn in strikes and militancy came after 1910, it underpinned the challenge to these narrow organisational and ideological horizons.[87] The leadership of the Labour Party was thrown heavily on the defensive despite a rhetorical shift to the left as the strikes and related actions raised the fundamental question of what direction the labour movement should move in. When Tom Mann and others were arrested for the famous leaflet calling on troops not to fire on striking workers the disillusioned ILP'er Leonard Hall saw it as a litmus test,

> the little crowd of dried Tories who have for years been labelling themselves "socialists" - even "Revolutionary Socialists" with the capital "R" (have been) tumbling over each other since the "mutiny" prosecutions to disclaim and repudiate any connection or even sympathy with the disreputable and unholy thing "Syndicalism".

But this view of the role of the Labour Party and the ILP was not just that of a radicalised left-winger. Lloyd George expressed the same thought; he argued that 'Syndicalism' and 'Socialism' (by which he meant the Labour Party) were 'mutually destructive', 'the best policeman for the Syndicalist is the Socialist':

> There is this guarantee for society, that one microbe can be trusted to kill another, and the microbe of Socialism, which may be a very beneficient one, does at any rate keep guard upon the other, which is a very dangerous and perilous one. I have, therefore, no real fear of the Syndicalist.[88]

NOTES

1. *Annual Report on Strikes and Lockouts for 1900*, PP 1902, pp.36-7. All unattributed strike statistics have been drawn from these annual reports.
2. E.H. Hunt, *British Labour History 1815-1914* (London, 1981), p.306.
3. A. Reid, 'Politics and Economics in the

Formation of the British Working Class: a response to H.F. Moorhouse', *Social History*, 3(3), 1978, pp. 347-63; J. Melling, 'The Workplace and the Rise of Labour', *Bulletin of the Society for the Study of Labour History*, 42, 1981, pp.44-8.

4.   K.G.J.C. Knowles, *Strikes: A Study in Industrial Conflict*(Oxford, 1952), p.xii; B.Holton, *British Syndicalism 1900-1914: Myths and Realities* (London, 1976), p.77.

5.   Benson, *supra*; M. Mann, *Consciousness and Action Among the Western Working Class* (London, 1973), p.30.

6.   J. Cronin, *Industrial Conflict in Modern Britain* (London, 1979), *passim*; J. Cronin, 'Strikes 1870-1914', in C. Wrigley (ed.), *A History of British Industrial Relations 1875-1914* (Brighton, 1982), pp. 79-98.

7.   P. Stearns, 'Measuring the Evolution of Strike Movements', *International Review of Social History*, xix (1), 1974, pp.1-27.

8.   S.W. Creigh, 'The Origins of British Strike Statistics', *Business History*, xxiv(1), 1982, pp. 95-106.

9.   G. Bevan, 'The Strikes of the Past Ten Years', *Journal of the Royal Statistical Society*, xlii (1), 1880, pp.35, 37, 52, 58.

10. *Strikes and Lockouts for 1888*, PP 1889, p.3.

11. R. Price, *Masters, unions and men: Work control in building and the rise of labour 1830-1914* (Cambridge, 1980).

12. M. Silver, 'Recent British Strike Trends: A Factual Analysis', *British Journal of Industrial Relations*, xi(1), 1973, pp.66-104.

13. G. Ingham, *Strikes and Industrial Conflict: Britain and Scandinavia* (London, 1974), pp.26-8; E. Batstone, I. Boraston and S. Frenkel, *The Social Organisation of Strikes* (Oxford, 1978), ch.2.

14. H. Llewellyn Smith, 'Strikes and Lockouts', *Encyclopaedia Britannica*, xxxiii (London, 1902 ed.), p.1,024.

15. K. Burgess, *The Origins of British Indus-trial Relations* (London, 1975), p.228.

16. Calculated from S.J. Chapman and T.S. Ashton, 'The Size of Businesses, mainly in the Tex-tile Industries', *Journal of the Royal Statistical Society*, lxxvii (5), 1914, table xxvii, p.548.

17. Calculated from *British Labour Statistics, Historical Abstract 1886-1968* (London, 1971), table 197. The official strike data in this table and table 4.2 differ from others quoted in this paper in

that they refer to Great Britain and Northern Ireland instead of Great Britain and Ireland and the numbers of strikers refers to both those directly and indirectly affected at plants on strike. These differences are necessary as this is the only series that distinguishes coalmining.

18. H.A. Turner, *Is Britain Really Strike Prone?: A Review of the Incidence, Character and Costs of Industrial Conflict* (Cambridge, 1969), p. 18.

19. J.W. Cunliffe, 'Modern Industrial Warfare', *Westminster Review*, cxl (2), 1893, pp.109-14. This is an interesting contemporary comparison of the two strikes.

20. W.H. Abraham, 'The Hull Strike', *The Economic Review*, 3, (4), 1893, p.359.

21. A. Gouldner, *Wildcat Strike* (London, 1955), p.65.

22. P. Stearns, 'The Unskilled and Industriali- sation; a Transformation of Consciousness', *Archiv für Sozial Geschichte*, xvi, 1976, pp.264-7.

23. For comparative data of this kind see Ingham, *Strikes* and especially W.Korpi and M.Shalev, 'Strikes, Power and Politics in Western Nations, 1900-1976', *Political Power and Social Theory*, 1, 1980, pp.301-34.

24. E.J. Hobsbawm, 'Economic Fluctuations and Social Movements since 1800', *Economic History Review*, v (1), 1952, pp.1-25.

25. It may well be that future research will show that earlier strike waves occurred. It should also be noted that Cronin in the works cited in footnote 6 uses the Board of Trade series from 1888 as if it is consistent therefore making unreliable comparisons between the strike wave of 1888-91 and later periods

26. J. Schooling, 'Strikes and Lock-outs, 1892- 1901', *Fortnightly Review*, n.s. 75, 1904, pp.849-63.

27. Cronin, *Industrial Conflict, passim*.

28. R. Hyman, *Strikes* (London, 1977; 2nd ed.), p.173; E. Batstone, 'Strikes and Sociologists', *Bulletin of the Society for the Study of Labour History*, 28, 1976, pp.86-90; R. Stern, 'Methodologi- cal Issues of Quantitative Strike Analysis', *Industrial Relations*, 7 (3), 1978, pp.32-42.

29. R. Bean and D.A. Peel, 'Business Activity, Labour Organisation and Industrial Disputes in the United Kingdom, 1892-1938', *Business History*, xvii (2), 1976, pp.205-11; see also C. Ragin, S.Coverman and M. Hayward, 'Major Labour Disputes in Britain, 1902-1938: the Relationship between Resource

Expenditure and Outcome', *American Sociological Review*, 42 (2), 1982, pp.238-52.

30. P.K. Edwards, 'The "Social" Determination of Strike Activity: an Explanation and Critique', *Journal of Industrial Relations*, 21 (2), 1979. For attempts to apply the 'social' analysis historically see Stearns, 'Measuring', and P. Stearns, *Lives of Labour* (London, 1975), ch.4-6, 9.

31. For an introduction to this, see C. Mulvey, *The Economic Analysis of Trade Unions* (Oxford, 1978) and for the steps in the development of the argument see J. Hicks, *The Theory of Wages* (London, 1932); O.C. Ashenfelter and G.E. Johnson, 'Bargaining Theory, Trade Unions and Industrial Strike Activity', *American Economic Review*, 59 (1), 1969, pp.33-49; D. Sapsford, 'The Theory of Bargaining and Strike Activity', in D. Sapsford *et.al.* (eds.), *Strikes, Theory and Activity* (Bradford, 1982).

32. The most common approach has been to relate strike activity to economic conditions; see, for example, E. Phelps Brown, *The Growth of British Industrial Relations* (London, 1959); H. Pelling, *Popular Politics and Society in Late Victorian Britain* (London, 1968); Hunt, *Labour History*; E. Hopkins, 'An Anatomy of Strikes in the Stourbridge Glass Industry, 1850-1914', *Midland History*, ii (1), 1973, pp.21-31.

33. Pelling, *Popular Politics*, pp.149-51; William Collison claimed that between 1893-1909 his strike breaking National Free Labour Association broke 680 strikes. This represents only 7% of all recorded strikes and is usually regarded as a grossly exaggerated claim. Pelling himself in an earlier work has noted the difficulties employers had in using blacklegs, *A History of British Trade Unionism* (Harmondsworth, 1963), p.110.

34. See Cronin, *Industrial Conflict*, ch.2 for a critique.

35. This is the technical problem of multi-collinearity in econometric work.

36. Those which include the period before 1914 are D. Sapsford, 'The United Kingdom's Industrial Disputes (1893-1971); A Study in the Economics of Industrial Unrest (unpublished Univ. of Leicester M. Phil. Thesis, 1973); D. Sapsford, 'A Time Series Analysis of the United Kingdom's Industrial Disputes', *Industrial Relations*, 14 (2), 1975, pp.242-9; Bean and Peel, 'Business Activity'; Ragin, Coverman and Hayward, 'Labour Disputes'; Cronin, *Industrial Conflict*.

37. Batstone, Boraston and Frenkel, *Strikes*, p.1.

38. M. Jones, 'The Llechwedd Dispute, Blaenau Ffestiniog', *Llafur*, 1 (4), 1975, p.6

39. Batstone, Boraston and Frenkel, *Strikes;* M. Gutman, 'Primary (Informal) Work Groups', *Radical America*, 6 (3), 1972, pp.78-88; Price, *Masters;* N. Nicholson and J. Kelly, 'The Psychology of Strikes', *Journal of Occupational Behaviour*, 1 (4), 1980, pp. 275-84.

40. J. Hills, W. Ashley and M. Woods, *Industrial Unrest: A Practical Solution* (London, 1914), p.39

41. *Strikes and Lockouts for 1913*, PP 1914-16, p.xvi.

42. P. Joyce, *Work, Society and Politics: The culture of the factory in later Victorian England* (London, 1982), ch.2.

43. There was significant tension between union officials and rank and file workers from the late 1870s; Burgess, *Origins*, pp.264-93.

44. Conflict sharpened as competition increased at the end of the 1870s. In 1877 and 1878 there were partial textile strikes in Bolton and Oldham (the latter unofficial) and in late 1878 a more general nine week stoppage affecting some 70,000 which led to riots after which 68 were tried and convicted. In 1884 some 18,000 weavers were on strike for 8 weeks, in 1885 25,000 spinners and weavers in Oldham were involved in a three month dispute and then in 1892-3 500,000 struck for 20 weeks in the 'cotton war'. If the claim that in Oldham alone between 1883-1893 spinners were involved in some 3,000 disputes in some 300 mills is correct the image of deference seems to pall a little. Joyce, *Work*, ch.2; Llewellyn Smith, 'Strikes', p. 1,030; Burgess, *Origins*, pp.266-71.

45. J. White, 'Cotton', in Wrigley (ed.), *Industrial Relations*, p.227 notes that between 1888-1892 9.2% of strikes in textiles ended with hands being replaced.

46. R. Bean, 'The Liverpool Dock Strike of 1890', *International Review of Social History*, xviii (1), 1973, p.63.

47. Knowles, *Strikes*, pp.219-20; Nicholson and Kelly, 'Psychology', p.281.

48. Llewellyn Smith, 'Strikes', pp.1,026-7.

49. *Strikes and Lockouts for 1895*, PP 1896, p.64. For discussions of unofficial action see Burgess, *Origins*; Price, *Masters*; V. Gore, 'Rank and File Dissent', in Wrigley (ed.), *Industrial Relations*, pp.47-73; K. Brooker, 'The Northamptonshire Shoemakers' Reaction to Industrialisation: some Thoughts', *Northamptonshire Past and Present*, vi (3),

1980, pp.151-9.

50. Llewellyn Smith, 'Strikes', p.1,027;
Jones, 'Llechwedd'.

51. Llewellyn Smith, 'Strikes', p.1,026; the
Reports on Strikes and Lockouts for the 1890s contain
information on strike pay in many strikes.

52. C. Pearce, *The Manningham Mills Strike,
Bradford December 1890 - April 1891* (Hull, 1975),
pp.59-67. This is one of the few studies of individual strikes that is sensitive to the issues raised
here.

53. This happened in the Manningham Mills
strike; Pearce, *Manningham*, pp.19, 50.

54. E. Jacques and C.H. Piret, 'La Saisie du
Sens de l'Action: Questions/Problèmes de méthode a
propos de l'Analyse', *Recherches Sociologiques,*
5 (1), 1974, pp.105-114; D. Geary, 'Identifying
Militancy: the Assessment of Working Class Attitudes
Towards State and Society', in R.J. Evans (ed.),
*The German Working Class 1888 - 1933: the Politics
of Everyday Life* (London, 1982).

55. W. McCarthy, 'The Reasons Given for Striking: an Analysis of Official Statistics, 1945-1957',
*Bulletin of the Oxford University Institute of Sta-
tistics,* 21, 1959, pp.17-29; P.L. Robertson, 'Demarcation Disputes in British Shipbuilding before 1914',
International Review of Social History, 20 (2), 1975,
pp.220-35.

56. Bean, 'Liverpool', p.67.

57. R.O. Clarke, 'The Dispute in the British
Engineering Industry 1897-1898: an Evaluation',
Economica, n.s. xxiv (94), 1957, pp.128-37; N.Todd,
'Trade Unions and the Engineering Industry Dispute
at Barrow-in-Furness, 1897-1898', *International
Review of Social History,* 20 (1), 1975, pp.33-47;
J. Hinton, *The First Shop Stewards Movement* (London,
1973).

58. Mann, *Consciousness*, p.13. My argument
here has benefited from an interesting critique of
Mann (though without accepting its conclusions);
M.R. Smith, 'The Effects of Strikes on Workers: a
Critical Analysis', *Canadian Journal of Sociology,*
8 (4), 1978, pp.457-72.

59. Schooling, 'Strikes', pp.860-61; J.R.
MacDonald, *The Socialist Movement* (London, 1912),
p.50; P. Snowden, *Socialism or Syndicalism* (London,
1913), pp.33,222-3; *The Industrial Syndicalist,* 1
(7), January 1911, pp.20-33.

60. *The Industrial Syndicalist,* 1 (6), December
1910, p.10; J. Hinton, *Labour and Socialism: A
History of the British Labour Movement 1867-1974*

(Brighton, 1983), p.69. The terms defensive/offensive are not used here in their restrictive nineteenth century sense of for/against new conditions.

61. Knowles, *Strikes*, p.151; on differences in strike proneness, see Cronin, *Industrial Conflict*, ch.7.

62. Compiled from *Abstract of Labour Statistics in the United Kingdom*, for 1904, 1909, 1913. These appear to contain the final revisions in a much revised series. Each year a small number of workers went on strike more than once. The only year in which this had a serious impact was 1912 in coal-mining when it affected some 106,000 workpeople.

63. Holton, *British Syndicalism*, pp.20, 76-77.

64. K. Forchheimer, 'Some International aspects of the strike Movement: the Results of Labour Disputes', *Bulletin of the Oxford University Institute of Statistics*, 10 (9) 1948, pp.294-304.

65. Holton, *British Syndicalism*, p.123.

66. E. Durkheim, *Suicide* (London, 1952). It should be stressed that Durkheim himself did not make this connection. S. Stack, 'The Effect of Strikes on Suicide: a National Analysis', *Sociological Focus*, 5 (2), 1982, pp.135-46.

67. O. Anderson, 'Did Suicide Increase with Industrialisation in Victorian England', *Past and Present*, 86, 1980, pp.149-73.

68. G. Stedman Jones, *Outcast London: A study in the relationship of classes in Victorian Society* (Oxford, 1971), ch.17.

69. There is a long standing but limited sociological debate around the 'Kerr-Siegel hypothesis' which attempts to link strikes to community character. For a historical critique see Cronin, *Industrial Conflict*, ch.7. L. Hollern Lees, 'Strikes and the Urban Hierarchy in Early Industrial Towns, 1842-1901', in J.E. Cronin and J. Schneer (eds.), *Social Conflict and the Political Order in Modern Britain* (London, 1982) also attempts to make some links but within a framework which stresses the institutionalisation of industrial relations.

70. Stedman Jones, *Outcast London*, ch.19; M. Blanch, 'Nation, Empire and the Birmingham Working Class, 1899-1914' (Unpublished Univ. of Birmingham Ph.D. Thesis, 1975), p.336.

71. J. McHugh, 'The Belfast Labour Dispute and the Riots of 1907', *International Review of Social History*, 27 (1), 1977; Holton, *British Syndicalism*, ch.6, 14.

72. Pearce, 'Manningham', pp.36-49; see also K. Laybourn, 'The Manningham Mills Strike: Its Importance in Bradford History', *The Bradford*

Antiquary, xlvi, 1976, pp.7-35. For a similar
though less intense polarisation in 1890 see H.
Hendrick,'The Leeds Gas Strike, 1890', *Thoresby
Society Publications*, liv (2), 1974), pp.78-98.

73. N. Scotland, 'Rural War in Late Victorian
Norfolk', *Norfolk Archives*, xxxvii (6), 1981, pp.
82-7; A. Howkins, 'Edwardian Liberalism and Industrial Unrest: a Class Analysis', *History Workshop*,
4, 1977, pp.143-62.

74. D. Smith, 'Tonypandy 1910: Definitions of
Community', *Past and Present*, 87, 1980, pp.158-84;
K. Brooker, *The Hull Strikes of 1911* (Hull, 1979);
H. Hilkins, 'The Liverpool General Transport Strike
of 1911', *Transactions of the Historical Society of
Lancashire and Cheshire*, 113, 1961, pp.169-95;
Holton, *British Syndicalism*, ch.6; *Wolverhampton
Express and Star*, Jan. - May 1913.

75. See C. Wrigley, 'The Government and Indus-
trial Relations', and R. Davidson, 'Government
Administration', in Wrigley (ed.), *Industrial
Relations*, pp.135-86.

76. Ingham, *Strikes*, *passim*.

77. G. Askwith, *Industrial Problems and Disputes* (London, 1920), p.228; E. Wigham, *Strikes and
the Government 1893-1981* (London, 1982), ch.1.

78. G. Marshall, 'The Armed Forces and Indus-
trial Disputes in the United Kingdom', *Armed Forces
and Society*, 5 (2), 1979, pp.271-3; R. Neville,
'The Yorkshire Miners and the 1893 Lockout: the
"Featherstone Massacre"', *International Review of
Social History*, 21 (3), 1976, pp.337-57.

79. McHugh, 'Belfast', pp.8-13; Smith, 'Tonypandy', pp.159-60; M. Daunton, 'Inter-Union Relations on the waterfront: Cardiff 1888-1914',
International Review of Social History, 22 (3),
1977, pp.350-78; Hilkins, 'Liverpool'. Two batta-
lions were put on alert in June 1911 after bitter
battles with police in Hull; see Brooker, *Hull
Strikes*, p.20; P. Addison, 'Winston Churchill and
the Working Class, 1900-1914', in J. Winter (ed.),
The Working Class in Modern British History
(Cambridge, 1983).

80. McHugh, 'Belfast', p.15.

81. H. Collins, 'The Marxism of the Social
Democratic Federation', in A. Briggs and J. Saville
(eds.), *Essays in Labour History* (London, 1971) II,
pp.47-69; W. Kendall, *The Revolutionary Movement
in Britain 1900-1921* (London, 1969), p.29.

82. MacDonald, *Socialist*; Snowden, *Socialism*;
Labour Leader, Oct. 2-23, 1913; R. Miliband, *Parli-
mentary Socialism* (London, 1972), pp.32-8.

83. For examples of the significance of local SDF involvement in strikes in one area see Brooker, 'Northamptonshire Shoemakers'; K. Brooker, 'James Grimble and the Raunds Strike of 1905', *Northamptonshire Past and Present*, vi (5), 1983, pp.275-9.

84. S. Yeo, 'A New Life: The Religion of Socialism in Britain 1883-1896', *History Workshop*, 4, 1977, pp.5-56.

85. R. Tressell, *The Ragged Trousered Philanthropists* (London, 1965), p.46; J. Young, 'Militancy, English Socialism and *The Ragged Trousered Philanthropists*' (mimeo, 1982).

86. Holton, *British Syndicalism*; Kendall, *Revolutionary Movement*; R. Challinor, *The Origins of British Bolshevism* (London, 1977); D. Morris, 'The Origins of the British Socialist Party', *North West Labour History Society Bulletin*, 8, 1982-3.

87. Hinton, *Labour and Socialism*, ch.4-5.

88. L. Hall, 'My Version of "Syndicalism"', *The Syndicalist*, May 1912, p.2; *Hansard*, March 19, 1912, p.1,774.

Chapter Five

LEISURE

Hugh Cunningham

I

The image of the years before 1914 as a golden age
derives much of its impetus from the history of
leisure. Particular forms of leisure, most notably
music hall, cricket and the seaside holiday, are
seen as enjoying in these years their golden age,
and more generally the period, and particularly the
Edwardian part of it, is conceived to have been more
leisured, more easily-paced, than those which came
before or after it.[1]
    In another perspective these years are seen as
the beginning of the age of 'mass' leisure, when a
new level of demand for leisure goods and services
within the working class was matched, on the supply
side, by major changes in technology, investment and
organisation. The word 'mass', of course, often en-
capsulates a critical moral comment as well as a
description of the marketing of leisure.[2]
    These two perspectives, that of the golden age
and of mass leisure, have their merits, but they
need to be seen as the product of the peculiar historiography of leisure, and of the sources upon
which it has been based. The mainstream historiography of leisure falls broadly into two categories;
on the one hand histories of production and perform-
ance, and on the other histories of moral attitudes.
The first category is constructed out of sources
which celebrate the role of the star - W.G. Grace or
Marie Lloyd[3] - or of a genre, or which, looking at
the leisure industries, demonstrate the accumulation
of capital, the increase of seating capacity, the
number of excursionists, and so on. The second
category focuses on the abundance of concern about
the morality of working class leisure, evident in
Parliamentary Papers, newspapers, journals and

books; it directs our attention to drinking, prostitution, gambling, crowd behaviour, and Sunday observance. The emphasis of both categories is on what is public, observable and measurable - and correspondingly, to a large extent, on what is masculine. In our period the most accessible sources require particularly careful handling, for the increase in the quantity of printed material can itself give an impression of an increase in the quantity of and concern about leisure. There is an obvious danger in assuming that because we can count more football matches or whatever, then more were happening; there is a less obvious danger in assuming that things which were not reported and written about did not happen at all. We need to guard against the possibility that there are conclusions built into the nature of the evidence.

This chapter seeks to circumvent the problems inherent in the sources by first surveying the evidence for the emergence of mass leisure at a national or macro level, and then counterposing to this an examination of leisure opportunities and of the structure of leisure from below, from the perspective of the family life cycle, gender, community and region. Finally the changes which did occur will be placed in two contexts: on the one hand an ideological commentary about working class leisure which both inherited much from the past and sought to structure the new leisure within a larger concern about war, empire and democracy; and on the other a major expansion of the leisure class itself during this period.

II

The argument that this period saw the birth of mass leisure is most naturally sustained by citing aggregate evidence for the country as a whole - sometimes enlivened by suitable local examples. There can be no doubt that this type of evidence points at the very least to the conclusion that there was a widening of opportunities for leisure within the working class. It is most conveniently surveyed by examining, first, the demand for leisure, then the supply of leisure, and finally the outcome in a new social organisation of leisure.

The increase in demand for leisure, though it undoubtedly occurred, is perhaps most subject to qualification. Three factors need to be considered. First, to what extent was there an increase in the hours free from work on a daily, weekly and annual

basis? Secondly, to what extent was there an increase in real incomes to allow of a greater expenditure on leisure? And thirdly, insofar as there
was an increase in time or money, how much of it was
spent on leisure, rather than, say, on overtime or
better food?

The period is given a certain unity by the fact
that major reductions in daily and weekly hours of
work occur immediately before and after it rather
than during it. The early 1870s saw the widespread
establishment of the nine-hour day. The struggle
for an eight-hour day from the 1880s onwards was
only very partially successful. Reductions in
normal hours through the period were piecemeal and
insubstantial, and may have been offset by increases
in overtime and a decrease in leisure on the job.
'Sky-larking and horse-play', as Alfred Williams
noted of a Swindon railway factory in 1915, 'are not
nearly as common and frequent as they were formerly.'[4] Moreover, if a 54-hour week was the norm
established in the 1870s there were numerous and
enduring exceptions to it. For agricultural labourers, for example, 'the hours of labour in the summer
months are usually 11 or 12 per day, with intervals
of 1½ to 2 hours for meals; in a few cases the working time on Saturdays is slightly reduced, but this
is not general.'[5] As to the notorious case of shop
assistants, the long campaign to reduce hours was
largely ineffective. The House of Lords Select
Committee in 1901 confirmed that many assistants
worked 80-90 hours per week, and the 1904 Shop Hours
Act was permissive and ineffective. The only real
advance was the achievement of a half-holiday in
1911 - though with some exceptions.[6] In addition to
these relatively well-documented cases, there were
many other workers whose conditions and hours of
work defy neat tabulation - seasonal, migratory and
casual workers, dockers, workers in the sweated
trades, domestic servants. For all such, and indeed
for unemployed married women, a regular 54-hour
working week with a Saturday half-holiday was at
best a distant dream; it had absolutely no foundation in the reality of their lives.

There can be no doubt, however, that one regular period of time, the Saturday half-holiday, was
becoming more widely available for leisure during
this period. Not only was the Saturday half-holiday
spreading at the expense of St. Monday; perhaps more
significant, work was ending earlier on Saturdays.
Thus for textile workers legislation laid down a
Saturday half-holiday beginning at 2.00 p.m. in 1850,

reduced to 1.00 p.m. in 1874 and to noon in 1901.
The majority of workers did not gain the Saturday
half-holiday through legislation, but through trade
union pressure, and demand grew in the 1890s to
leave off work at noon. The engineering trades on
the Tyne and Wear, for example, obtained a 'twelve
o'clock' Saturday in 1890. The increasing universality of the Saturday half-holiday and its growing
length undoubtedly gave an edge to the demand for
leisure in this period, and had demonstrably important effects in, for example, the spread of organised sport. Once again, however, many workers, as
noted above, failed to benefit from it.[7]

Besides the possibilities for leisure daily and
weekly, this period also saw changes in the pattern
of annual holidays - though once again they are not
very major changes. As far as the law was concerned
there was no advance on the 1875 Holidays Extension
Act whose chief impact, of course, was to spread the
institution of the first Monday in August as a
holiday. August Bank Holiday was particularly important in southern England giving at least one
break in a calendar from which holidays had largely
been excluded. Elsewhere traditional holidays continued, whether in the form of the Lancashire Wakes
Weeks or of more sporadic holidays for special
events like the races in the rest of the north and
midlands; the August Bank Holiday had less of an
impact. The day trip remained by far the most
common form of holiday, but in the Lancashire textile industry and to a lesser extent in the Yorkshire woollen industry up to a week on holiday had
become a possibility by the turn of the century. It
was, however, with rare exceptions, a week without
pay. Only in 1911 did the trade union movement begin to press for holidays with pay for all workers,
and the impact of the demand before 1914 was
slight.[8] The extension of holiday time suggests an
increase in demand for leisure, but at the same time
it must be recognised that some enforced holidays
were in effect unemployment. In the Swindon railway
factory many workmen were 'indifferent to holidays.
Many hundreds of them would never have one at all if
they were not forced to do so by the constitution of
the calendar and the natural order of things.' More
sharply still, workmen in Lancaster enjoying four
weeks annual holiday without pay at Easter, Whitsun,
August and Christmas, often described the experiences as 'lock-outs'. As John Walton has des-
scribed, only in the Lancashire textile industry was
the availability of holiday time matched by the

resources to enjoy it for a time-span longer than one or at most two to three days.[9]

Overall, then, the increase in the time available for leisure in this period was marginal, and subject to much qualification. What can be said about income? The general picture is of a rise in real wages of approximately one third in the last quarter of the century, followed by stagnation or decline in the period up to the First World War. Qualifications, of course, are necessary: unemployment, underemployment, occupational structures, regional and more localised variations, the level of means for supplementing income, for example through allotment produce, all contribute to a more complex and generally less blandly optimistic picture - as of course do the numerous investigations of poverty and of family budgets.[10]

None of these qualifications should obscure the fact that there was a substantial increase in working class spending power in the last quarter of the nineteenth century. Unfortunately there is no reliable means of calculating how much of it was spent on leisure. Food, clothing, and household goods and furniture had equal if not more pressing claims, and for some of these at least there is evidence of increased expenditure.[11] Such figures as there are (and they are often little better than guesses) do suggest an increase in total expenditure on leisure goods and services even in the period of stagnant real income in the early twentieth century, but part of that increase may be due to a disproportionate rise in expenditure on leisure among the leisure classes. Within the working class, as to an even greater extent within society as a whole, there was a significant decline in the proportion of income absorbed by alcohol, but even at the end of the period expenditure on alcohol dominated total expenditure on leisure goods and services, forming over half.[12]

In reality there was an infinite number of gradations in the extent to which working class people could participate in expenditure on leisure, but in the attempt to estimate overall demand it is probably fair to conclude that expenditure on leisure, apart from alcohol, was scarcely possible at all for one third of the working class; that about half were able to participate fairly fully, and the remainder intermittently and on no more than a daily basis. Of course these static figures take no account of the movements of the life cycle, but they do alert us to the fact that the increase of demand from within the working class was restricted by a variety of factors, and that many of 'the masses' played no part in the mass market for leisure.

An increase in the supply of leisure, particularly commercial leisure, seems at first glance less open to doubt. The major expansion of the seaside holiday industry, the birth of the cinema, and the incursion of commercial modes of supply, particularly into football, all point to a major increase in the volume of supply together with a greater dependence on the market in the provision of it.[13] The cinema perhaps provides the most dramatic evidence that this was the case. By 1914 there were between 3,500 and 4,500 cinemas in Great Britain, with an average of 22 picture theatres for every town with a population over 100,000. From its inception in 1896 this thoroughly commercialised industry had quickly brought the experience of film, on a regular basis, within the reach of every town dweller. Its impact could be sudden and dramatic. Middlesborough, for example, which in 1907 had only two theatres and two music halls, by 1911 had ten music halls, all of them showing moving pictures - it was the chapter on recreation which required revision between the first and second editions of Lady Bell's *At the Works*.[14] The impact of commercial leisure stretches beyond the more obvious leisure industries. Activities which previously had been pursued without a business structure now came within the ambit of the market. Most notoriously this was the case with sport, where both professionalism and limited liability spread, but it is also observable in the growing dominance of commercial entertainment and of business modes of management in the working men's clubs.[15]

Four qualifications, however, need to be made to the notion that commercial entertainment was the only force transforming the supply of leisure for the people, or that it operated in one direction only. The first is that in some sections of commercial supply there was contraction not expansion. The number of pubs, the key locale for so much working class leisure, declined, and correspondingly the number of persons per licence increased.

Stricter fire regulations and licensing policies led, too, to a reduction in the number of music halls. The new London County Council reduced the number of places licensed for music or music and dancing from 348 in 1889 to 189 in 1891, and of these 189 only 39 were music halls (the remainder included 34 public houses which may have approximated to music halls, but also 95 Town Halls

Table 5.1: On Licences in England and Wales, 1875-
1915 [16]

	Number of on licences	Persons per licence
1875	109,346	223
1886	103,593	251
1896	101,903	285
1906	98,894	329
1915	86,626	416

and Assembly Rooms). There was a reduction, too, in
the number of venues for horse racing. It is possible, of course, for a reduction in the number of
outlets to be consonant with an overall increase in
supply - the pubs, the music halls and the race
courses which survived may have been bigger, and
this is certainly likely. But at ground level what
people were likely to be conscious of was a pub,
music hall or race course closed down, or transfor-
med in its function, from, say, music hall to
cinema.[17]
The second qualification is linked to the first.
Commercial and market forces were subject to a number of restrictions of which the most serious was
licensing. The state had increasing powers to regulate the provision and content of leisure; it had
no hesitation in acting to maintain public safety
and to uphold public morals, and in both ways restrained the full development of market forces.
Partly in response to this the market regulated itself, both by conforming to those norms which it
shared with the state, and by controlling, in
certain spheres, the pursuit of profit. This control over the pursuit of profit did not restrict the
quantity of supply, but it points to the difficulty
of separating out commercial and non-commercial
sources of supply.[18]
The third qualification is that much of the
increase in the supply of leisure in this period
catered not for the working class or for the masses
but for the wealthy or relatively wealthy. In
central London, for example, according to Charles
Booth, 'all places of amusement are very largely
supported by the rich or by strangers visiting
London.' Some of the most significant increases in
supply in the period - in shooting, for example, or

in land-hungry golf, or tennis - were for the rich.[19]

Finally, and most important, non-commercial supply of leisure, though less spectacular than commercial, remained of crucial importance. The dividing line between the two, as we have seen, is less than clear cut. A seaside municipality building sea defences and promenades was clearly acting to enhance the commercial prosperity of the town.[20] In most towns, however, expenditure on leisure was a continuation of what had started in the mid nineteenth century. Libraries, parks, museums and baths became facilities which in this period any town of size recognised it ought to possess. Sometimes the initial outlay came from a philanthropist; Bristol was typical in acquiring a municipally owned library, museum and art gallery between 1895 and 1905, all of them through private benefactions. By 1913 Carnegie had made grants amounting to almost two million pounds to libraries in the United Kingdom, and this kind of private donation together with ratepayers' money meant that 60 percent of the population was within reach of a public library in 1914 compared to 23 percent in 1885. Despite their rules and regulations and sometimes forbidding appearance these libraries were used, and used mainly, by the working class.[21]

There remained the vast range of leisure activities for the working class supplied without thought of profit and without expectation that the rates or tax payer might provide financial support. Many of the suppliers of these services felt themselves to be living in difficult times, short of members and short of money. They were tempted either to become purist and inward-looking, accepting a minority and limited status, or to try to keep up membership by softening its obligations. These were the kind of dilemmas faced by temperance organisations, YMCAs, and so on. Their sense of distress, however, should not obscure the major role which such organisations played in the provision of leisure right up to 1914. In Rochdale, for example, the churches and chapels, with their annual Whit walks and outings, and their regular tea parties, bazaars, concerts, lectures, classes and debating societies probably provided the main structure for the leisure time of their members. Besides this continuity of provision there were new initiatives in this period of which by far the most prominent were the numerous and successful endeavours to provide organised leisure for young people, starting

with the Boys' Brigades in 1884, and growing to include the Lads' Brigades, the Girls' Friendly
Society, and the Boy Scouts. It is true that finance
for the uniform was often a problem, and there was a
familiar difficulty in reaching below the better off
among the working class, but as the memories of many
working class people show, these institutions and
others like them, for example Sunday Schools, at the
very least rivalled the commercial and public suppliers of leisure in the period up to 1914.[22] It was
these voluntary organisations, too, which provided
some of the new initiatives, necessarily for minori-
ties, which helped to expand leisure opportunities
during the period. The coop movement, YMCAs, the
Pleasant Sunday Afternoon Association, and the
Clarion Clubs all had recreational offshoots, many
of them bringing working class and lower middle
class town dwellers together in a discovery or re-
discovery of the countryside.[23]

Outside the relatively narrow circles of their
spiritual descendants these developments have
attracted little attention. The focus of historians,
as of commentators and photographers of the time,
has been on the seaside resorts, the music hall and
cinema, football and Bank Holidays. The development
of these forms of leisure is often seen as marking
the beginning of the age of mass leisure. Besides
the evidence of growth in supply and demand there
are three types of argument used to suggest that the
coming together of supply and demand resulted in a
new social organisation of leisure.. The first is
the amount and the structure of investment in the
leisure industries. Research here has scarcely
developed beyond the point of citing random figures:
£650,650 as the capital value of the sixteen leading
London music halls in 1892, and £776,200 for 36
provincial halls; £6 million estimated to represent
the capital value in 1887 of the nation's 1,310
places of amusement (200 theatres, 950 concert halls,
galleries, public halls and gardens, 160 music
halls); £2 million in the Moss Empires music hall
syndicate formed in 1900; over £11 million invested
in cinema by 1914; £500,000 in the 1890s for Blackpool's Tower, Alhambra and Gigantic Wheel; £30
million invested in joint stock cycle companies by
1903.[24] It is not easy to see any obvious pattern
in such figures. It is probable, though we have no
means of knowing for certain, that the total capital
investment in leisure industries was increasing
during our period, but it is worth noting three
points in qualification. First, there was substan-

tial investment before our period, in music halls,
piers and hotels for example in the 1860s.[25] Second,
investment in leisure is not a history of continuous
and profitable expansion. There were many disas-
ters, many setbacks, possibly a tendency for investment in entertainment to be counter-cyclical.[26]
Third, it is a mistake to assume from the example of
music hall that the tendency was always towards the
concentration of ownership. Thus in cinema after
1910 the tendency was towards a greater number of
smaller companies. There continued, too, a considerable amount of small-scale enterprise in popular entertainment aimed at a working class audience.
As Booth put it, 'especially in poor neighbourhoods,
the old-fashioned style of sing-song still continues
in force.' In York, too, Rowntree found that 'Only
about a dozen public-houses have music licenses, but
there is music and singing in a great many others.'[27]
Counting licences will not necessarily tell us
what was actually happening. And that small-scale
licence holder, the publican, remained crucial in
the supply and organisation of recreation and entertainment - a key figure in the spread and organisation of football in the north east, of boxing, of
outings, and of betting.[28] The notion that entertainment for the people was being provided by a
handful of self-made millionaires, in the same way
as Lipton was providing groceries or Boots medicines,
bears at best an approximation to the truth.

The second type of argument relates to the
number of people employed in the entertainment industries. The census figures suggest that whilst
the population rose on average 0.8 percent a year
between 1871 and 1911, employment in the arts and
entertainment increased by 4.7 percent a year. This
evidence seems to point to a major increase in the
supply of entertainment. It probably needs to be
treated with much scepticism. The Registrar-
General was all too aware of the difficulty of allo-
cating people to particular jobs in this field, and
of defining the entertainment industries; were
'musicians', for example, performers or teachers or
a combination of both? Much of the work was part-
time; of some 7,000 football professionals in 1914
only 2,500 were full-time. Much of it, too, provided employment for the working class, but not
entertainment: there was, for example, a substantial
increase in the number of gamekeepers from 12,633 in
1881 to 17,148 in 1911 and the figures under-record
the extent of the increase.[29]

The third and critical argument is that a

characteristic of the age was the growth of spectatorship and of consumption of leisure goods and
services. It is figures for these which most plausibly lead historians to talk of an age of mass
leisure. The growth of spectatorship was perhaps
the most notable change. In horse racing it was not
uncommon to find crowds of 10,000 to 15,000 rising
at Bank Holiday events to 70,000 or 80,000. The
average football cup tie attendance is reckoned to
have risen from 6,000 in 1888-9 to 12,800 in 1895-6,
to over 20,000 in the first round in 1903. Spectatorship was not confined to sports; 70,000 people,
for example, watched the 1907 Crystal Palace Brass
Band Championships. It is important not to fall
into the trap of assuming that there were no spectators of anything before about 1870 - on the contrary
cricket, prizefighting, horse racing, pedestrianism,
and even events like Volunteer Field Days attracted
spectators in tens of thousands in the earlier nineteenth century. Nor should we exaggerate the proportion of the masses who were mass spectators:
football spectators probably accounted for no more
than three or four percent of the population. What
it does seem plausible to suggest, however, is
greater regularity of spectatorship - weekly during
the season, rather than sporadic - and it is in this
respect that football is so important.[30]
     The growth and regularity of spectatorship was
dependent on ease of travel, and the numbers travel-
ling grew rapidly. The estimated annual number of
visitors to Blackpool in season rose from one million in 1883 to two million in 1893 to four million
in 1914. There was a regular large-scale exodus
from the industrial towns, particularly in Lancashire; in Accrington half the population stayed away
for a week in 1905. But travel as a form of leisure
consumption was not confined to such towns; even in
southern England agricultural workers, like George
Sturt's Bettesworth, might go on an annual day
excursion.[31]
     There was, too, increasing purchase of leisure
goods, for example newspapers, bicycles and pianos.
All of these, of course, found a substantial market
within the middle classes, but there is significant
evidence that they were within the reach of the
better-off among the working class. Ehrlich, for
example, calculates that by 1910 there were between
two and four million pianos in Britain, one for
every ten or twenty people, and concludes that 'even
the lowest estimates imply that ownership was by no
means confined to the middle classes.'[32]

It is this kind of evidence, coupled with figures for levels of investment and the visible presence of leisure facilities in the shape of music
halls, cinemas, piers, sports grounds, public
libraries, temperance halls and so on, which point
most obviously to a new age of mass leisure. Urbanisation, improvements in urban transport systems,
the application of technology to the provision of
leisure and an undoubted if modest and interrupted
rise in the level of working class demand, add
further plausibility to the idea. Our task now is
to assess the impact of this new level of leisure
provision on the lives of working people. It will
be done at two levels, first by examining at an individual and family level the amount of leisure time
which was taken and the ways in which it was spent,
and secondly by looking at the context in which the
new leisure became available.

III

The increase and reorganisation of the supply of
leisure did not mean that leisure was, as it were,
permanently on tap. On the contrary leisure time
was heavily structured, moulded by three cycles.
The first of these, as crucial in the study of
leisure as in that of poverty, was the life cycle.
Leisure expectations as well as the opportunities to
fulfil them varied according to age.
   In childhood time for play was universal, and
yet what is remarkable about working class childhood leisure in these decades is the very limited
degree to which it was affected by or came into contact with the leisure industries. All observers of
working class children at play, and all autobiographical memories of childhood, stress both the
traditionalism of children at play and their ability
to fill time without resort to the purchase of the
means of enjoyment. 'There were no bought pleasures' as Flora Thompson noted of her Oxfordshire
childhood. Toys were in short supply. Dolls, hoops,
marbles, and tops were in most cases the limit of
equipment specifically designed for play. 'Indoors',
as Mrs Pember Reeves noted in south London, 'there
are no amusements. There are no books and no games,
nor any place to play the games should they exist.'
The street was the playground for both boys and
girls, boys running around, playing at soldiers,
perhaps more adventurously creating a tramcar or an
ambulance out of an old box on wheels. Girls,
typically, played hopscotch or skipped.[33]

144

Some variety was introduced into children's leisure in three forms. First itinerant entertainers, losing their markets among adults, increasingly performed for the young. The punch and judy men, and the penny freak shows, still lining Shoreditch High Street at the end of the century, scraped a living from the halfpennies and pennies of the children of the poor. Secondly, of course, children might participate in family outings to the seaside or more locally - though sometimes with less than happy memories. And thirdly, and probably most important of all, the churches and chapels and Sunday Schools provided an annual structure to children's leisure, with their tea parties and outings as a reward for attendance. The famous Whit Walks, the parades of the Sunday School scholars, provided a focal point in the year, the preparations for it taking many weeks. By the early twentieth century summer could be one treat after another, comprising for one twelve year old daughter of a country labourer two Sunday School treats, one circus, one fair, one co-operative tea and two picnics.[34] Of these three forms of leisure only the second, which was not specifically for children, was dependent on any innovations in the supply of leisure. Right at the end of the period, it is true, children began to be able to take advantage of the cinema, but the extent to which they were able to do so was probably exaggerated; as Pember Reeves put it, 'Boys and girls who earn money probably spend some of it on picture palaces; but the dependent children of parents in steady work at a low wage are not able to visit these fascinating places - much as they would like to.'[35]

The 'boys and girls who earn money' had entered a second stage in the life cycle when the opportunities for spending money on leisure were increasing at the same rate as the concern of the authorities about the manner of its spending. It is all too easy to exaggerate the opportunities. Many young people - girls, for example, sent away to domestic service - had little leisure time, and the money they earned was sent back to the family home. In rural areas, particularly in winter, leisure for the young was characterised by boredom. In the East Riding, reported Rowntree and Kendall, 'there is nothing in the way of amusement for the young people.'[36] In the larger urban centres, however, it becomes plausible to talk of a 'youth culture' in which there were recognised styles of dress, activities and meeting places for young people. To contemporary

145

commentators the latter seemed to be making the
transition to adulthood too quickly; their means
were inadequate to the time at their disposal and to
the offerings of the leisure industries, and they
resorted, or so the crime figures suggested, to
gambling, trespass, loitering, dangerous play, malicious mischief and wilful damage - and were arrested,
sometimes in groups, for so doing. These crime
figures probably do not reflect a real increase in
juvenile crime, and oral, autobiographical and diary
evidence suggests that the leisure of such young
people was marked by sexual restraint, and by frequent attendance at football matches, theatres,
music halls and cinemas. It was they above all who
benefited from innovations in the supply of leisure
before the First World War.[37]

Marriage, and more particularly the appearance
of children, marked a new phase in the life cycle in
which the opportunities for leisure, especially
for women, sharply contracted. In the numerous and
earnestly detailed budgets of poor families there is
no margin for entertainment. A married man with a
family on under thirty shillings a week 'must never
smoke, he must never take a glass of ale; he must
walk to and from his work in all weathers; he must
have no recreations but the continual mending of his
children's boots; he must neither read nor go to
picture palaces nor take holidays, if he is to do
all that social reformers expect of him when they
theoretically parcel out his tiny income.' Needless
to say these counsels of perfection were not adhered
to. Typically men kept back a proportion of their
wage for themselves, and although some of it might
be spent on fares or clothing, the bulk of it probably went on alcohol. For women, but also for men,
marriage meant that life became more home-centred,
as did any leisure that it offered. 'The pleasures
of a married man among the poor,' wrote Miss Loane,
'are chiefly connected with his children. When they
are too old to interest him much - fortunately they
are never too young! - he falls back on papering,
painting, gardening, carpentry, joinery, and wood-
carving.' Such a pattern of life was hardly typical
- the usual complaint was that married men spent too
little time with their families - but it suggests
the remoteness of the world of the leisure industries to many of the 'masses'. For many married men
the allotment absorbed more hours than the music
hall, or even the pub. For married women life
centred on the home. As a consequence, as Lady Bell
put it, wives 'have no definite intervals of

146

leisure.' 'At first sight', agreed Miss Loane, 'one is inclined to say that there are no pleasures for poor married women independently of their children', and those she could think of on second thoughts were talking to the neighbours, reading, and attending 'that much ridiculed institution Mothers' Meetings.'38

The pattern of the life cycle suggests that greater opportunities for leisure should have occurred as the children grew up and became wage-earners. The opportunities may theoretically have been there, but there is little evidence that they were taken. Habits had been formed, patterns of behaviour by then established, which were not easily broken. The leisure industries were for the young; the middle aged typically disapproved of innovations to the leisure patterns of their youth, and fell back on the offerings of the pub, enlivened by the occasional excursion. As for the old, their pleasures, as Miss Loane put it, 'are scarce, although they need them more than the young and enjoy them quite as much.'39

The life cycle was one way in which leisure time was structured. Equally important was an annual cycle. We have seen already how it gave a time structure to the lives of children, but it was also vital in the lives of adults; indeed as holiday periods became better recognised they exercised a greater influence on the family sense of time and on the family economy. The year was broken into segments, the dividing points being Christmas or New Year, Easter and/or Whitsun, and holiday time, either the August Bank Holiday or the Wakes Week or equivalent break. Time was measured by these events and the family economy geared towards saving in anticipation of them or extra work to make up for time lost and debts incurred. Undoubtedly the most important event was the summer holiday, the longest break from work and the most expensive, for it involved not simply time lost, expenditure on travel, and for the fortunate a guest house, but also new clothing. There can be no doubt that one of the major changes in the pattern of leisure in the later nineteenth and early twentieth centuries was the increasing formalisation of this annual structuring of time, and in particular the degree to which, spreading from Lancashire, it gave rise to the expectation of a summer holiday. It became the central point of the year, the event by which other occasions were measured.40

The third cycle which structured people's time

was a weekly one. As with the annual cycle it takes
on in this period a universality previously lacking.
By and large Monday ceased to be a holiday - though
as a workday it was, as it continued to be, a day
noted for absenteeism and low productivity. Pay day
- Friday or Saturday - had always been the point
around which the week and the family economy revol-
ved, but now it was much less associated with that
frantic, sometimes all night work, which had characterised the domestic worker in the early period of
industrialisation. Work was more evenly paced,
heading towards the pay packet and the Saturday
half-holiday, with the Saturday afternoon the time
devoted to playing or watching sport. This weekly
structure for those in regular paid employment was
paralleled in the home by a cycle which started with
washday on Monday, and worked towards its climac-
teric of cleaning on Fridays. These two work
cycles, paid and unpaid, might be consummated in the
pub on Saturday evening, leaving Sunday as a day of
some anti-climax. 'Sunday', wrote Alfred Williams,
'is the day of complete inactivity with most of the
workmen, and it is possible the weakest and the
least enjoyed of all. If the weather is dull and
wet a great number stay in bed till dinner-time, and
sometimes they remain there all day and night, till
Monday morning comes.' There were of course more
active Sundays than this - the Sunday dinner a focal
point, for some of course church, chapel and Sunday
School, perhaps a visit to or from relatives, the
possibility of an excursion or even the cinema - but
perhaps the chief characteristic of Sunday was that
it was a day of recuperation, and one therefore
which brought the working class into contact with
the providers of mass leisure in one major form
only - the Sunday paper.[41]

These three cycles structuring the time of the
working class point to two rather different conclusions. In the first place mass leisure impinged
on working class life relatively rarely, and much
more at certain points in the life, year or week
than at others. Secondly, however, it was the
prospect or the memory of leisure which gave shape
to those lives, years and weeks. One could of
course put this the other way around: the work gave
shape to the leisure, but in fact, as people experienced it and expressed it, the moments of leisure
structured time. On a daily basis the clock or the
factory hooter might dominate people's lives, but
beyond that time was measured by the opportunities
for leisure.

This study of the structuring of time must be qualified in two ways. The first qualification has already been made implicitly, but needs to be made explicit. In each of these cycles there was likely to be a markedly different experience for men and women, with women enduring greater constraints on their opportunities for leisure at almost all points in every cycle - the one possible exception being the relative freedom enjoyed by young unmarried women in full-time employment. For married women who were not in employment - the majority - the Saturday half-holiday was meaningless, and for those who were employed it had to be devoted to housework. Women amongst the poor, wrote Miss Loane, 'generally abjured, from the very day of their marriage, all pleasures but those of a strictly domestic nature' (though there were some signs of change amongst younger married women). If family budgets allow something for the 'luxuries' of the man, they make none at all for the woman. As Preston women put it, 'It was all bed and work.' Mass leisure impinged on the lives of most working class women only very intermittently, and in some of its most celebrated forms - for example, football and indeed almost all sport - it had the effect of increasing the distinctness of the experience of men and women.[42]

The second qualification is not easy to quantify, but important nonetheless. Cutting across the three cycles was a fourth one, the trade cycle. In individual lives, and in particular years, it could play havoc with any notion of a known, knowable and secure pattern of leisure. Not only at a national level, but also in particular industries, upturns and downturns, short-time, lock-outs and strikes added an unwelcome element of uncertainty to the prospect of leisure. Historians of leisure have scarcely begun to assess the impact of these cycles in the availability of work, indeed they have generally completely ignored them. At a local level there is some evidence. The spread of the seaside holiday amongst Lancashire textile workers, John Walton argues, owed something to the relative rarity of lay-offs, and hence the greater possibility of regular saving. A depression in the cotton industry resulted, in Rochdale in 1909-11, in a smaller number of people leaving for a holiday at the seaside. There may still have existed, too, an earlier pattern of response to the cycle of boom and trade, with more drunkenness in booms than in depressions.[43] This scattered evidence does not get us very far, but there is in general no reason to

expect that leisure was in any way protected from
the known insecurities of working class life -
insecurities which of course extended beyond the
family and trade cycles to, for example, health.
What it would be interesting to know is whether expenditure on leisure was the first casualty in any
curtailing of the family budget.

The structuring of the time of the working
class by leisure was paralleled by a structuring of
space. Leisure began to replace work in giving
shape to the boundaries and contours of the known
world - the world, that is, which had been experienced rather than learned through geography books.
The journey to and from work allowed of no devia-
tion. One went and one came back, a route and a
routine boringly familiar. Or, alternatively, work
was in the home, involving no journey. Leisure,
too, as a child, started in the home, but quickly
expanded outwards, first to the street, then to the
neighbourhood, to waste space, perhaps a park, or in
summer, for boys, to a canal or river to swim in,
often to a rival neighbourhood, involving a struggle
for territorial space, then to the local theatres,
music halls and cinemas each with their different
ethos. Eventually it would take in the local pubs
and beerhouses, and the local 'parade' for courting.
Punctuating this process would be excursions outside
this familiar world to amenities which served the
whole town - the zoo, perhaps, or the museum, or the
annual fair - and further afield to the countryside,
perhaps by bicycle, or to some historical site, or
of course to the seaside.[44] How far one went, of
course, depended on the starting point. In rural
Oxfordshire St. Giles's Fair in Oxford might be the
centre point of the year as well as the ultimate
point in the known world. Starting in a city one
could go further - but rarely very far. The mass
market for leisure was a series of regional ones at
least so far as holiday-making was concerned. In
some respects London was becoming a national centre,
the location for the supreme tournaments for brass
bands as well as for football players. Apart from
this, however, the known world was the region, and
it was known not through work but through leisure.[45]

Leisure structured space in two other ways. In
the first place it was probably more important than
the geography lesson in giving working class people
an idea of the world beyond the region, and in particular beyond Britain. At the fairground, in the
peepshow and later in the cinema people formed their
images of the world they did not know.[46]

In the second place, in leisure people learned the politics of space. Private space was quite easily recognisable, fenced by notices threatening to prosecute trespassers. The politics of public space were more complex, for public spaces were controlled by regulations which might or might not be enforced. Sometimes, but not always, the police turned a blind eye to boys swimming in the rivers and canals. In the street, the key playground for working class children, they were in this period harsh in their response to football and to games of chance which might have in them an element of gambling. More formal areas of public space, like parks, were, as one commentator put it, 'very well for sedate and elderly people. They are useful to foster-mothers, slave girls hugging babies about, and a boon for nurses with perambulators. But what of Tom, Dick and Harry, who have just commenced work; what of them?' For them the park, regulated by bye-laws and closing at a respectable hour, presented a mode of life quite alien to that they had learned in the street.[47] Even common land, increasingly protected by law and given the royal seal of approval when the Queen opened Epping Forest to the public in 1882, was controlled by restrictions and increasingly invaded by a new and unwelcome type of user, the golfer. In the countryside itself the working class rambler was quickly at odds with the upper class shooter, and the first rumblings can be heard of the struggles which were to reach a crescendo in the inter-war period. Space was fundamental to the enjoyment of leisure, and working class people could not be unaware of the disadvantages in which they were placed in respect to access and use. One of the attractions of the pub was still, as in the first half of the century, that it was open and accessible, making no stipulations as to dress or respectability.[48]

Besides the pub, one of the most important but rarely noted spaces for leisure was the home and its surroundings. One of the paradoxes of the age of mass leisure was that it was accompanied by an increase in the amount of family, individual and face-to-face community leisure. As Miss Loane put it:

> My acquaintances among the poor, and they are numerous, ... seldom enter theatre, dancing saloon, music hall, or concert room; they seem to have little or no connection with the vast crowds hanging round football and cricket matches, or on the outskirts of racecourses;

they are not often to be found listening to
improving lectures, nor attending political
meetings, nor crowding into police-courts, and
except very early and very late in life, they
are not even regular attendants at church or
chapel. Such enjoyments as they have seem to
me to be of an entirely domestic nature; if not
'sacred' they are at least 'home-felt delights',
and most of them can be savoured in solitude,
or at any rate in solitude *à deux*.

Family-based leisure, centred in the home, so often
depicted as a consequence of radio and television,
can be seen in more than embryo in our period. It
owed much to the increasing comfort of working class
homes. It took many forms; do-it-yourself activity,
playing with children, music, talking, even 'doing
absolutely nothing', 'a pleasure which is almost entirely a lost art among the upper classes.' Certainly home-based leisure, as an ideal and an actuality,
was not confined to the middle classes; the problem
is that the sources do not often draw our attention
to it.[49]
Outside the home participant competitiveness
was a leading feature of much working class leisure
in this period: individuals competed against individuals, pubs against pubs, clubs against clubs. The
same pattern of competitiveness can be seen in
billiards, bowls, boxing, brass bands, choral societies, fishing, horticulture, pigeon fancying and
racing, rabbit coursing, rifle shooting, and whippet
racing. The rewards were sometimes material, beef
or beer or a clock, sometimes a silver cup or plate,
chiefly perhaps the honour and self or group satis-
faction of winning. At its roots this competitiveness was local - intra - or inter-community - but it
increasingly in our period reached up to the regional and then the national level.[50] How can we
explain this participant competitiveness? There is
no reason to look beyond the obvious explanation
that in leisure, much more than in work, individuals
and groups could gain some sense of achievement and
control - for these competitions were for the most
part organised by and for the working class.

IV

These types of activity receive relatively little
attention in the middle class commentaries which are
the source for so much of the history of leisure.
They existed, indeed, in happy isolation from that

commentary. Yet that commentary, that ideology, formed a context within which much working class leisure was carried on, and could affect by its propaganda and sometimes by resulting legislation the forms and structures of that leisure. Four different components of that ideology may be isolated, two of them essentially inherited from the past, two of them coming to the fore in our period.

The chief inheritance from the past was a concern about the morality of working class leisure. This concern had become institutionalised in the early and mid nineteenth century in temperance, Sabbatarian, animal welfare, and youth organisations. The concern varied from an emphasis on the reformation or conversion of the individual to a policy of establishing legislative constraints on the behaviour of the working class. These one-issue campaigns often operated in isolation from, and sometimes in disagreement with, each other but they had in common a desire to modify by persuasion or by the force of law types of behaviour within the working class which were not consonant with respectable norms. Of course they had, and made much of, any working class adherents, but essentially they were movements of one class acting as it was persuaded in the interests of another. These types of activity all continued, and neither their methods nor their language shifted to any great degree. They sometimes saw themselves as, and sometimes were, in decline (both Sabbatarians and temperance workers, for example, felt that the spirit of the times was against them), but equally they were capable of new initiatives and new directions.[51] The most notable of these was the focus on gambling, coming to the fore from the 1870s. By the early twentieth century gambling had come to be seen as of equal status with drinking. The remedies suggested were familiar ones: the mobilisation of public opinion, a tightening-up of the law, but also the provision of counter-attractions. 'We want, indeed,' wrote Seebohm Rowntree, 'in every town people's palaces, where people can be thoroughly at home, and where they can spend a social evening pleasantly and rationally.' The extent of gambling was in fact almost certainly exaggerated, but the campaign against it was indicative of the fact that forms of working class leisure were still subject to attack on the basis of their immorality.[52]

The second inheritance from the past was the belief that class divisions might be superseded or at least softened in leisure. This ideology was at

153

its height in the mid Victorian period, but a residual belief in it remained, and it was often at the
forefront of a number of attempts to repatronise
occasions which had once been thought irredeemable.
In the countryside in particular this was a new era
of gentry and lady patronage - of Whitsun, of fairs,
of maypole dancing. There was perhaps a shift of
emphasis from class conciliation between adults
(when, as with working men's clubs, patronage and
the message it carried might be rejected) to a more
authoritarian relationship in which the class of the
patron was reinforced by age: the events patronised
were increasingly for children who were neither
likely nor in a position to reject what was offered
- often food.[53] Beyond this small-scale institutionalisation of the belief in class conciliation
through leisure there remained broader hopes that
sport might be a new location for the meeting of the
classes.[54]

It was the commercialism creeping into sport
that formed the focus for the third component in the
middle class ideology of leisure. It would be quite
wrong to suggest that there was any middle class
unanimity on the issues that surrounded professionalism - any more than there was on temperance - but
there can be no doubt that it became the centre of
commentary and concern, forming by and large a hostile context for the development of working class
sport, and hence exacerbating class relationships.
From the middle class perspective the distinction
between leisure and business, or more precisely between sport and business, was becoming muddied, and
it left them unhappy. In the working class perspective there was no tradition of unbusinesslike
sport, and hence no real problem or issue. Undoubtedly, however, the middle class ethos left its
imprint, most obviously on cricket, but also on
football.[55]

It was sport, too, which was at the centre of
the final component in the middle class ideological
spectrum: the concern at the relationship between
leisure, empire and war. This became of significance during and after the Boer War, and by 1905 had
become a '"hackneyed" subject'. The issue was a
simple one: did sport prepare people for an imperial
and military role, or was it a distraction from it?
Was Price Collier right in claiming that '... the
governing races of today are races of sportsmen',
or did the truth lie with Kipling's gibes about
flannelled fools and muddied oafs? These were the
terms of the debate - and not, for example, whether

there ought to be *any* relationship between sport,
empire and war. If sport was not preparing people
for war, then it ought to be, or it ought to be
abandoned in favour of rifle shooting. This debate,
like the one about professionalism, so permeated
thinking about sport in the early twentieth century
that it is difficult to imagine that anyone connected with sport, certainly any of the players, remained unaffected by it. The response of sportsmen
in the early part of the First World War confirms
that this was so.[56]

The working class, then, went about their
leisure, knowingly or unknowingly, within constraints
which were largely set by the middle and upper
classes. Sometimes, as with the restrictions on
gambling, drinking and Sunday leisure, these constraints had the force of law - and might, indeed,
meet with the approval of some of the working class.
In other instances the pressures were of a different
kind, inserting a moral or political content into
activities which for the working class were of a
simpler nature: for enjoyment, or as work, or an un-
problematic combination of the two - as with fishing
and gardening.[57]

There was one further context within which
working class people enjoyed their leisure: they did
so in awareness of the fact that the dominant feature of the age was the expansion of leisure for the
leisured. The leisure class, already in 1868, as
Trollope noted, the largest and wealthiest ever
known, expanded in size, in the range of its activities, and in the flamboyance of its pursuit of
pleasure. The 'luxury' it engendered provoked hostility from labour spokesmen who either deplored its
corrupting influence on the working class or hoped
that 'the pomp and arrogance of wealth and luxury'
might sow the seeds of its own downfall.[58]

V

This socialist picture of the leisure history of the
period may be set alongside the two we noted at the
beginning: the golden age and mass leisure. They
have this in common: they are all pictures constructed by people who observe, spectate and publicise
but do not fully participate in the activities they
describe. Some of them are nostalgic (the golden
age), some critical (mass leisure and socialist
theory), but all are produced from a position off-
stage, on the bye-lines, or even further removed.
They offer perspectives on the leisure of the age,

but each is an imaginative and to some extent imaginary construction of reality.

From yet another perspective, that of working class experience, none of these constructions bears much weight. No golden age could be apparent to those whose lives were cut across by the life and trade cycles. Mass leisure was not obvious to those who, if they participated in crowds, did so as members of a family or a community; nor did working class people feel themselves to be merely 'consumers' of leisure - they also produced it, particularly in that participatory competitiveness which we have stressed. Even the luxury of the rich could be observed with tolerance and without resentment.[59] For about one third of the working class, indeed, leisure had no meaning at all, except as something enjoyed by others. For the majority there was, in varying degrees and at varying stages in their lives, an increase in the ability to pay for leisure, more time for it, and an increase in the quantity of leisure activities on offer, whether through the market, or by state or voluntary agencies. But this growth in the opportunities for leisure was matched in working class experience by the structuring of leisure to the point where it took on the force of custom. The times for leisure, daily, weekly, annually and through the life cycle, became more fixed; the places for leisure - home, street, pub, the seaside, the public facility, places where you paid to spectate and places where you were encouraged to participate - acquired a fixed quality so that you knew what to expect and how to behave in each. Children, young people, men and women learned early on that they would enjoy different leisure experiences - and that males would enjoy more than females. Possibly leisure became not only more separated from work, but also more valued than work. Although the particular structure varied from one part of the country to another, and at different income levels within the working class, the crucial point is that in all areas and at all levels leisure acquired the quality of routine. It was subject, too, to common pressures. Arching over and linking together the separate histories of music hall, film, sport, the seaside holiday, the pub, and home leisure were pressures which became encapsulated in our understanding of the meaning of leisure: the expansion of market forces; the licensing role of the state; the pervading concern about the morality of leisure activities; the pressures of family obligation; the structuring of leisure by work; the

captivating example of the leisure class. None of
this was entirely new. The moulding of leisure in
the way we have described had its origins in the
preceding age, and it survives into the present.
What was distinctive about the period 1875-1914 was
that during it the structuring of leisure acquired
the force of custom.

NOTES

1. W. Macqueen-Pope, *Twenty Shillings in the
Pound* (London, 1948); R. Mander and J. Mitchenson,
British Music Hall (London, 1965), part three, 'The
Golden Age'; Patrick Morrah, *The Golden Age of
Cricket* (London, 1967); David Frith, *The Golden Age
of Cricket 1890-1914* (Guildford, 1978); Tonie and
Valmai Holt, *Picture Postcards of the Golden Age*
(London, 1971); John K. Walton, *The English Seaside
Resort: A Social History 1750-1914* (Leicester, 1983),
pp.64-6.
2. Asa Briggs, *Mass Entertainment: The Origins
of a Modern Industry* (Adelaide, 1960); W. Hamish
Fraser, *The Coming of the Mass Market, 1850-1914*
(London, 1981), ch. 6, 14; Asa Briggs, 'The Lan-
guage of "Mass" and "Masses" in Nineteenth Century
England',in David E. Martin and David Rubinstein
(eds.), *Ideology and the Labour Movement* (London,
1979),pp.62-83.
3. See W.F. Mandle, 'W.G. Grace as a Victorian
Hero', *Historical Studies,* 19, 1980-1, pp.353-68;
Eric Midwinter, *W.G. Grace: His Life and Times*
(London, 1981); D.F. Cheshire, *Music Hall in Britain*
(Newton Abbot, 1974), pp.60-81.
4. M.A. Bienefeld, *Working Hours in British
Industry* (London, 1972), pp.82-161; S. and B. Webb,
Industrial Democracy (London, 1920), p.353; Peter N.
Stearns, *Lives of Labour* (London, 1975), pp.193-228,
256; G. Howell, *Trade Unionism Old and New* (London,
1891), pp.170-205; Stephen Yeo, *Religion and Voluntary Organisations in Crisis* (London, 1976), p.374;
Alfred Williams, *Life in a Railway Factory* (London,
1915), pp.5, 267-73, 292-3, 302, 304. Cf.Benson,
supra.
5. B. Seebohm Rowntree and May Kendall, *How
the Labourer Lives* (London, 1913), p.32.
6. Wilfred B. Whitaker, *Victorian and Edwardian
Shopworkers* (Newton Abbot, 1973).

7.   B.L. Hutchins and A. Harrison, *A History of Factory Legislation* (London, 1966), p.195; Monica Hodgson, 'The Working Day and the Working Week' (Unpublished Univ. of London M.Phil. Thesis, 1974), pp.172-4; Webbs, *Industrial Democracy*, p.352; D.A. Reid, 'The Decline of Saint Monday, 1766-1876', *Past and Present*, 71, 1976, pp.76-101.

8.   John K. Walton, 'The Demand for Working-Class Seaside Holidays in Victorian England', *Economic History Review*, xxxiv (2), 1981, pp.249-65; J.A.R. Pimlott, *The Englishman's Holiday* (London, 1947), pp.155-7; from 1891 all employees of W.D. & H.O. Wills of at least one year's standing were allowed one week's paid holiday - see B.W.E. Alford, *W.D. & H.O. Wills and the Development of the U.K. Tobacco Industry 1786-1965* (London, 1973), p.288.

9.   Williams, *Railway Factory*, pp.245-6; Elizabeth Roberts, 'Working-Class Standards of Living in Barrow and Lancaster, 1890-1914', *Economic History Review*, xxx (2), 1977,pp.308-9; Walton, *Seaside Resort*, p.188; Walton, 'Demand for Working-Class Seaside Holidays'.

10.   Roberts, 'Working-Class Standards of Living in Barrow and Lancaster', and 'Working-class standards of living in three Lancashire Towns, 1890-1914', *International Review of Social History*, xxvii (1), 1982, pp.43-65; A.A. Hall, 'Wages, Earnings and Real Earnings in Teeside: A Re-assessment of the Ameliorist Interpretation of Living Standards in Britain, 1870-1914', *International Review of Social History*,xxci(2) 1981,pp.202-19; E.H. Hunt, *Regional Wage Variations in Britain 1850-1914* (Oxford, 1973); D.J. Oddy, 'A Nutritional Analysis of Historical Evidence: The Working-Class Diet, 1880-1914',in Derek Oddy and Derek Miller (eds.), *The Making of the Modern British Diet* (London, 1976), pp.214-31; W.H. Beveridge, *Unemployment: A Problem of Industry* (London, 1909).

11.   Fraser, *Mass Market*.

12.   For some figures, and an interpretation of them, see A.R. Prest, *Consumers' Expenditure in the United Kingdom 1900-1919*(Cambridge, 1954), and John Myerscough, 'The Recent History of the Use of Leisure Time',in I. Appleton (ed.), *Leisure Research and Policy* (Edinburgh, 1974), pp.8-11. On alcohol see A.E. Dingle, 'Drink and working-class standards of living in Britain 1870-1914',in Oddy and Miller (eds.), *Modern British Diet*, pp.117-34.

13.   Walton, *Seaside Resort*; Rachael Low and Roger Manvell, *The History of British Film*, vols. I and II (London, 1948);Tony Mason, *Association*

Football and English Society 1863-1915 (Brighton, 1980).

14. Low and Manvell, *British Film*, esp. vol 2, pp.19-23, 50-2; Briggs, *Mass Entertainment*, pp.15-16; Lady Bell, *At the Works* (London 1st ed.,1907; 2nd ed., 1911), pp.184-5; cf. Paul Wild, 'Recreation in Rochdale, 1900-40' in John Clarke, Chas Critcher and Richard Johnson (eds.), *Working Class Culture* (London, 1979), pp.150-9.

15. T.G. Ashplant, 'London Working Men's Clubs, 1875-1914' in Eileen and Stephen Yeo (eds.), *Popular Culture and Class Conflict 1590-1914* (Brighton, 1981), pp.241-70.

16. George B. Wilson, *Alcohol and the Nation* (London, 1940), p.380.

17. *Select Committee on Theatres and Places of Entertainment*, PP 1892, vol. xviii, Q. 4,207, App. 2; Wray Vamplew, *The Turf* (London, 1976), p.46.

18. Penelope Summerfield, 'The Effingham Arms and the Empire: Deliberate Selection in the Evolution of Music Hall In London', and Eileen and Stephen Yeo, 'Perceived Patterns: Competition and Licence versus Class and Struggle', in E. and S. Yeo (eds.), *Popular Culture*, pp.209-40, 298-302; Peter Bailey, *Leisure and Class in Victorian England* (London, 1978), pp.164-8; Edward J. Bristow, *Vice and Vigilance: Purity Movements in Britain since 1700* (Dublin, 1977), pp.125-228. For the control of profit in sport, see J.R. Lowerson, 'Middle Class Sport, 1880-1914', in *Aspects of the Social History of Nineteenth-Century Sport* (The Proceedings of the Inaugural Conference of the British Society of Sport History, School of Physical Education, University of Liverpool, 1982), pp.1-22, and Mason, *Association Football*, pp.42-9.

19. Charles Booth, *Life and Labour of the People in London* (London, 1902), final volume p.53; Lowerson, 'Middle Class Sport'.

20. Walton, *Seaside Resort*, pp.128-55; Richard Roberts, 'The Corporation as Impresario: the municipal provision of entertainment in Victorian and Edwardian Bournemouth', and John K. Walton, 'Municipal government and the holiday industry in Blackpool, 1876-1914', in John K. Walton and James Walvin (eds.), *Leisure in Britain 1780-1939* (Manchester, 1983), pp.137-85.

21. H.E. Meller, *Leisure and the Changing City, 1870-1914* (London, 1976), p.66; Thomas Kelly, *A History of Public Libraries in Great Britain* (London, 1973), pp.28-9, 115-23; Yeo, *Religion and Voluntary Organisations*, pp.188, 374.

22. Yeo, *Religion and Voluntary Organisations*, pp.184-209; Wild 'Recreation in Rochdale', pp.141-2; J.O. Springhall, *Youth, Empire and Society* (London, 1977); B. Harrison, 'For Church, Queen and Family: The Girls' Friendly Society 1874-1920', *Past and Present*, 61, 1973, pp.107-38; Robert Roberts, *A Ragged Schooling* (London, 1978), pp.87-9.

23. Howard Hill, *Freedom to Roam: The Struggle for Access to Britain's Moors and Mountains* (Ashbourne, 1980), pp.26-41; David Prynn, 'The Clarion Clubs, Rambling and the Holiday Associations in Britain since the 1890s', *Journal of Contemporary History*, 11, 1976, pp.65-77.

24. *Select Committee on Theatres*, PP 1892, App. 26 and Q. 1,188; Bailey, *Leisure and Class*, p.168; Briggs, *Mass Entertainment*, pp.15-16; Walton, *Seaside Resort*, p.175; David Rubinstein, 'Cycling in the 1890s', *Victorian Studies*, 21, 1977, p.55.

25. The capital value of the 16 leading London music halls in 1866 was estimated at £362,000, *Select Committee on Theatrical Licences and Regulations*, PP 1866, vol. xi, App. 3; Walton, *Seaside Resort*, pp.92, 163-4.

26. Walton, *Seaside Resort*, pp.174-5, 220-1; Mason, *Association Football*, pp.44-9.

27. Low and Manvell, *British Film*, vol. 2, pp. 19-22; Booth, *Life and Labour*, final volume, p.53; B.S. Rowntree, *Poverty, A Study of Town Life*, (London,4th ed.,1902), pp.310-13; for contrasting views on development in music hall in London, see Summerfield in E. and S. Yeo (eds.), *Popular Culture*, pp.209-40, and *S.C. on Theatres*, PP 1892, Q. 4,208.

28. Alan Metcalfe, 'Organized Sport in the Mining Communities of South Northumberland, 1800-1889', *Victorian Studies*, 25, 1982, pp.482-6; Stan Shipley, 'Tom Causer of Bermondsey: A Boxer Hero of the 1890s', *History Workshop*, 15, Spring 1983, pp. 30, 43-6; Rowntree, *Poverty*, pp.212-3; R. McKibbin, 'Working-class gambling in Britain 1880-1939', *Past and Present*, 82, 1979, pp.159-60.

29. John Lowerson and John Myerscough, *Time to Spare in Victorian England* (Hassocks, 1977), p.21; Michael Baker, *The Rise of the Victorian Actor* (London, 1978), pp.24-5, 109, 225; *1911 Census*, PP 1913, vol.lxxviii, pp.345, 349 and Table 26; Wray Vamplew, 'Playing for Pay: The Earnings of Professional Sportsmen in England 1870-1914', in Richard Cashman and Michael McKernan (eds.), *Sport, Money, Morality and the Media* (Kensington, New South Wales, n.d.), p.124.

30. Vamplew, *Turf*, p.136; Mason, *Association*

Football, pp.138-43; Dave Russell, 'Popular musical culture and popular politics in the Yorkshire textile districts, 1880-1914', in Walton and Walvin (eds.), *Leisure in Britain*, p.100; Hugh Cunningham, *Leisure in the Industrial Revolution* (London, 1980), pp.26-7, 113, and *The Volunteer Force* (London, 1975), pp.70-3; Roy Hay, 'Soccer and Social Control in Scotland 1873-1978', in Cashman and McKernan (eds.), *Sport*, pp.223-47.

31. Walton, *Seaside Resort*, p.31, and 'Residential amenity, respectable morality and the rise of the entertainment industry: the case of Blackpool 1860-1914', *Literature and History*, 1, 1975, p.77; Wild, 'Recreation in Rochdale', pp.145-6; Allan Redfern, 'Crewe: leisure in a railway town', in Walton and Walvin (eds.), *Leisure in Britain*, pp. 126-7; George Sturt, *A Memoir of a Surrey Labourer* (1907; repr. Firle, 1978), pp.50-1.

32. Raymond Williams, *The Long Revolution* (London, 1961), pp.199-206; Rubinstein, 'Cycling', pp.51, 58; Prest, *Consumers' Expenditure*, p.139; C. Ehrlich, *The Piano* (London, 1976) pp.91-107; Rowntree, *Poverty*, pp.73, 148, 150, 288.

33. John Burnett, *Destiny Obscure: Autobiographies of childhood, education and family from the 1820s to the 1920s* (London, 1982), pp.240-1; Flora Thompson, *Lark Rise to Candleford* (London, 1954), pp.34, 157-9; M. Pember Reeves, *Round About a Pound a Week* (1913; repr. London, 1979), pp.191-2; Raphael Samuel, *East End Underworld: Chapters in the Life of Arthur Harding* (London, 1981), pp.32-3; Thomas Holmes, *London's Underworld* (London, 1912), pp.163-85; cf. Roberts, *supra*.

34. Samuel, *East End Underworld*, pp.35-6; Burnett, *Destiny Obscure*, p.301; M. Loane, *The Next Street But One* (London, 1907), pp.39-40.

35. Reeves, *Pound a Week*, p.192.

36. Rowntree and Kendall, *How the Labourer Lives*, pp.228, 233; cf. M.F. Davies, *Life in an English Village* (London, 1909), pp.276-83; Thompson, *Lark Rise*, p.284.

37. Burnett, *Destiny Obscure*, pp.252-7; Paul Thompson, *The Edwardians* (London, 1975), pp.68-73; Arnold Freeman, *Boy Life and Labour* (London, 1914), pp.108-60; Williams, *Railway Factory*, pp.58-9; John R. Gillis, 'The Evolution of Juvenile Delinquency in England 1890-1914', *Past and Present*, 67, 1975, pp. 96-126; P.N. Stearns, 'Working Class Women in Britain, 1890-1914', in M. Vicinus (ed.), *Suffer and be Still* (Bloomington, 1972), p.111; cf. Roberts, *supra*.

38. Reeves, *Pound a Week*, p.152; Loane, *Next Street*, pp.38-41; Bell, *At the Works*, pp.191, 236.

39. Loane, *Next Street*, p.40; George Sturt, *The Bettesworth Book* (1901; repr. Firle, 1978), pp.46-7; *Surrey Labourer*, pp.50-1, 308-9; J. Ramsay MacDonald, 'Gambling and Citizenship', in B. Seebohm Rowntree (ed.), *Betting and Gambling* (London, 1905), pp.132-3.

40. Williams, *Railway Factory*, pp.245-51; Walton, 'Demand for Working-Class Seaside Holidays'.

41. Williams, *Railway Factory*, pp.251-4; Jeremy Seabrook, *Working-Class Childhood* (London, 1982), pp.202-8; Booth, *Life and Labour*, final volume, pp. 47-9; on Sunday cinema, Bell, *At the Works*, p.186.

42. Stearns, 'Working-Class Women', pp.111-3; M. Loane, *An Englishman's Castle* (London, 1909), p.13; Roberts, 'Working-Class Standards of Living in Three Lancashire Towns', p.52; E.H. Phelps Brown, *The Growth of British Industrial Relations* (London, 1959), p.69.

43. Walton, 'Demand for Working-Class Seaside Holidays', p.253; Wild, 'Recreation in Rochdale', p.146; Roberts, 'Working-Class Standards of Living in Barrow and Lancaster', p.319; cf. Mason, *Association Football*, p.148.

44. See above n.33 and 34 and Robert Roberts, *The Classic Slum* (Manchester, 1971) pp.121-4 and *A Ragged Schooling*, pp.11-21.

45. S. Alexander, *St. Giles's Fair, 1830-1914* (History Workshop Pamphlet No. 2, Ruskin College, Oxford, 1970), pp.20-3; Walton 'Demand for Working-Class Seaside Holidays'; J.F. Russell and J.H. Elliot, *The Brass Band Movement* (London, 1936), p. 176; Mason, *Association Football*, p.141.

46. Alexander, *St. Giles's Fair*, pp.47-58; Freeman, *Boy Life*, p.134; Low and Manvell, *British Film*, vol.I, pp.43-74; vol.II, p.145.

47. Samuel, *East End Underworld*, pp.38-9; Holmes, *London's Underworld*, pp.168-76; Gillis, 'Juvenile Delinquency'.

48. Hill, *Freedom to Roam*, pp.18-49; John Lowerson, 'Battles for the Countryside', in Frank Gloversmith (ed.), *Class, Culture and Social Change: A New View of the 1930s* (Brighton, 1980), pp.268-77; Lord Eversley, *Commons, Forests and Footpaths* (London, revised ed.,1910); Geoffrey Cousins, *Golf in Britain* (London, 1975), p.23; Anthony Delves, 'Popular Recreation and Social Conflict in Derby 1800-1850',in E. and S. Yeo (eds.), *Popular Culture*, pp.98-9.

49. Loane, *Englishman's Castle*, pp.32-60; M.J.

Daunton, 'Public Place and Private Space: The
Victorian City and the Working-Class Household',
in Derek Fraser and Anthony Sutcliffe (eds.), *The
Pursuit of Urban History* (London, 1983), pp.212-33;
James Walvin, *Leisure and Society 1830-1950* (London,
1978), pp.106-9; cf. Hugh McLeod, 'White Collar
Values and the Role of Religion', in Geoffrey
Crossick (ed.), *The Lower Middle Class in Britain
1870-1914* (London, 1977), p.71.

   50. Metcalfe, 'Organized Sport'; Russell and
Elliot, *Brass Band Movement*; Russell, 'Popular
Musical Culture', pp.111-2; Redfern, 'Crewe', pp.
127-32; Bernard Waites, 'Popular culture in late
nineteenth and early twentieth century Lancashire',
in The Open University, *The Historical Development
of Popular Culture in Britain* (Milton Keynes, 1981),
pp.98-101, 103-08; Shipley, 'Tom Causer', pp.40-53;
James Mott, 'Miners, weavers and pigeon racing', in
Michael Smith, Stanley Parker and Cyril Smith (eds.),
Leisure and Society in Britain (London, 1973), pp.
86-96; John Benson, *British Coalminers in the Nineteenth Century: A Social History* (Dublin, 1980), pp.
156-7; Loane, *Next Street*, pp.137-8; Burnett,
Destiny Obscure, pp.309-10.

   51. John Wigley, *The Rise and Fall of The
Victorian Sunday* (Manchester, 1980); A.E. Dingle,
*The Campaign for Prohibition in Victorian England:
The United Kingdom Alliance 1872-1895* (London, 1980);
Yeo, *Religion and Voluntary Organisations*, pp.203-9;
Brian Harrison, *Peaceable Kingdom*(Oxford, 1982),
esp. ch. 2 and 3; J.B. Brown, 'The Pig or the Stye:
Drink and Poverty in late Victorian England',
International Review of Social History, xviii(3),
1973, pp.394-5.

   52. James Greenwood, *The Seven Curses of London*
(London, n.d.), pp.377-419; Booth, *Life and Labour*,
final volume, pp.56-9; Rowntree, *Betting and Gambling*, p.183.

   53. Cunningham, *Leisure in Industrial Revolu-
tion*, pp.110-30; Alun Howkins, 'The Taming of
Whitsun: the Changing Face of a Nineteenth-Century
Rural Holiday', in E. and S. Yeo (eds.), *Popular
Culture*, pp.187-208; C. Torr, *Small Talk at Wreyland*
(Cambridge, 1918), p.58.

   54. For the hope that the classes would come
together in leisure, see Price Collier, *England and
the English* (New York, 1909), pp.206, 248, 264-5,
331-2; Yeo, *Religion and Voluntary Organisations*,
p.187; Russell, 'Popular musical culture', p.104.
For evidence that in sport in particular there were
pressures against class mixing, see Lowerson,

'Middle Class Sport'; Meller, *Leisure and City*, pp.226-36; Bailey, *Leisure and Class*, pp.124-46.

55. Mason, *Association Football*, pp.69-81; W.F. Mandle, 'The Professional Cricketer in England in the Nineteenth Century', *Labour History*, 23, 1972, pp.1-16; 'Games people played; cricket and football in England and Victoria in the late nineteenth century', *Historical Studies*, 15, 1973, pp. 511-35.

56. J.H.M. Abbott, *An Outlander in England* (London, 1905), pp.256-64; Collier, *England*, p.241; Mason, *Association Football*, pp.251-5; Vamplew, *Turf*, pp.62-73; Morrah, *Golden Age of Cricket*, p.249.

57. For the combination of work and pleasure see Roberts, 'Working-Class Standards of Living in Three Lancashire Towns', pp.55-8; Rowntree and Kendall, *How the Labourer Lives*, p.173. Gardening and fishing were to become two major leisure industries in the twentieth century, but very little is known about the extent to which working class people were able to participate in them before 1914; on gardening, see Stephen Constantine, 'Amateur Gardening and Popular Recreation in the 19th and 20th Centuries', *Journal of Social History*, 14, 1981, pp.387-406, and S. Martin Gaskell, 'Gardens for the Working Class: Victorian Practical Pleasure', *Victorian Studies*, 23, 1980, pp.479-501.

58. T. Veblen, *The Theory of the Leisure Class* (1899; London, 1925); A. Trollope (ed.), *British Sports and Pastimes* (London, 1868), p.18; MacDonald, 'Gambling and Citizenship', pp.117-34; Standish Meacham, *A Life Apart: The English Working Class 1890-1914* (London, 1977), p.218.

59. M. Loane, *From Their Point of View* (London, 1908), p.64.

Chapter Six

COMMUNITY VIOLENCE

David Woods

I

When the Criminal and Judicial Statistics for
England and Wales were reorganised in 1893 the
Criminal Registrar took the opportunity to review
criminal trends over the previous twenty years. He
noted that indictable crimes of violence against the
person had 'diminished to a marked degree' and that
the same tendency to diminution was observable in
terms of summary trials of violence, where the
average number had dropped from 402 trials per
10,000 people in 1874-8 to 268 per 10,000 people in
1889-93.[1] In his Report for 1896 the Registrar
noted particularly 'the fairly steady decline in
assault proceedings' and that in 1894 the total
number of common assaults had fallen below 60,000
for the first time since proper statistics had been
kept in 1857.[2] By 1899 the Registrar was convinced
that there had been 'a considerable decline absolutely and a still greater decline in proportion to
population.' Although he admitted that the 'unknown
element' was large he thought that 'on the whole the
facts seemed to indicate a great change in manners:
the substitution of words without blows for blows
with or without words; an approximation in the manners of different classes, a decline in the spirit
of lawlessness.'[3] The Report for 1908 returned to
the same theme, with the Registrar noting over a
period of fifty years an 'enormous diminution of
assaults ... a gratifying improvement reflecting the
general amelioration of manners.'[4]
     Most contemporary observers agreed with these
conclusions. In papers presented to the Royal
Statistical Society, Leoni Levi and George Grosvenor
referred to the overall decline in crime and in
crimes of violence against the person in the last

decades of the nineteenth century.[5] A.C. Hall went
so far as to argue in his book, *Crime and its Relation to Social Progress*, that the old and most
serious kinds of crime showed a greater and more
continuous diminution in England that in any other
great nation and R.F. Quinton referred to the improvements that had taken place as 'both gratifying
and remarkable.'[6]

Modern historians of crime have generally
agreed that there was a long-term decline of criminal activity in the second half of the nineteenth
century. As far as the incidence of community violence is concerned, Gatrell and Hadden point to a
sustained decline from the 1860s onwards and to the
emergence by 1890 of what may be called a policed
society.[7] In a recent study Gatrell has highlighted
the record decline in all crimes of violence against
the person observing that, when adjusted to population, the criminal statistics demonstrate that
assaults against the police fell by 64 percent between the late 1850s and 1914, and that total
assaults fell by 71 percent over the same period.
As he points out, 'this is an extraordinary decline
for a historian to contemplate from the vantage
point of the late twentieth century.'[8]

It is the intention of this chapter to explore
the nature and extent of community violence in the
period c.1870-1914, during which there would appear
to have been a real change in the social behaviour
of the working class. The notion of community
violence encompasses a wide range of criminal activity, but it is proposed here to examine in particular the indices concerning common assaults, assaults
upon the police, and aggravated assaults on women
and children.[9] A study of community violence does
present particular problems to the historian because of the absence of first hand evidence.
Although there is a vast range of literary evidence
- parliamentary papers, police reports, watch committee minutes, the observations of prison chaplains
and governors, magistrates, lawyers, charity workers,
clergymen and journalists - much of it is exclusively the experience of the middle class. These
observers saw everything through the lens of middle
class morality and respectability and through the
interests of their own value system. Further, most
of the evidence is essentially impressionistic
rather than statistical and scientific. However
because of their immediacy of reference, these
sources can be of great value to the historian. On
the other hand, a study based on criminal statistics

is also fraught with difficulties. J.J. Tobias
states flatly that 'criminal statistics have little
to tell us about crime and criminals in the nineteenth century', and he lists a whole series of ob-
jections to their use, such as changes in the law
and the practice of the courts which make comparison
pointless, the level of unrecorded crime or the
'dark figure', the variable use which judges and
magistrates made of their powers, the effect of the
new police force, and the problem of unreliable returns from some police districts.[10] However, other
studies contradict this view, most notably Gatrell
and Hadden's work on the interpretation of criminal
statistics in the nineteenth century. Although they
accept that two deficiencies cannot be overcome;
that the 'actual' extent of criminal behaviour can
never be fully quantified, and that legal and police
developments over a period of time must affect the
consistency of the recorded incidence of criminal
activity, they are convinced that the statistics can
be used to plot long-term trends in the incidence of
criminal activity.[11] In their examination of 'Crime
in Nineteenth Century Wales', Jones and Bainbridge
have further demonstrated the value of statistical
evidence and they conclude that in the final analysis no study of nineteenth century crime can afford
to ignore it.[12] Perhaps we may accept the comment
of R.D. Storch in his review essay on urban crime
that 'criminal statistics throw back a skewed picture, but just as what is reflected in a funhouse
mirror is an accurate image - if the viewer controls
for its propensity to distort the body - so too
long-term series of criminal statistics hold out the
hope of being interpreted.'[13]

For the study of community violence there are
particular, long term series of criminal statistics.
From 1857 the judicial and criminal statistics were
published in an enlarged form and included information from police districts of the number of people
committed to trial for indictable and summary
offences. Common assaults, which were assaults involving no aggravating circumstances, had been
classed as summary offences since 1828. The maximum
penalty that could be imposed by the magistrates was
two months imprisonment. In 1853 an act was approved 'for the better prevention and punishment of
aggravated assaults on women and children' which
provided that assaults on any female or any male
child under fourteen occasioning actual bodily harm
could be punished by summary conviction. The magistrates were given the power to imprison offenders

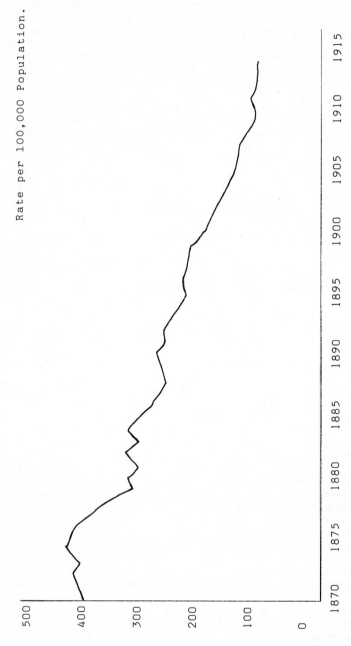

Figure 6.1: Assaults in England and Wales, 1870-1914

Rate per 100,000 Population.

for up to six months with or without hard labour, or impose a fine not exceeding twenty pounds. Assaults on police officers were also usually tried summarily, the maximum penalty being six months imprisonment. All assaults which involved malicious and unlawful wounding and grievous bodily harm were tried on indictment. There are, therefore, three specific indices of assault and it is possible to construct a graph illustrating long-term and short-term trends in community violence.

For England and Wales the evidence does point to a real and steady decline in the incidence of all forms of assaults which, allowing for increases in population, were reduced by two thirds between 1870 and 1914. There were some short-term increases during this period, particularly in the mid 1870s, but after this date the trend is one of steady decline. However, a major problem underlying assault statistics in particular concerns the unknown element, or 'dark figure', which is probably very large especially in the statistical series of common assault and aggravated assaults on women and children. The Criminal Registrar admitted this in his Report of 1896: 'when it is remembered how little is required to constitute which is strictly speaking an assault in the eyes of the law, it will be recognised that only a small proportion of the acts so characterised ever come before a Court of Justice.'[15] There is an inevitable gap between the real incidence of these assaults and the number of trials that are actually recorded. In communities where fighting and brawling were traditional ways of settling disputes, the courts were not likely to be used unless the assault was unprovoked or particularly brutal. The Stipendiary Justice of Salford recognised this in his evidence to the Select Committee on Intemperance in 1877. 'Generally speaking common assaults are the result of a complaint upon the part of the assaulted person, and very frequently brought forward without the intervention of the police at all, or the party comes out and finds the policeman where he is.'[16] In cases of aggravated assaults on women and children it is very possible that the vast majority of cases never reached the trial stage. Even when wives brought a charge against their husbands they often withdrew it. The Leeds Stipendiary cited an example of being sent for at midnight to take the deposition of a woman supposedly dying of kicks and blows to her head. The woman recovered and the man was charged with an indictable offence. Yet the case did not commence

169

because the wife feared that her husband would get a substantial prison sentence.[17] Frances Power Cobbe put it very well when she wrote that:

> as a general rule it is said that wives will often tell their stories to the constables at the moment of her arrest, and can frequently be induced to attend in court the day or two after their injuries and while still smarting from their blows and kicks and 'cloggings', but if a week be allowed to elapse ... the wife is almost certain in the interval to have relented, or to have learned to dread the consequences of bearing testimony ...[18]

However, although common assaults and aggravated assaults on women and children are underestimated in the statistics, assaults on police officers provide accurate data because the crime in question, by definition, had to be committed in the presence of a police officer. The incidence of police assault can, therefore, be used as a measurement of one aspect of community violence and as a guide to the transition from disorderly to orderly societies. Even here though the figures may be distorted by changing patterns of policing at local level. If watch committees ordered the police to undertake new duties such as greater surveillance of public houses and beer houses, or crackdowns on public drunkenness and brawling in the streets, the more likely it was that conflict and friction would occur especially in overcrowded, slum districts where there was little liking for the police anyway.

Of course, all criminal statistics are affected by the fact that attitudes to certain offences change over time. Magistrates, police forces and watch committees might well be influenced by the demand from 'respectable' citizens for action to stamp out certain types of offences. At any given time at a community level there may have been a particular onslaught on brawling, rowdiness, and disorderly conduct which on a short-term basis would result in higher arrests and trials. However, we are concerned here with long-term trends in particular and it is a reasonable assumption that the real rate of assaults would maintain a consistent relationship with the unknown rate, and that changing local police practice would only have short-term effects. It is only by using national statistics as a guide and turning to local and regional case studies that confirmation of trends in the incidence and patterns of violence can be established. A closer view is necessary in order to test out the suggested transition from 'rough' to 'respectable' communities in this period and to examine whether there was a real decline in 'the spirit of lawlessness'.

Certainly at mid century and beyond, violence was still a prominent feature of working class life in many towns. Engels had argued that with the extension of the proletariat crime had increased and that society was in a state of visible dissolution:

> In this country social war is under headway, everyone stands for himself, and fights for himself against all comers ... it no longer occurs to anyone to come to a peaceful understanding with his fellow men; all differences are settled by threats, violence, or in a law court.[19]

There were particular problems of law and order in rapidly expanding industrial communities such as Merthyr Tydfil which had a notorious reputation for criminal violence. In the 1860s common assault was still the largest entry in the town's criminal records and assaults in general accounted for between a quarter and a third of all charges.[20] However, although many of these 'frontier' towns can be described as rough societies with plenty of fighting and casual violence, David Philips suggests that in the Black Country 'there was little to show that people feared for their lives, or felt themselves unable to use the roads at night.'[21] In the large cities such as Manchester and Birmingham recent research has revealed that certainly until the end of the 1870s a high degree of casual violence was accepted as a normal part of life among large sections of the community with the courts becoming involved only when the 'norm' was exceeded. Charles de Motte argues that there was a large sub-culture of violence in Manchester with street muggings, street fights and pitched battles, unprovoked assaults, kicking and 'clogging', disorderly conduct and wife beating, very much everyday events.[22] Similarly Barbara Weinberger demonstrates that in the poorest areas of Birmingham, drunken brawls, Saturday night disturbances, street battles, attacks on bailiffs, poor rate collectors and policemen, and domestic assaults were characteristic and indicative that violence was very much a way of life.[23] In London also, in the middle decades of the nineteenth

century, high rates of casual violence persisted.
Henry Mayhew noted the tendency to violence amongst
certain groups of workers such as the costermongers
where 'everybody practises fighting, and the man with
the largest and hardest muscle is spoken of in terms
of the highest commendation. It is often said in
admiration of such a man that he could muzzle half a
dozen bobbies before breakfast.'[24] There were fears
that the 'residuum' would swamp society in this
period. 'London was seen as the Mecca of the dissolute, the lazy, the mendicant, the 'rough' and the
spendthrift.'[25]

By the early 1870s the government was suffi-
ciently alarmed by reports of an 'epidemic of violence' in the country to set up an enquiry into the
state of the law relating to brutal assaults.
Questionnaires were sent out to judges, recorders,
and magistrates and although the main thrust of the
enquiry was concerned with whether the law was suf-
ficiently stringent to deal with assaults many
replies described the state of violence in local
districts. In County Durham there was said to be a
strong increase in the number of brutal assaults and
community violence although this was blamed on 'the
continual, rapid increase of population of a very
rough character from all parts of the country,
attracted by very high wages.'[26] In Derbyshire
there had been an increase in violence since 1872,
blamed on the fact that the bulk of the population
was composed of colliers and nailers who were enjoying high wages. There had been an increase in
Staffordshire also which was similarly attributed to
the increase in wages leading to drunkenness and to
shorter hours which increased time and opportunity
for 'domestic and out-door brawling.' The Stipendiary of Swansea thought that 'there had been a
great change in the temper of great numbers of the
labouring classes which had increased the risk of
quiet persons in public houses and roads and
streets', and from Merthyr the Stipendiary reported
that 'there are many assaults accompanied with great
and brutal violence upon men, such as kicking and
biting', which he believed should be tried indic-
tably rather than summarily.[27] In Birmingham there
were over 100 men in the borough gaol for committing
acts of violence and the Recorder believed that this
'epidemic of brutality' could have been put down
from the first if the punishment of flogging had
been added to imprisonment. The Chairman of the
Middlesex Quarter Sessions reported that there was a
'class of persons who habitually committed assaults

of brutal violence and who were prone to biting,
kicking and wounding with dangerous weapons.'[28] The
same reports of an increase in brutal assaults come
from towns all over the country, from Wolverhampton,
Newcastle, Wigan, Leeds and Liverpool in particular.
Generally, the Report gives the impression that
community violence was on the increase in the early
1870s and this is borne out by the criminal statistics. Apart from deficiencies in the law, the contemporary explanation seems to be the good state of
trade which in its turn had produced high wages
leading to drunkenness and violence. The connection
between drunkenness and violent crime was stressed
repeatedly by contemporaries and further evidence
was given to the Select Committee on Intemperance
(1877). The Swansea Stipendiary Justice claimed
that all violent assaults took place under the influence of drink and the Chief Constable at Durham
blamed drunkenness for at least two thirds of
them.[29] The Chief Constable of Staffordshire presented a paper to the Committee comparing the incidence of drunkenness with that of assault in the
county between 1861 and 1876, demonstrating a
positive correlation.[30] With regard to the national
statistics, drunkenness offences slowly declined
until the end of the 1860s, reached a peak in the
mid 1870s, and overall decreased slowly after this
although periods of good trade and high wages produced short-term increases. The figures for assaults
also reached a peak in the mid 1870s and then
declined until the end of the century and beyond indicating the importance of relating trends in drunkenness to those in community violence.[31] Drink
played a very important part in Victorian and Edwardian society and as Kitson-Clark comments, its
results 'were patent in disgusting forms in most of
the streets and market-places of Britain ... in the
background there was always present the degradation,
the cruelty, particularly to the sick and defence-
less which resulted from drunkenness.'[32] Most expenditure on beer and spirits came from the working
classes and John Burnett estimates that an average
working class household spent between fifteen and
twenty pounds a year on drink and that many families
spent a third or even half their income in this
way.[33] Such consumption had a direct impact on the
incidence of street fighting, common assault,
attacks on the police, wife beating and cruelty to
children. Over the period drink expenditure began
to level out from a peak of over fifteen percent in
1876 to under nine percent by 1910, a change brought

about mainly by alternative lines of expenditure but also no doubt by temperance campaigning and stricter licensing legislation, which must have helped to reduce the incidence of community violence.[34]

II

To test out more fully the nature and extent of community violence in this period it is proposed to examine in depth one particular area, the industrialised and urbanised region known as the Black Country, with reference to the incidence of common assault, police assault, and aggravated assaults on women and children; and compare it to the national picure where appropriate. This region covers the area of south Staffordshire and north east Worcestershire, some 100 square miles, containing within it the four major towns of Wolverhampton, Walsall, West Bromwich and Dudley, as well as numerous small townships. The Black Country's economy was centred on the iron and coal trades and its population was almost entirely working class.[35]

In Wolverhampton and Walsall the general trend of common assault follows the national pattern. The peak years for this offence were the mid 1870s when the rate of proceedings exceeded ten trials per 1,000 population. By the 1890s this rate had been halved in Wolverhampton and reduced by 75 percent in Walsall. The trend over the period and the close correlation between drunkenness and assault can be illustrated by reference to the decennial averages.

An examination of the nature of common assault in this period reveals a great range and variety of cases; neighbourhood squabbles, disputes between husband and wife, arguments at work or in the public house, street fighting and rowdyism, and challenges to authority in the form of such figures as bailiffs, nuisance inspectors, and school attendance officers. Magistrates in the Black Country towns frequently expressed their determination to put down 'public brawling', 'ruffianism', and 'drunken rowdyism' which was said to be of common occurrence and to include both sexes. In 1875 the editor of the *Walsall Free Press* commented that

> Birmingham and the Black Country have for
> several years past obtained an unenviable noto-
> riety for brutal assaults ... nor can our town
> plead innocent of such cases. Almost every
> Saturday night scenes of the most disgraceful
> kind can be witnessed ... it is a well known

Table 6.1: Drunkenness and Common Assault Proceedings per 1,000 of the Population in Wolverhampton and Walsall,1860s-1890s [36]

| | Common Assault | | Drunkenness | |
	Wolverhampton	Walsall	Wolverhampton	Walsall
1860s	8.64	7.14	6.7	3.8
1870s	9.45	9.81	9.09	7.97
1880s	7.14	4.35	7.45	4.0
1890s	5.28	2.52	5.75	3.18

fact that no Saturday night passes without one or more cases being taken to hospital to have their wounds, injured in drunken rows, attended to ...[37]

In one Saturday night disturbance in Kate's Hill, Dudley, a crowd of 300 gathered to watch a drunken brawl. 'The disturbance was so great and the shrieks and cries of murder so loud that the school-master rang the school bell to alarm the police.'[38] Fighting seemed to be the most common way of settling disputes in these towns and one observer, who had been a curate in Walsall, remembered that 'open air fighting was normal in the town ... the good people, however, were as a rule content with raw fists and not much harm was done.' When he moved to London he was surprised at first never to see fighting in the streets ...'Londoners were tough enough, it was merely a difference in social customs.'[39] Certainly, drunken fighting in the streets was common with magistrates complaining that crowds were treating these exhibitions as entertainment instead of doing all they could to put a stop to such proceedings. However Will Thorne, remembering his Birmingham youth in the 1870s, remarks that this drinking and fighting should not be magnified or misjudged. 'We were healthy, normal human beings, fond of fair play, we had little amusement and little opportunity to enjoy the better things of life. If these fights sometimes took place, it was no fault of ours, but rather of the system of society we lived under - a system that made us work long hours of brutalising toil for little money; a system that had no care as to the slums we slept in, the food we ate, or the education we received...'[40]

Many common assault cases stemmed from neighbourhood disputes where the sheer frustration of
trying to get a living in miserable, overcrowded
conditions often meant that a chance word could set
off a quarrel which ended in blows. Such disputes
were of a common occurrence and took place without
reference to the courts, but some caught the eye of
a passing policeman or left the aggrieved party so
indignant that the offence was reported and a complaint lodged. The Wolverhampton police court
reporter commented that:

> Neighbours, like their dogs and cats will fight
> and quarrel and they are never satisfied until
> they have aired their dirty linen in the Police
> Court ... it was often a hard matter to keep
> them from fighting even in court. They turn
> up the whites of their eyes and take deep sighs
> when the "naughty hussies" tell lies about one
> of the other, and wonder that they "baint
> ashamed to stand there and kiss the book" ...
> Sometimes they'll produce an apron full of
> brickbats, a broom stall, a poker, a frying pan,
> and a paper full of hair that had been pulled
> off the head in the struggle.
> Generally, there's about six of one and half a
> dozen of the other in these quarrels, and if
> the case is dismissed the complainant has to
> pay costs, and then another shindy follows.[41]

Some of these women were of a particularly fearsome
disposition; there was Bridget Murphy of Cox's Yard,
Walsall known as the 'Queen of Hell Fold', because
of her disorderly conduct, who had seized another
woman by the hair, striking and abusing her; and
Caroline Piper of West Bromwich, 'a terror to her
neighbours because of her violent and overbearing
conduct'. She had quarrelled with a neighbour and
picked up a brick and struck her with it causing a
severe wound.[42]
Neighbourhood quarrels and assaults were common
amongst the London working class also. Octavia Hill,
who managed a court in Marylebone, noted the endless
opportunities of collision and the tension that
built up in dirty, close quarters and Charles Booth
recorded his impressions of tenement life with its
constant disputes over common rights and duties and
the ferocity of washing day disputes.[43] In her
article on neighbourhood sharing in London before
the First World War Ellen Ross points out that
women's neighbourhood relationships often generated

tension and anger and that public fights between women seem to have been a regular occurrence on the poorest streets.[44]

Violence was also common in or around public houses and beer houses. Landlords, fearing to be prosecuted for 'permitting drunkenness', were attacked by those they refused to serve, and drunken quarrelling often occurred in these places with jugs, spittoons and pokers being used as handy weapons. Sometimes, these quarrels escalated into full scale conflict such as the case of the Felves and McNallys who had been drinking together on a Sunday afternoon in a Wolverhampton public house. The Felves brothers refused to buy the McNallys any more drinks and late that afternoon they were set upon by the whole McNally clan shouting 'kill all the Englishmen'. A crowd of some 60 people assembled and cinders, brick-ends and other missiles were thrown injuring the Felves brothers.[45] Most of these disputes were less dramatic than this, consisting of an exchange of blows after an argument and only coming to the notice of the police by accident or mischance.

Assaults committed in the work place, either between workers themselves or by masters on apprentices, constitute another type of common assault. Workers paid on piece work would take exception to some articles being rejected as sub standard; James Wilcox, a tinner of Hill Top, West Bromwich, assaulted the foreman for 'scratching' some of his work, and John Bucknall, a shingler, assaulted the overlooker after being accused of making inferior iron.[46] Apprentices were in a very difficult position with regard to any punishment their masters might inflict on them. Such punishment may well have been regarded as 'proper correction' rather than illegal assault. For this reason, assaults by masters were unlikely to come before the courts, and those that did were almost always dismissed; there was the Walsall lad who had been knocked about badly by his master, but it was counter-claimed that he was 'inattentive, impudent and violent and that slight correction was necessary.'[47] Girls in domestic service were equally at the mercy of their employers who regarded 'proper correction' as their right and duty. One girl had been beaten so badly by her mistress that there were severe weals on her arms and legs. The defendant contended that the girl had lied to her and gone out of the house without permission, but she was fined five shillings with costs.[48]

The police court cases do demonstrate that
sections of the working class in these Black Country
communities were generally not well disposed to outside interference in their lives. Police, bailiffs,
public health inspectors, School Board officials
were all unwelcome visitors to the yards, courts and
backstreets and were often met with hostile resistance. After the introduction of compulsory education, attendance officers were a particular target,
at best being scorned and cursed and at worst
physically attacked. One of the Dudley attendance
officers offered his resignation in October, 1876
because

> he found the work so rough, and he met with so
> much insult and abuse that he couldn't stand
> it. He had been threatened three times in one
> day and if he was to do his duty his life was in
> danger. One man had said he would do three
> months in Worcester (prison) for him, and
> another threatened to break his nose. In one
> district, a woman raised the whole neighbour-
> hood against him.[49]

When the children were in school, parents did not
readily accept the rights of school teachers to discipline their children and some rushed to the school
to take direct vengeance on those who had punished
their offspring. Some waited for the teachers outside the schools, abusing, threatening and punching
them. A member of the Walsall School Board urged a
strict policy of prosecuting for assault in all such
cases 'as it seemed to be the understanding of the
parents of children in some localities that if a
child was punished they would have their revenge.'[50]
Bailiffs were the common enemy. Attempts to evict a
family or carry out a distraint for rent often led
to physical resistance which was the workers' way of
fighting back. To use the courts would cost money
and it was unlikely that the verdict would go in
their favour. Other public officials were simply
carrying out the policies of the borough councils
but as front line representatives of that authority
they faced the resentment of working class communities.

III

Like the incidence of common assault, the rate of
assaults on police in England and Wales declined in
this period, by some 60 percent between 1870 and

1914, allowing for population increase. However, in the 1870s there was an upsurge of assaults on the police, reflected both in national and local statistics, as R.D. Storch shows in his analysis of ten police districts. On the evidence of this survey 'no significant diminution takes place in this offence until 1876-1880.'[51] In Birmingham, assaults on the police peaked in 1867-8 and 1872-4 and they remained at a generally higher level throughout the seventies than they had been in the previous decade. Further, these assaults were of a more violent nature and often took the form of mob attacks.[52] In Manchester, there seems to be a trend to greater violence against the police between 1867 and 1876 with no permanent decline until 1883.[53] David Jones records that in London the trend was slightly different with a high plateau of offences until the mid 1860s and a lower one thereafter with peaks in 1872 and 1881. He cites a police report for 1872 which estimated that each metropolitan officer was injured once every two years.[54] In the Black Country the peaks of police assaults in Wolverhampton occurred between 1858 and 1862 and 1875 and 1879 including a record number of 107 assaults in 1878. It was not until the 1880s that the rate fell consistently below the 1858 level. In Walsall, the peaks are similar (1858-62, 1874-5) but there is a steady decline from 1876.[55]

The *Report on Brutal Assaults* (1874) suggested that part of the problem was caused by the magistrates' courts which did not seem prepared in the sentencing to create an effective deterrent against police assault despite the fact that assaulting a policeman in the execution of his duty could be punished summarily by a twenty pound fine or six months imprisonment, which was a more severe sentence than could be imposed for common assault on a private citizen. The Chairman of the Middlesex Quarter Sessions, Sergeant Cox, reported that 'assaults on the police were so frequent, brutal and dangerous that they should not be dealt with by magistrates, but sent to Quarter Sessions. This would make intelligible to the disorderly a fact that they do not now recognise that the law looks upon an assault upon a policeman in the execution of his duties as a very much more grave offence than an ordinary assault.'[56] A plea for stricter sentencing had also been made some years before by J.H. Elliott who argued that:

the person of the humblest police officer ought

to be as safe as that of a judge or bishop, protected by unusual severity. No man should be allowed to resist him or raise a hand against him. The civilization of a country is low indeed, while such grievous cruelties inflicted on policemen, especially by street ruffians, are but slightly punished, regarded with apparent indifference by the public or as considered to be equitably compensated for in their wages.[57]

Despite these views, an analysis of sentencing for police assault in Wolverhampton in 1878 demonstrates that magistrates were not pursuing a deterrent policy.

Table 6.2: Sentencing for Police Assault, Wolverhampton Borough, 1878 [58]

107 Cases, 101 Convictions (90 Males, 11 Females)		
Above six months (indictable)	-	1
6 months	-	1
3 months	-	10
2 months	-	12
1 month	-	34
14 days	-	7
Fines	-	34
Other Punishments	-	2
		101

Police-community relationships in this period were largely determined by the fact that social class was the basis of police treatment of citizens. There were no complaints of oppression from the middle classes - rather that the police were inefficient in coping with the problems of urban crime and behaviour. The working class, however, were more likely to see the police 'as masters instead of servants', the upholders of a hierarchical social order which meant one law for the rich and another one for the poor. Most of the hostility directed against the police from within the working classes resulted from what was felt to be interference in neighbourhood and recreational life, such as drinking, gambling and prize fighting.[59] Surveillance of public houses and beer houses was particularly detested, and often

resulted in violent clashes and it is significant
that the limitations on hours of drinking imposed by
the Licensing Acts of 1872 and 1874 and enforced by
local watch committees and police forces occur at
the same time as a general increase in police
assault cases.

A detailed analysis of police court proceedings
in the Black Country reveals three basic reasons for
police assault over and above the fact that the
police were regarded as unwelcome intruders in some
working class neighbourhoods: individual resistance
to being arrested; attempts to protect and rescue
members of the community being arrested; and assault
as a result of 'unwarranted' police interference.

Resistance to arrest seems to have been the
most common cause of police assault, the great majority of cases occurring when the person being arrested was drunk. It could be argued that many of the
assaults were the result of a loss of control rather
than a dislike of the police although it is likely
the two went together. Many cases refer to prison-
ers 'struggling and kicking in a savage manner', or
'kicking and biting'. However, some were arrested
for making a noise and 'refusing to go home' or
'move along' and here there was real resentment
often leading to blows. There seems little doubt
that certain characters were moved on and arrested
because they were well known to the police as
'nuisances'. In any dispute and disturbance they
were arrested first. John Stevens of Canal Street,
Wolverhampton, with nineteen previous convictions,
was arrested for being drunk and disorderly and resisted with great violence. Inspector Thomas described the prisoner as 'a very rough fellow who had
threatened to stab a policeman and was a perfect
terror to the neighbourhood ... the worst character
in Wolverhampton.'60

The tradition of rescuing a prisoner or preven-
ting an arrest was still a feature of police-
community relations in the Black Country as elsewhere. The idea of rescue had a certain legitimacy
especially when it concerned close friends, or community loyalties.61 When Patrick Joyce was arrested
after a Saturday night disturbance in Wolverhampton
in 1874, the two policemen were 'followed by a large
mob', among whom was Richard Joyce, brother of the
arrested, who 'endeavoured to incite the mob to
attack the constables and release his brother.' The
mob did so, injuring the policemen, one having his
leg severely fractured.62 Sometimes the entire
neighbourhood became involved in a rescue,

especially in those areas where there was already a
great deal of hostility towards the police. One
Saturday night in February 1879, the West Bromwich
police attempted to arrest a drunken man who had
'refused to go home and had used obscene language.'
A crowd of 200 quickly gathered and forced the
policemen to take refuge in a butcher's shop with
their prisoner. 'While they were there the mob,
which had been unruly all along, remained yelling
and hurling stones into the shop.' When the police
superintendent arrived and the drunken man was
brought out, the mob charged forward felling the
superintendent with a brick. Eventually, the
prisoner was got to the police station, the mob
following all the way. The editor of the *West
Bromwich Weekly News* commented that 'the riot had
been noticeable for one peculiarity - the police had
borne the whole brunt of the savage mob and received
no assistance from the inhabitants.'[63] In another
incident in Wolverhampton in August 1884, wholesale
community resistance greeted the attempt to arrest
a woman for being drunk and disorderly on 'Irish
Row', Willenhall Road. Bridget Regan was seen at
11.15 p.m. to be drunk and P.C. Purchase had

> endeavoured to persuade her to go into her own
> home, but as soon as she got in she came out
> and renewed the disturbance. He put her in
> several times and on one occasion kept the door
> closed for five minutes. The prisoner then
> came out with a poker and struck him with it on
> the side. With the assistance of P.C. Thompson
> they tried to take her into custody, but this
> they could not do owing to the obstruction of
> some 1500 people who had by then collected. A
> number of men hustled and struck at the offic-
> ers and finally dragged them into a house.
> They kept them there some time and it was 12.20
> p.m. before the officers could get away with
> the prisoner in their custody. Both officers
> were maltreated by the mob and the language
> towards them was of the most gross and indecent
> character.[64]

Certainly the Irish communities in general resented
the presence and attention of the police. Charles
Booth referred to one area in Limehouse, known as
the Fenian Barracks, which 'had a very bad name with
the police for violence, sending, we are told more
police to hospital than any other block in London...
and being Irish if one of their number is taken by

the police a rescue is attempted.'65
    The last category of police assaults concerned
those who attacked the police as a result of 'unwarranted' interference in their lives. Prostitutes
in particular felt that they were unduly harassed,
as did vagrants and working class youths. Some
assaults in this category resulted directly from resentment at being driven off the streets for little
apparent reason except noise or disturbance, as in
the case of one Dudley labourer who refused to 'move
on' and hit the policeman in the course of the
argument. He defended himself stoutly in court and
stated that 'he had fought for his country and had
a perfect right to knock a policeman down.'66 As
R.D. Storch comments, the imposition of the 'move
on' system was 'an attack upon a traditionally sanc-
tioned freedom ... and a keenly felt sense of humi-
liation.'67 Some assaults on the police had no
immediate provocation except the latter's very
presence in certain areas. In many streets and
slums the police were an alien force, regarded as
despots, and fair game for attack if they put themselves in a vulnerable position. The police themselves recognised this state of affairs and seldom
ventured into such districts, unless they were with
others. Even 'doubling up' offered little security.
In May 1879, two policemen passing through Guns Lane,
West Bromwich, 'were set upon by a mob and beaten
almost insensible, one of their assailants using a
belt with a heavy buckle. They were both wounded
severely and unable to move.'68 The Salford Stipendiary noted in 1877 that many police attacks were
not mere rough conduct which almost every drunken
person was given to but 'premeditated assaults,
something serious and determined', and if arrest was
attempted 'they use the police in a very brutal
manner, kicking with their clogs and beating
them.'69 Some streets were scenes of violently open
warfare especially on Saturday nights. In Birmingham
'gangs of youths terrorised certain neighbourhoods,
pelting and stoning the police on sight',70 and so
frequent was stoning the police in Stafford Street,
Wolverhampton, that the Chief Constable referred to
the conduct of that street as 'almost unbelievable
and a disgrace to every civilized town.'71
    It would appear from studying these police
assault cases that the majority of offences were
committed in those areas where the police were regarded at best as unwelcome intruders and at worst
as hated despots. In the poorest and most deprived
parts of these Black Country towns, assaulting and

baiting the police seemed to be the only way of
fighting back against the persistent monitoring and
control of the streets. Active resistance and hostility to the police seems to have been widespread
in the 1870s, and Weinberger has shown that in
Birmingham assaults were not confined to the lowest
social stratum, that all the manual strata were well
represented and that although 'a distinction can be
made between the roughs who assaulted the police and
the respectable who did not, this distinction does
not differentiate between social layers as such but
rather between the position and expectation of different groups of people within them.'[72] Yet in the
Black Country, Birmingham and everywhere else the
rate of assaults against the police declined substantially from about 1880 and by the 1890s in east
London, apart from the rough cockney Irish, it was
said that 'nearly everyone speaks well of the
police', and 'relations were noticeably friendly.'[73]
It would appear that by the end of the nineteenth
century the vast majority of the working class had
acquiesced in police authority and the only resistance to them came from persistently antagonistic
groups such as the dispossessed slum dwelling poor,
the Irish, juvenile street gangs and those of the
criminal sub-culture. Of course acquiescence does
not mean consent and in Robert Roberts' Salford
slum the poor in general looked upon the policeman
with fear and dislike and 'watched him passing with
suspicion and his disappearance with relief.'[74]
Part of this acquiescence may have been associated
with fear but part was also due to changing attitudes from the police who began to use greater dis-
cretion in performing their duties. 'The police
have grasped the fact that to treat people roughly
is the surest way to make them disorderly', said one
witness and in many rough districts policing became
increasingly a matter of expediency.[75] As long as
there was public order on the main streets the
police were usually prepared to connive at some gambling and drinking offences and as to rows and
fights 'the police don't as a rule see them, and
don't want to ... The disorderly people might be
locked up constantly, but what would be the good of
it?'[76] At the end of the nineteenth century Charles
Booth concluded that it was the policy of the London
police to be too easy rather than too exacting,
realising that 'police practice can only go just a
little ahead of the morality of the district. In
all they do to suppress rowdyism they must have the
moral support of the better class of the neighbours

if they are to be successful.'[77] The confrontation
techniques of the 1870s had been replaced by a much
more restrained approach, made possible of course by
the increasing orderliness of the population.

IV

The third index of community violence that needs to
be identified is that of aggravated assaults on
women and children which were recorded separately in
the criminal statistics and defined as those
assaults 'attended with circumstances of particular
outrage or atrocity.' In 1853 Parliament had re-
sponded to pressure that the law was insufficient to
protect women and children from violent assaults by
approving legislation which gave magistrates the
power to imprison offenders for up to six months
with or without hard labour. The offender could
also be bound over to keep the peace for a period of
up to six months after the end of the sentence.
However, many of these cases of family assault were
classed as 'common' rather than 'aggravated' and
thus the quantification of such assaults is a very
difficult exercise. Further, this type of offence
is a classic instance of the 'dark figure' of crime,
occurring mainly in private and largely unreported
by the victims. Neighbours and friends would rarely
intervene directly in family quarrels and even if
they did they would hardly be likely to involve the
police. Thus long-term trends in this offence are
extremely difficult to assess although the statistics do indicate a decline relative to population.
Aggravated assaults tried summarily reached a peak
of about 3,000 offences annually in the mid 1860s
and had dropped to under 1,000 offences annually by
the middle of the Edwardian period.[78]
    By the early 1870s there was growing concern
among magistrates and middle class reformers about
the brutality inflicted on women. The *Report on Brutal Assaults* (1874) considered whether changes in the
law would improve the situation and particularly
whether the imposition of flogging would act as a
deterrent. However, there were several arguments
against this. The Manchester Stipendiary stated
that if flogging was introduced the women would not
give evidence because 'their chief desire is to get
what they term a "protection order" or to have their
husbands bound over to keep the peace.'[79] Similarly
the chairman of the North Riding Quarter Sessions
argued that in brutal assaults upon wives 'the
better feeling often returns in sober moments; the

attachment of the wife is not extinguished, and
although compelled for her own security to give
evidence against a brutal husband whose conduct is
to be punished by imprisonment there would be a
greater reluctance if flogging were to result.'80
The issue was raised again at the Congress of the
National Association for the Promotion of Social
Sciences in Liverpool in 1876, when Sergeant Pulling
exposed the amount of brutality taking place in that
city and the ineffectiveness of the law. 'The ill-
usage of women was systematic and little hindered by
the supposed strong arm of the law making the lot
of a married women whose locality is the "kicking
district" simply a duration of suffering and sub-
jection to injury and savage treatment, far worse
than that to which the lives of savages are used.'
The law seemed designed not to repress crime but to
discourage the complainant and to overcome this he
suggested the appointment of a Public Presecutor,
the taking of depositions from wives, and flogging
for second convictions.81 In 1878 Frances Power
Cobbe revived interest in the subject of wife beating through her article in the *Fortnightly Review*
entitled 'Wife Torture in England', which included
proposals for new legislation. She contended,
although without much evidence, that dangerous wife
beaters belonged almost exclusively to the artisan
and labouring classes:

> Colliers, puddlers and weavers have long earned
> for themselves in this matter a bad reputation
> ... in the worst districts of London four-
> fifths of the wife-beating cases are among the
> lowest class of Irish labourers ... There are
> also various degrees of wife-beating in the
> different localities. In London it seldom goes
> beyond a severe thrashing with a fist, a suf-
> ficiently dreadful punishment it is true but
> mild in comparison to the kickings, tramplings
> and "purrings" with hobnailed shoes and clogs
> (of the North) ... it is in the centres of
> dense mercantile and manufacturing populations
> that this offence reaches its climax.82

Due to the pressure exerted by Frances Cobbe and
others, there passed in 1878 the Matrimonial Causes
Act which allowed a wife who had suffered from an
'aggravated assault' to obtain a separation order
through the Magistrates Courts with maintenance and
custody of children under ten. However the granting
of a separation order was no guarantee of safety, as

men often sought revenge. For example William Henshaw, a hawker of Wolverhampton, on the same day that his wife had been granted a separation order, pursued her into an entry and then kicked her until she fell, for which he was sentenced to six months hard labour.[83] All this meant that a woman still had to weigh up carefully the consequences of taking her husband before the courts. In the Black Country, the magistrates were usually very reluctant to grant a separation order unless there had been previous assaults of the same nature. When women asked for such an order, the usual practice was to adjourn the case for one or two months to see how the marriage progressed. Therefore, a wife 'qualified' for separation and maintenance only through a series of brutal assaults. Another limitation on the wife's freedom of action was the level of maintenance granted by the court. Many awards amounted to only five or six shillings a week. Obviously, separation might put an end to a hellish existence for some women, but the problem of subsistence must have deterred many except the most desperate, especially those with large families to consider.

Throughout the period women faced great problems if they sought to use the courts to redress their grievances. The fear of revenge, a lack of knowledge of the law, unwelcome publicity, the impoverishment of the family, must have combined to produce a massive deterrent. Perhaps the biggest deterrent for a wife was the fear of subsequent revenge. What was to happen to a wife when the husband came out of prison determined to make her suffer for having summoned him in the first place? Although the law did provide for an offender to be bound over to keep the peace, this provision seemed to be hardly used at all in the Black Country except in the case of a man with previous convictions. Another problem was that a woman would usually have to apply for a summons before the man came to court, which would cost her two shillings unless her injuries were so evident as to induce the magistrate to issue the summons without charge.

When the summons was served the woman had to face the consequences. James Dance, a bricklayers' labourer of West Bromwich, 'flew at his wife' when this happened and 'although she was weak and nearly famished for want of food, he kicked, struck, and bit her, and behaved like a madman.'[84]

Very often the woman sought to withdraw the charge when the matter came to court. As the Wolverhampton police court reporter observed:

the women in the witness-box with broken hands,
faces and arms black and blue, and blood flow-
ing from wounds, the result of brutality on
the part of their husbands, but despite this he
had seen them and heard them with tears in
their eyes, plead for those who had cruelly
ill-used them and asked that the charge might
be withdrawn. They had perjured themselves
that their 'better halves' might receive the
more merciful consideration of the court, and
have said they merely took the summons out in
the heat of the moment...[85]

Thomas Holmes, a London police court missionary,
noticed the same thing. 'I see women with bruised
and battered faces, I see their cuts and wounds and
putrefying sores, I hear stories of devilish cruelty,
and I hear the poor, bruised women pleading that
their husbands may not be punished for their
cruelty.'[86] This reluctance to substantiate charges
made may have resulted from the fear of subsequent
revenge but more likely it was a matter of economic
consideration. The loss of the wage-earner in
prison meant absolute poverty unless the woman
worked herself and this would be almost impossible
where there were young children. The only alternative was to seek help from her family or her neighbours whose own resources were likely to be limited.
Thus the workhouse might be the only solution. As
Davidoff points out, once a woman married she shared
the basic precariousness of all working class
families - a dependence on a man's wage. 'Her deference was to his paternalistic status - hers was a
complete physical subordination with physical
coercion often the source of the husband's control
... Having a good husband or a "real bad un", was,
in a sense, to be accepted as a stroke of fate in
just the same way as the wife accepted the good of
the family survival over her individual interests.'[87] Domestic circumstances, then, gave working class women little option but to struggle on
and put up with their wretchedness - 'the absolute
rule for all sub-affluent marriages was like it or
lump it.'[88]
    From studies of court cases at a local level
some idea can be gained of the extent of violence,
and the sources of tension that led to conflict between the sexes as well as some sense of the attitude of working class communities towards such
violence. In her study of crimes of violence between working class men and women in London, Nancy

Tomes concludes that 'based on a neighbourhood perspective, whatever his or her personal experience, no working class individual could escape exposure to acts of violence between the sexes.' Similarly Ellen Ross refers to an East End culture 'where husband and wife violence was incredibly frequent.'[89] The most dangerous place in nineteenth century Manchester, according to David Jones, was the home, with plenty of evidence from court cases and newspapers of brutality 'underlining the ferocity which sprang from irreconcilable marriage and tense common-law relationships.'[90] The most common reasons behind these assaults in the Black Country would appear to be drunkenness, money problems, the alleged failure of the woman to perform her housekeeping functions adequately, and jealousy. However, it should be stressed that in some cases the husband assaulted his wife for no apparent reason which may reinforce the idea of 'customary coercion' as part of a behavioural norm among certain sections of the working class. 'Within marriage, violence was viewed as normal because it was seen as serving a disciplinary function ... the working class community recognised violence or threats of violence as legitimate means of maintaining the husband's superiority in the family.'[91] Some offenders before the court defended themselves on these grounds. A Wolverhampton labourer, Thomas Fitzgerald, accused of hitting and kicking his wife in Queen Square, replied that 'he thought it was his right to chastise her and get her home as she had had beer', and a Walsall man sentenced for assaulting his wife explaimed to the magistrates, 'Do you call this a land of liberty when a fellow ain't at liberty to thrash his own wife?'[92]

Drink was a very important factor in most of these cases. A man often assaulted his wife because he was already drunk or wanted the means to get into that condition. Wives lived in fear of their husbands' return from the public house; some of them were said to be 'mad with drink' when they arrived back. In some cases drunkenness and temper led to extreme acts of violence such as attacks with razors, pokers and any handy weapon as well as with fists and feet. The need to get money for drink led to other assaults. John Dasey, a Walsall miner, had demanded money from his wife for drink but she had told him to sell his pigeons. He took them to a public house, sold them, returned drunk and kicked her until she was insensible. The surgeon reported 'that he had literally danced upon her and that she

was in a very weak condition.' This was one of the
few cases which resulted in a maximum sentence of
six months hard labour.[93] The general pressure of
living on a precarious budget led to many quarrels
and assaults. The wife had the ultimate responsibility of feeding the children and she was often
desperate to get money from her husband. In one
Dudley case, Frederic Wood, a basket maker, had been
followed to the public house by his wife because
'the family had no victuals or fire and he had sold
a blanket and was drinking the proceeds.' He refused to give up the money and when his wife followed him through the town he turned and kicked her
violently, saturating her clothes with blood.[94]

Whatever the immediate cause of assault, many
cases studied reveal a pattern of coercion which had
existed for years. Frances Cobbe noted that 'the
suffering wives take it for granted that a husband
is a beating animal and may be heard to remark when
extraordinarily ill-treated by a stranger, - "that
they never were so badly used, no not by their own
'usbands".'[95] Similarly Thomas Holmes found in
London that 'wife-beating was so common among a
certain class that plenty of wives take it as a
perfect matter of course, and did not appear to mind
very much unless they were seriously damaged.'[96]
This pattern of coercion and often resigned acceptance continued on into the first decades of the
twentieth century. A St. Helens woman born during
World War I referred to the way her own father and
many others behaved.

> Men were tyrants... There was an awful lot of
> wifebeating and women were the underdogs... My
> mother slept in the outside lavatory at times.
> The men that didn't drink and behaved like that
> were the worst of all ... The wifebeating came
> from the Victorian era. When it happened,
> women went to neighbours' houses. Then the
> husband would come and kick the door down to
> get the wife out ... It was just a way of
> life.[97]

In assessing the incidence of family assaults and
its under-representation in the criminal statistics
one must be wary of over compensating and assuming
it to be general practice in many working class
families, especially as the evidence is fragmentary.
However, it would appear that the physical coercion
of families by the husband would have been considered by contemporaries to be unremarkable, if not

customary. The authority of the father was accepted and if there were blows they were part of the marriage bond and were not the business of neighbours or of the police.[98] As Nancy Tomes remarks of the London working class, 'in a community where physical violence occurred frequently, these crimes were deviant not in their nature but in the level of their violence.'[99] The idea that the physical coercion of wives and families was perceived as the masculine prerogative of matrimony rather than as a potential criminal offence is given some support by the fact that in the Black Country police court cases a wide range of occupations and of social strata were involved.[100] Undoubtedly poverty, drunkenness, and wretched living conditions played a part but the helpless dependence of women was a very important factor. Jack London, in *The People of the Abyss* (1903), thought that in the lowest social classes the idea of male domination was at its strongest:

> A woman of the lower ghetto classes is as much the slave of her husband as is the Indian squaw ... the men are economically dependent upon their masters, and the women are economically dependent on the men. The result is that the woman gets the beating that the man should give his master and she can do nothing.[101]

This helpless dependence of women together with a likely acceptance of 'reasonable' coercion makes it exceptionally difficult for the historian to make any judgement on the scale of such violence. Women would not bring their husbands to court unless they were suffering from repeated and excessive violence. Although Tomes claims for London a true decline in all forms of aggravated assaults upon women between 1853 and 1889 which 'seems to reflect a real change in behaviour' the statistics are not convincing. As we have seen the national indices of aggravated assaults also appear to be declining steadily in this period but this may be misleading because an increasing number of women were making use of other legal remedies. Women would stop short of getting warrants served on their husbands but as the law changed in the late nineteenth century women took other action. The Matrimonial Causes Act of 1878 did provide women with the opportunity of getting a separation order from the magistrates and when this Act was strengthened in 1895 with the provision that women suffering from persistent violence could leave

their husbands and then apply to the magistrates
within whose jurisdiction they lived for a summons
for separation and maintenance, a flood of applica-
tions resulted which, as Margaret May suggests,
'provides a clearer gauge of matrimonial misery
hidden by previous measures.'[102]   In the first year
after the passing of the Summary Jurisdiction
(Married Women) Act of 1895, 5,314 maintenance
orders were granted in England and Wales and by the
1900s between seven and eight thousand orders were
made annually.[103]   The problem of the battered wife
continued to receive attention in the Edwardian
period and further evidence was supplied to the
Royal Commission on Divorce and Matrimonial Causes
which was set up in 1909, although ultimately no
changes in the law resulted from it.[104]   However,
it is still true that the real incidence of this
offence remained largely hidden in this period -
just as it continues to be in the late twentieth
century.

     Included in the statistical tables for aggra-
vated assaults are assaults on children under fourteen. Although children were supposed to be protected by the Act of 1853, in practice the authority
and right of parents to discipline and chastise
their children as they pleased was not seriously
challenged until the end of the nineteenth century.
Violence inflicted on children was commonplace
throughout Victorian society and the difficulty was
to make a distinction between legitimate and un-
acceptable violence. The courts usually became involved only when there was cruelty on a horrific
scale such as a Wolverhampton case in 1884 when
Henry Phillips, a wheelwright, had tied up his
eleven year old son and beat his naked flesh with a
clothes line, rubbing salt into the wounds.[105]   It
was not until the 1880s that the question of cruelty
to children became a subject of national concern and
in April 1883 the first society for the prevention
of cruelty to children was established in Liverpool,
followed by Bristol and Birmingham in the same year
and London, Glasgow and Hull in 1885.[106]   In London,
Benjamin Waugh, a Congregational minister, was made
the first secretary of the society and he campaigned
determinedly for a change in the law. In an article
written jointly with Cardinal Manning entitled 'The
Child of the English Savage', he reported on the
first year's work of the London society. The problem facing the society was that 'cruelty is done
chiefly where its doer is most secure from detection,
and where no one has the right to follow them.'

The article pleaded for new legislation 'to place the children of the savage on the same level as his dog', an ironical reference to the fact that legislation had existed to protect animals for some sixty years.[107] By 1889, 31 towns and cities had joined societies to protect children from cruelty and in May of that year they amalgamated to form the National Society for the Prevention of Cruelty to Children. Largely because of the evidence these societies provided, Parliament approved in 1889 the Prevention of Cruelty to Children Act known as the Children's Charter. This Act gave police and magistrates the power to intervene in domestic circumstances where they suspected cruelty to children and if necessary to remove a child from a suspect home. The ill treatment of children was punishable by three months to two years imprisonment and fines of £25 to £100. In 1894 the Act was amended to protect children up to sixteen and the definition of cruelty was broadened.[108] This legislation helped to make visible the extent of cruelty to children although the figures include 'neglect' as well as 'violence'. Between 1893 and 1914 there was an annual average of some 3,400 summary prosecutions for cruelty in England and Wales.[109] These figures would have been a great deal higher if the National Society had not pursued a policy of prosecuting and removing the child only as a last resort, relying on a system of warnings supervised by the inspectors. By 1897-8 the Society was dealing with 25,000 complaints a year. In his Report for 1899 the Criminal Registrar addressed himself to the question of cruelty to children observing that prosecutions were increasing because of the existence of an active Society and because of strong public opinion which favoured carrying out the law. He referred to various reports of the National Society which indicated that presecutions for 'violence' as opposed to 'neglect' had averaged 40 percent in the 1880s but this had been reduced to around 20 percent in the 1890s. The places alleged to have the highest proportion of crimes of violence against children in 1894-5 were London with 29 percent, Birmingham 23 percent, followed by Newcastle and Leeds at twenty percent. The Assistant Criminal Registrar had worked out his own local cruelty table using the criteria of murder of children under one year of age, prosecutions for cruelty to children, and numbers of children abandoned under two years of age, although it was admitted that too much stress could not be laid on the figures.

Table 6.3: Cruelty to Children per 100,000 Population in Selected English Towns, 1889 [110]

Towns greater than 88,000 population

Liverpool	103.48
Wolverhampton	47.80
Newcastle	43.72
Manchester	32.31
Salford	26.51

Towns between 34,000 and 88,000 population

Bootle	77.11
Wigan	58.18
Warrington	53.49
Stockport	45.56
St. Helens	38.31

Referring to Edwardian Salford, Robert Roberts recalled that the punishment of children seemed to be widespread and severe:

> no one who spent his childhood in the slums during those years will easily forget the regular and often brutal assaults on some children perpetrated in the name of discipline and often for the most venial offences ... Whenever my mother heard of a heinous case, as with the woman who boasted in the shop, "My master (husband) allus flogs 'em till the blood runs down their back!" she quietly "put the Cruelty man on". In its city windows the NSPCC displayed photographs of beaten children and rows of confiscated belts and canes. Gallantly as it worked, the Society hardly touched the fringe of the problem.[111]

V

Was there a real change in the social behaviour of the working classes in this period? There does seem to have been a watershed in the incidence of community violence around about 1880. In the middle of the 1870s common assault, drunkenness and assaults on police officers had reached very high levels. There was enough government concern to set up investigations into brutality (1874) and drunkenness

(1877) and to strengthen the law with regard to aggravated assaults on women. From approximately 1880 onwards the indices of community violence showed a marked decline, suggesting a substantial change in public order in most areas, although it has always to be remembered that many domestic assaults would be unreported. Clearly there was much less casual violence by the beginning of the twentieth century and there was much less disorderly conduct in the streets. The figures for both common assault and police assault continued to decline throughout the Edwardian period and the latter index particularly provides an accurate guide to the development of new standards of discipline and control. Contemporary observers and social investigators noted the steady improvement in the 'habits and the morals' of most of the working class. Evidence given to the Royal Commission on the Housing of the Working Classes (1884-5) referred to improvements in manners, sobriety and public order.[112] Charles Booth, in his survey of the London working class, cited police evidence as being practially agreed that the people were much less rowdy than formerly: 'totally different people to what they were thirty-three years ago said one who had joined the force then.' He concluded that there was less drunken rowdiness and despite outbursts of 'hooliganism', much less street violence and 'such scenes of open depravity that occurred in years gone by do not happen now.'[113]

Although there may have been a decline in the 'spirit of lawlessness' as the Criminal Registrar observed in 1899, it is important to bear in mind the specific social strata that this can be applied to. Thomas Wright, a journeyman engineer, writing in 1868, had divided the working class into three main sections: the educated workman, the intelligent artisan, and what he termed the lower working class. 'The working man of the latter type has more in common with the roughs - he lives in low, disreputable neighbourhoods, his household is genuinely dirty and overcrowded, he habitually loafs about street corners and public houses when not at work. He is usually given to drunkenness and often to wife-beating. He allows his children to hang as they grow.'[114] It can be argued that violence was mainly the prerogative of this section of the working class, in particular casual and unskilled labourers who lived alongside paupers, vagrants and those of the criminal sub-culture. Over the period this stratum was increasingly reduced and isolated to join an under class or 'residuum' whilst the

vast majority of the working class became increasingly respectable and law abiding, accommodated and
controlled by various state agencies.[115] This residuum remained both hostile to authority and
largely untouched by the attempts of the state to
improve it. Crowded together in particular courts,
streets and slums, these people did not accept the
'civilising' message and continued to act according
to behavioural norms received over many generations.
In their world the police and other strangers remained alien and unwelcome, fighting and brawling
was normal, and family violence customary. Of
course within the slum itself there were many social
gradations and each family earned its status from
its conduct, 'its manners and morals being judged
before a mass public tribunal.' Robert Roberts reminds us that in 'examining the standards of the
Edwardian lower orders one always has to bear in
mind that street disturbances, gutter fighters, and
general destroyers of the peace come from comparatively small sections of the community.'[116]
     If there was, as appears likely, a real change
in the incidence of community violence in this
period to what can this be attributed? It can be
argued that material wretchedness had a debasing
effect both morally and physically and that as en-
vironmental and economic conditions improved so did
standards of behaviour. However, poverty still
existed on a considerable scale in Edwardian Britain
and improvements in the standard of living of the
working class were only marginal and for those at
the bottom of the social scale it is difficult to
detect any improvement at all. In any case economic
conditions are not always a satisfactory indication
of community violence and many contemporaries noted
increases in violence as a result of prosperity and
high wages rather than the reverse. It does not
appear that the criminal law was a more effective
deterrent to disorderly conduct than it had been in
the mid nineteenth century because apart from alterations in the law relating to assaults on women and
children there was little change. The application
of the law is a different matter and here one does
sense a determination on the behalf of magistrates
and watch committees to put down violence and rowdyism and to 'civilise' their communities through the
imposition of new standards of respectability. The
main instruments of this new urban discipline were
the police whose strength and efficiency increased
gradually throughout the period. By the end of the
nineteenth century the authorities had succeeded in

their mission and public order in the streets was a reality. However, although this may help to explain the decline in common assault and police assault, many other assaults were carried out in private and were not subject to police control.

Perhaps the answer is to be seen in the increasing number of state, philanthropic and evangelical agencies and controls at work in late Victorian and Edwardian Britain which helped to make the transition from rough and potentially disorderly communities to stable, settled and socially disciplined communities. The agencies that assisted in this process included reformatories and industrial schools, compulsory education after 1870, boys' and girls' clubs, the temperance movement, the Salvation Army, the Church Army, missions of all kinds, the Charity Organisation Society, the University Settlement Movement, the National Society for the Prevention of Cruelty to Children, and successive waves of clergymen, charity workers, court missionaries and social investigators concerned to identify social problems and obtain improving legislation. Faced with this offensive the great mass of the working class may have become docile and, as Stedman Jones argues, developed a culture 'which no longer reflected any widespread class combativity ... and was no longer threatening or subversive but conservative and defensive.'[117] The benefits of compulsory education in particular were stressed by contemporaries. Walter Besant wrote of east London in 1901 that 'there was a consensus that the influence of the schools had been to humanise the people in a manner actually visible to all. The results are before us. The children of today are in every respect better than they were twenty years ago,' and Charles Booth referred to the importance of the schools as agents of discipline 'where rules of proper behaviour have been inculcated.'[118] Society seemed to be slowly improving and as Edward Carpenter observed in 1905: 'Looking around us we see all the elements of a free human society preparing. Education, widespreading, is bringing a knowledge of the conditions and necessities of mutually helpful social life even to the least instructed. It is bringing also a far reaching sense of human dignity and equality.'[119]

NOTES

1. *Criminal Registrar's Report*, 1893, pp.73-5.
2. *Criminal Registrar's Report*, 1896, p.17.
3. *Criminal Registrar's Report*, 1899, p.37.
4. *Criminal Registrar's Report*, 1908, p.14.
5. G. Grosvenor, 'Statistics of the Abatement of Crime in England and Wales during the Twenty years ending 1887-1888', *Journal of the Royal Statistical Society*, 53, 1890 and L. Levi, 'A Summary of Indictable and Summary jurisdiction offences in England and Wales, 1857-1878', *Journal of the Royal Statistical Society*, 43, 1880.
6. A.C. Hall, *Crime and its Relation to Social Progress* (London, 1902), p.358; R. Quinton, *Crime and Criminals (1876-1910)* (London, 1910). However, according to H. Zehr, *Crime and the Development of Modern Society* (London, 1976) assault rates in France and Germany rose between 1832-1910, the opposite of what happened in England and Wales.
7. V.A.C. Gatrell, and T.B. Hadden, 'Criminal Statistics and their Interpretation', in E.A. Wrigley (ed.), *Nineteenth Century Society: Essays in the use of quantitative methods for the study of social data* (Cambridge, 1972). See also T.R. Gurr, *Rogues, Rebels and Reformers, A Political History of Urban Crime and Conflict* (London, 1976).
8. V.A.C. Gatrell, 'The Decline of Theft and Violence in Victorian and Edwardian England', in V.A.C. Gatrell, B. Lenman and G. Parker (eds.), *Crime and the Law* (London, 1980), pp.286-9.
9. Community violence could be said to include the indices of murder, manslaughter, felonies and malicious wounding and sexual assaults which were all indictable offences. However, serious acts of violence were comparatively rare and because of extraneous factors very little can be learned from the statistical trends in these offences. In this period less than 5 percent of criminal violence was tried on indictment.
10. J.J. Tobias, *Crime and Industrial Society in the 19th Century* (London, 1967), pp.14-21.
11. Gatrell and Hadden, 'Criminal Statistics', p.337.
12. D.J.V. Jones, and A. Bainbridge, *Crime in Nineteenth Century Wales* (S.S.R.C. Report, 1976), vol.I, pp.64-9.
13. R.D. Storch, 'The Study of Urban Crime', *Journal of Social History*, 4, 1979.
14. Indictable offences were those tried before a judge or bench of magistrates sitting with a jury,

with the jury responsible for the verdict. Summary offences were those tried by magistrates, sitting without a jury at petty sessions with both verdict and sentence being given by the magistrates.

15. *Criminal Registrar's Report*, 1896, p.17.
16. *Report from the Select Committee on the Prevention of Intemperance*, PP 1877, 3, p.33.
17. *Report on the State of the Law Relating to Brutal Assaults*, PP 1874, p.105.
18. F.P. Cobbe, 'Wife Torture in England', *Contemporary Review*, 32, 1878, p.81.
19. F. Engels, *The Condition of the Working Class in England* (Oxford, 1958), p.161.
20. D.J.V. Jones, *Crime, Protest, Community and Police in Nineteenth-Century Britain* (London, 1982), p.104. See also Jones and Bainbridge, *Crime*, pp. 147-23.
21. David Philips, *Crime and Authority in Victorian England: the Black Country, 1835-1860* (London, 1977), pp.283-4.
22. C. de Motte, 'The Dark Side of Town. Crime in Manchester and Salford, 1815-1875' (Unpublished Univ. of Kansas Ph.D. Thesis, 1976).
23. B. Weinberger, 'Crime and Society in Birmingham, 1860-1885' (Unpublished Univ.of Warwick Ph.D. Thesis, 1981). See also ·D.C. Woods, 'Crime and Society in the Black Country, 1860-1900' (Unpublished Univ.of Aston Ph.D. Thesis, 1979).
24. Henry Mayhew, *London Labour and the London Poor* (London, 1851), vol. I. p.16.
25. G. Stedman Jones, *Outcast London: A study in the Relationship between Classes in Victorian Society* (Oxford, 1971), p.12. For further details of violence in London see D.J.V. Jones, 'Crime in London: the evidence of the Metropolitan Police, 1831-1892', in Jones, *Crime, Protest, Community*, pp.121-4.
26. *Report on Brutal Assaults*, PP 1875, p.152.
27. *Report on Brutal Assaults*, PP 1875, pp.108, 111.
28. *Report on Brutal Assaults*, PP 1875, p.44.
29. *S.C. On Intemperance*, PP 1877, vol. III, p.305. See also evidence given by the Chief Constable of Manchester (p.171), the Liverpool magistrate R. Neilson, (p.100) and Superintendent Turner of the East End of London (p.229).
30. *S.C. on Intemperance*, PP 1877, Appendix O, p.393.
31. For further contemporary evidence on the connection between drunkenness and violent crime see

F. Peek, 'Intemperance: Its Prevalence, Effects and Remedy, *Contemporary Review*,11, 1876 and F.W.Farrar, 'Drink and Crime', *Fortnightly Review*, 53, 1893. The Criminal Registrar noted that correspondence between the incidence of drunkenness and assault appeared to exist up to 1895 but since then there had been a divergence, *Criminal Registrar's Report*, 1905, pp.27-28.

32. G. Kitson-Clark, *The Making of Victorian England* (London, 1961), p.127.

33. J. Burnett, *Plenty and Want* (Harmondsworth, 1966), p.199.

34. A.E. Dingle, 'Drink and Working Class Living Standards in Britain', *Economic History Review*, xxv(4) 1972).

35. Of the total employed in 1881 only 7 percent in Wolverhampton and 5 percent in Walsall and West Bromwich could be described as being in middle class occupations. West Bromwich had 33 percent of its workforce employed in the coal and iron trades and Dudley 38 percent. Wolverhampton and Walsall had a greater diversity of trades although the iron industry and metal trades accounted for 28 percent of the Wolverhampton workforce.

36. Wolverhampton Central Library and Walsall Town Hall, Criminal and Judicial Statistics and Watch Committee Minutes for Wolverhampton and Walsall.

37. *Walsall Free Press*, August 21, 1875.

38. *Dudley Herald*, September 25, 1880.

39. W.S. Swayne, *Parson's Pleasure* (London and Edinburgh, 1934), p.138.

40. W. Thorne, *My Life's Battles* (London, n.d.), pp.45-6.

41. *Wolverhampton Chronicle*, May 4, 1887.

42. *Walsall Free Press*, July 20, 1867 and *West Bromwich Free Press*, June 17, 1876.

43. Octavia Hill, *Homes of the London Poor, Four Year Management of a London Court* (London, 1869), pp.30-1, 89-90; C. Booth, *Life and Labour of the People of London, First Series, Poverty*, vol. III, pp.37-42. See also J. White, *R thschild Buildings: Life in an East End Tenement Block, 1867-1920*

44. E. Ross, 'Survival Networks: Women's Neighbourhood Sharing in London before World War One', *History Workshop*,15,1983. The same pattern of neighbourhood quarrels is observed by Weinberger in Birmingham particularly in crowded courts sharing water taps and work houses; see Weinberger, 'Crime', pp.205-6.

45. *Wolverhampton Chronicle*, November 21, 1883.

46. *West Bromwich Free Press*, February 6, 1886 and *Wolverhampton Chronicle*, November 23, 1870.

47. *Walsall Free Press*, February 25, 1882.

48. *Walsall Free Press*, August 26, 1882.

49. *Dudley Herald*, October 21, 1876. See D. Rubinstein, *School Attendance in London 1870-1904* (Hull, 1969), pp.49-51, and J.S. Hurt, *Elementary Schooling and the Working Classes, 1860-1918 (London,* 1979), pp.155-6, for other examples of assaults on School Board visitors.

50. *Walsall Free Press*, July 20, 1889.

51. R.D. Storch, 'The Policeman as Domestic Missionary: Urban discipline and popular culture in Northern England, 1850-1880', *Journal of Social History*, 9, 1976, p.503.

52. B. Weinberger, 'The Police and the Public in Mid-Nineteenth Century Warwickshire', in V. Bailey (ed.), *Policing and Punishment in Nineteenth Century Britain* (London, 1981), pp.67-9.

53. Jones, *Crime, Protest, Community*, pp.154-5.

54. Jones, *Crime, Protest, Community*, pp.123-4.

55. Woods, 'Crime and Society', pp.235-9.

56. *Report on Brutal Assaults*, PP 1875, p.48.

57. J.H. Elliott, 'The Increase of National Prosperity and of moral agents compared with the state of crime and pauperism', *Journal of the Royal Statistical Society*, 31, 1868, pp.314-5.

58. Wolverhampton Central Library, Wolverhampton Watch Committee Minutes, Annual Report, 1878.

59. See W.R. Miller, 'Police Authority in London and New York City 1830-1870', *Journal of Social History*, 8, 1975; R.D. Storch, 'The Plague of the Blue Locusts: police reform and popular resistance in Northern England, 1840-1857', *International Review of Social History*, 20(1) 1975, and P. Cohen, 'Policing the Working Class City', in M. Fitzgerald, G. McLennan and J. Pawson (eds.), *Crime and Society: Readings in History and Theory* (London, 1981).

60. *Wolverhampton Chronicle*, June 26, 1878.

61. In Islington the local press recorded 146 incidents of affrays between police and community from 1880 to 1920, and in the 1920s collective self-defence against the police still existed; Cohen, 'Policing', pp.117-8.

62. *Wolverhampton Chronicle*, November 25, 1874.

63. *West Bromwich Weekly News*, February 26, 1879.

64. *Wolverhampton Chronicle*, August 20, 1884.

65. Booth, *Life and Labour of the People of*

London, Third Series, Religious Influences, vol. I, p.47. See also J.A. Jackson, *The Irish in Britain* (London, 1963), pp.58-62; L.H. Lees, *Exiles of Erin* (Manchester, 1979); J. Denvir, *The Irish in Britain* (London, 1892).

66. *Dudley Herald*, March 8, 1873.

67. Storch, 'Domestic Missionary', p.482.

68. *West Bromwich Echo*, May 31, 1879. See also W.R. Cockcroft, 'The Liverpool Police Force 1836-1902', in S.P. Bell (ed.), *Victorian Lancashire* (Newton Abbott, 1974), p.165.

69. *S.C. Intemperance, Drunkenness*, 3, p.33. For the ferocity of some attacks on the police see J. Bent, *Criminal Life: Reminiscences of 42 years as a Police Officer* (Manchester, 1892), pp.76-7.

70. Weinberger, 'Crime', p.69.

71. *Wolverhampton Chronicle*, December 12, 1877.

72. Weinberger, 'Crime', pp.73-4.

73. Booth, *Religious Influences*, vol. I, pp.52-3.

74. Robert Roberts, *The Classic Slum: Salford Life in the First Quarter of the Century* (Manchester, 1973), p.100. See also Standish Meacham, *A Life Apart: The English Working Class, 1890-1914* (London, 1977), p.18.

75. Booth, *Social Influences and Conclusion*, pp.140-141.

76. Booth, *Social Influences and Conclusion*, pp.132-3, 137.

77. Booth, *Social Influences and Conclusion*, pp.140-41.

78. *Judicial and Criminal Statistics for England and Wales*, 1857-1914.

79. *Report on Brutal Assaults*, PP 1875, p.108.

80. *Report on Brutal Assaults*, PP 1875, p.60.

81. *Transactions of the National Association for the Promotion of Social Sciences*, 1876, pp.345-61.

82. F.P. Cobbe, 'Wife Torture in England', *Contemporary Review*, 32, 1878, pp.58-9.

83. *Wolverhampton Chronicle*, November 27, 1890.

84. *West Bromwich Weekly News*, May 27, 1876.

85. *Wolverhampton Chronicle*, May 4, 1887.

86. T. Holmes, *Pictures and Problems from London Police Courts* (London, 1900), p.24.

87. L. Davidoff, 'Mastered for Life: Servant and Wife in Victorian and Edwardian England, *Journal of Social History*, 7, 1974, pp.418-9. See also I. Minor, 'Working Class Women and Matrimonial Law Reform, 1890-1914', in D. Martin and D. Rubinstein, (eds.), *Ideology and the Labour Movement* (London,

1979), pp.115-7.

88. G. Best, *Mid Victorian Britain, 1851-1875* (London, 1971), p.304.

89. N. Tomes, 'A Torrent of Abuse: Crimes of Violence between working class men and women in London, 1840-1875', *Journal of Social History*, 11, 1978, p.329; E. Ross, 'Fierce Questions and Taunts: Married Life in Working-Class London, 1870-1914', *Feminist Studies*, 8, 1982, pp.557, 591-2.

90. Jones, *Crime, Protest, Community*, pp.152-3. See also Bent, *Criminal Life*, pp.19-21.

91. Tomes, 'Torrent of Abuse', p.338.

92. *Wolverhampton Chronicle*, July 3, 1878; *Walsall Free Press*, May 22, 1869.

93. *Walsall Free Press*, September 28, 1872.

94. *Dudley Herald*, July 6, 1872.

95. Cobbe, 'Wife Torture'.

96. Holmes, *Police Courts*, p.73.

97. Charles Forman, *Industrial Town: Self Portrait of St Helens in the 1920s* (St Albans, 1979), pp.128-9. See also Florence Bell's comments on wife beating in Middlesborough, *At the Works* (1907; repr. New York, 1969), pp.238-9.

98. See A. Paterson, *Across the Bridges or Life by the South London River-Side* (London, 1911), pp. 30-31: 'sometimes there are blows of which she says nothing ...', W. Besant, *East London* (London, 1901), p.151; M. Loane, *An Englishman's Castle* (London, 1909),pp.108-9, 178-9, 188-9; and Raphael Samuel, *East End Underworld: Chapters in the Life of Arthur Harding* (London, 1981) where Arthur Harding states (p.21) that 'Victorian husbands of the working class were very ignorant and brutal in their treatment of women'.

99. Tomes, 'Torrent of Abuse', p.329.

100. In Birmingham wife beaters were also drawn from a wide area and across many occupations although the unskilled and metal workers predominated. Weinberger, 'Crime', pp.203-4.

101. Jack London, *The People of the Abyss* (London 1903), p.52.

102. M. May, 'Violence in the Family: an Historical Perspective', in J.P. Martin (ed.), *Violence and the Family* (Chichester, 1978), p.149. See also J.H. Potter, *Inasmuch: The Story of the Police Court Mission 1876-1926* (London, 1927), pp.67-80. At a local level in the industrial town of Walsall, with a population of approximately 85,000 in 1901, over 40 separation orders were made annually between 1900-1910.

103. However, appeals to the court for obtain-

ing the money frequently met with indifference. See Meacham, *Life Apart*, p.18.

104. Women's Co-operative Guild, *Working Women and Divorce* (London, 1911), particularly Appendix II, pp.59-63.

105. *Wolverhampton Chronicle*, March 19, 1884.

106. See I. Pinchbeck and M. Hewitt, *Children in English Society*, II, *From the Eighteenth Century to the Children's Act, 1948* (London, 1973); J. Walvin, *A Child's World: A Social History of English Childhood 1800-1914* (Harmondsworth, 1982); May, 'Violence'; J.S. Heywood, *Children in Care* (London, 1959); G.K. Behlmer, *Child Abuse and Moral Reform in England, 1870-1908* (Stanford, 1982).

107. B. Waugh, and H. Manning, 'The Child of the English Savage', *Contemporary Review*, 49, 1886. See also B. Waugh, 'Street Children', *Contemporary Review*, 53, 1888, and M.C. Tabor, 'The Rights of Children', *Contemporary Review*, 54, 1888. Mary Tabor referred to 'an appalling amount of semi-starvation, illtreatment and neglect to which children are subjected with impunity at the hands of drunken, dissolute, and idle parents.'

108. Pinchbeck and Hewitt, *Children*, pp.623-9; Behlmer, *Child Abuse*, chs. 4, 5.

109. *Judicial and Criminal Statistics, England and Wales*, 1893-1914

110. *Criminal Registrar's Report*, 1899, pp.43-5. By 1910 the N.S.P.C.C. found that only seven percent of its complaints could be attributed to violence; see Behlmer, *Child Abuse*, p.181.

111. Roberts, *Classic Slum*, p.45. See also Thea Thompson, *Edwardian Childhoods* (London, 1981).

112. *Royal Commission on the Housing of the Working Classes*, PP 1884-5; see evidence given by Sir E.W. Walker and Joseph Chamberlain.

113. Booth, *Social Influences and Conclusion*, pp.200-201.

114. T. Wright, *The Great Unwashed* (London, 1868), pp.24-5.

115. For a discussion on the nature of the English working class in this period see Meacham, *Life Apart*, pp.11-29.

116. Roberts, *Classic Slum*, p.24.

117. G. Stedman Jones, 'Working Class Culture and Working Class Politics in London, 1870-1900: Notes on the re-making of a working class', *Journal of Social History*, 7, 1974.

118. Besant, *East London*, p.332. Booth, *Social Influences*, p.202. See also D. Rubinstein, 'Socialization and the London School Board 1870-

1904', in P. McCann, (ed.), *Popular Education and Socialisation in the nineteenth century* (London, 1977).

    119. E. Carpenter, *Prisons, Police and Punishment* (London 1905), p.62.